A Tour of C++
Second Edition

A Tour of C++
Second Edition

Bjarne Stroustrup

Addison-Wesley

Boston • Columbus • New York • San Francisco • Amsterdam • Cape Town
Dubai • London • Madrid • Milan • Munich • Paris • Montreal • Toronto • Delhi • Mexico City
São Paulo • Sydney • Hong Kong • Seoul • Singapore • Taipei • Tokyo

For information about buying this title in bulk quantities, or for special sales opportunities (which may include electronic versions; custom cover designs; and content particular to your business, training goals, marketing focus, or branding interests), please contact our corporate sales department at corpsales@pearsoned.com or (800) 382-3419.

For government sales inquiries, please contact governmentsales@pearsoned.com.

For questions about sales outside the U.S., please contact intlcs@pearson.com.

Visit us on the Web: informit.com/aw

Library of Congress Control Number: 2018941627

This book was typeset in Times and Helvetica by the author.

ISBN-13: 978-0-13-499783-4
ISBN-10: 0-13-499783-2
Third printing, March 2019
2 2019

Contents

Preface **xi**

1 The Basics **1**

1.1 Introduction 1
1.2 Programs 2
1.3 Functions 4
1.4 Types, Variables, and Arithmetic 5
1.5 Scope and Lifetime 9
1.6 Constants 9
1.7 Pointers, Arrays, and References 11
1.8 Tests 14
1.9 Mapping to Hardware 16
1.10 Advice 18

2 User-Defined Types **21**

2.1 Introduction 21
2.2 Structures 22
2.3 Classes 23
2.4 Unions 25
2.5 Enumerations 26
2.6 Advice 27

3 Modularity 29

3.1 Introduction 29
3.2 Separate Compilation 30
3.3 Modules (C++20) 32
3.4 Namespaces 34
3.5 Error Handling 35
3.6 Function Arguments and Return Values 36
3.7 Advice 46

4 Classes 47

4.1 Introduction 47
4.2 Concrete Types 48
4.3 Abstract Types 54
4.4 Virtual Functions 56
4.5 Class Hierarchies 57
4.6 Advice 63

5 Essential Operations 65

5.1 Introduction 65
5.2 Copy and Move 68
5.3 Resource Management 72
5.4 Conventional Operations 74
5.5 Advice 77

6 Templates 79

6.1 Introduction 79
6.2 Parameterized Types 79
6.3 Parameterized Operations 84
6.4 Template Mechanisms 89
6.5 Advice 92

7 Concepts and Generic Programming 93

7.1 Introduction 93
7.2 Concepts 94
7.3 Generic Programming 98
7.4 Variadic Templates 100
7.5 Template Compilation Model 104
7.6 Advice 104

8 Library Overview **107**

8.1 Introduction 107
8.2 Standard-Library Components 108
8.3 Standard-Library Headers and Namespace 109
8.4 Advice 110

9 Strings and Regular Expressions **111**

9.1 Introduction 111
9.2 Strings 111
9.3 String Views 114
9.4 Regular Expressions 116
9.5 Advice 122

10 Input and Output **123**

10.1 Introduction 123
10.2 Output 123
10.3 Input 125
10.4 I/O State 127
10.5 I/O of User-Defined Types 128
10.6 Formatting 129
10.7 File Streams 130
10.8 String Streams 130
10.9 C-style I/O 131
10.10 File System 132
10.11 Advice 136

11 Containers **137**

11.1 Introduction 137
11.2 vector 138
11.3 list 142
11.4 map 144
11.5 unordered_map 144
11.6 Container Overview 146
11.7 Advice 148

12 Algorithms **149**

12.1 Introduction 149
12.2 Use of Iterators 150
12.3 Iterator Types 153

12.4 Stream Iterators 154
12.5 Predicates 155
12.6 Algorithm Overview 156
12.7 Concepts (C++20) 157
12.8 Container Algorithms 160
12.9 Parallel Algorithms 161
12.10 Advice 161

13 Utilities **163**

13.1 Introduction 163
13.2 Resource Management 164
13.3 Range Checking: span 168
13.4 Specialized Containers 170
13.5 Alternatives 174
13.6 Allocators 178
13.7 Time 179
13.8 Function Adaption 180
13.9 Type Functions 181
13.10 Advice 185

14 Numerics **187**

14.1 Introduction 187
14.2 Mathematical Functions 188
14.3 Numerical Algorithms 189
14.4 Complex Numbers 190
14.5 Random Numbers 191
14.6 Vector Arithmetic 192
14.7 Numeric Limits 193
14.8 Advice 193

15 Concurrency **195**

15.1 Introduction 195
15.2 Tasks and threads 196
15.3 Passing Arguments 197
15.4 Returning Results 198
15.5 Sharing Data 199
15.6 Waiting for Events 200
15.7 Communicating Tasks 202
15.8 Advice 205

16 History and Compatibility **207**

16.1 History 207
16.2 C++ Feature Evolution 214
16.3 C/C++ Compatibility 218
16.4 Bibliography 222
16.5 Advice 225

Index **227**

Preface

When you wish to instruct,
be brief.
– Cicero

C++ feels like a new language. That is, I can express my ideas more clearly, more simply, and more directly today than I could in C++98. Furthermore, the resulting programs are better checked by the compiler and run faster.

This book gives an overview of C++ as defined by C++17, the current ISO C++ standard, and implemented by the major C++ suppliers. In addition, it mentions concepts and modules, as defined in ISO Technical Specifications and in current use, but not scheduled for inclusion into the standard until C++20.

Like other modern languages, C++ is large and there are a large number of libraries needed for effective use. This thin book aims to give an experienced programmer an idea of what constitutes modern C++. It covers most major language features and the major standard-library components. This book can be read in just a few hours but, obviously, there is much more to writing good C++ than can be learned in a day. However, the aim here is not mastery, but to give an overview, to give key examples, and to help a programmer get started.

The assumption is that you have programmed before. If not, please consider reading a textbook, such as *Programming: Principles and Practice Using C++ (Second edition)* [Stroustrup,2014], before continuing here. Even if you have programmed before, the language you used or the applications you wrote may be very different from the style of C++ presented here.

Think of a sightseeing tour of a city, such as Copenhagen or New York. In just a few hours, you are given a quick peek at the major attractions, told a few background stories, and given some suggestions about what to do next. You do *not* know the city after such a tour. You do *not* understand all you have seen and heard. You do *not* know how to navigate the formal and informal rules that govern life in the city. To really know a city, you have to live in it, often for years. However, with a bit of luck, you will have gained a bit of an overview, a notion of what is special about the city, and ideas of what might be of interest to you. After the tour, the real exploration can begin.

This tour presents the major C++ language features as they support programming styles, such as object-oriented and generic programming. It does not attempt to provide a detailed, reference-manual, feature-by-feature view of the language. In the best textbook tradition, I try to explain a feature before I use it, but that is not always possible and not everybody reads the text strictly sequentially. So, the reader is encouraged to use the cross references and the index.

Similarly, this tour presents the standard libraries in terms of examples, rather than exhaustively. It does not describe libraries beyond those defined by the ISO standard. The reader can search out supporting material as needed. [Stroustrup,2013] and [Stroustrup,2014] are examples of such material, but there is an enormous amount of material (of varying quality) available on the Web, e.g., [Cppreference]. For example, when I mention a standard-library function or class, its definition can easily be looked up, and by examining its documentation, many related facilities can be found.

This tour presents C++ as an integrated whole, rather than as a layer cake. Consequently, it does not identify language features as present in C, part of C++98, or new in C++11, C++14, or C++17. Such information can be found in Chapter 16 (History and Compatibility). I focus on fundamentals and try to be brief, but I have not completely resisted the temptation to overrepresent novel features. This also seems to satisfy the curiosity of many readers who already know some older version of C++.

A programming language reference manual or standard simply states what can be done, but programmers are often more interested in learning how to use the language well. This aspect is partly addressed in the selection of topics covered, partly in the text, and specifically in the advice sections. More advice about what constitutes *good modern* C++ can be found in the C++ Core Guidelines [Stroustrup,2015]. The core guidelines can be a good source for further exploration of the ideas presented in this book. You may note a remarkable similarity of the advice formulation and even the numbering of advice between the Core Guidelines and this book. One reason is that the first edition of *A Tour of C++* was a major source of the initial Core Guidelines.

Acknowledgments

Some of the material presented here is borrowed from TC++PL4 [Stroustrup,2013], so thanks to all who helped completing that book.

Thanks to all who help complete and correct the first edition of “A Tour of C++.”

Thanks to Morgan Stanley for giving me time to write this second edition. Thanks to the Columbia University Spring 2018 “Design Using C++” class for finding many a typo and bug in an early draft of this book and for making many constructive suggestions.

Thanks to Paul Anderson, Chuck Allison, Peter Gottschling, William Mon, Charles Wilson, and Sergey Zubkov for reviewing the book and suggesting many improvements.

Manhattan, New York *Bjarne Stroustrup*

1

The Basics

The first thing we do, let's
kill all the language lawyers.
– Henry VI, Part II

- Introduction
- Programs
  Hello, World!
- Functions
- Types, Variables, and Arithmetic
  Arithmetic; Initialization
- Scope and Lifetime
- Constants
- Pointers, Arrays, and References
  The Null Pointer
- Tests
- Mapping to Hardware
  Assignment; Initialization
- Advice

1.1 Introduction

This chapter informally presents the notation of C++, C++'s model of memory and computation, and the basic mechanisms for organizing code into a program. These are the language facilities supporting the styles most often seen in C and sometimes called *procedural programming*.

1.2 Programs

C++ is a compiled language. For a program to run, its source text has to be processed by a compiler, producing object files, which are combined by a linker yielding an executable program. A C++ program typically consists of many source code files (usually simply called *source files*).

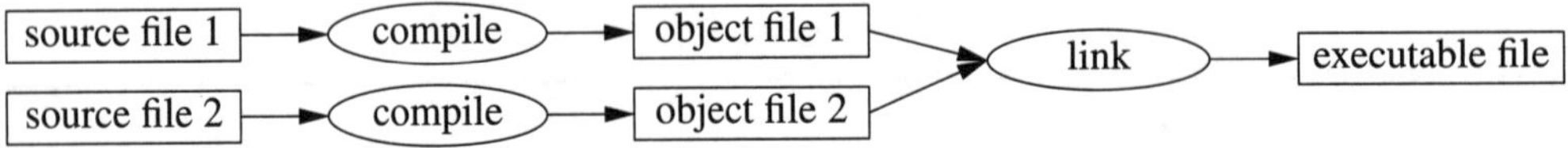

An executable program is created for a specific hardware/system combination; it is not portable, say, from a Mac to a Windows PC. When we talk about portability of C++ programs, we usually mean portability of source code; that is, the source code can be successfully compiled and run on a variety of systems.

The ISO C++ standard defines two kinds of entities:

- *Core language features*, such as built-in types (e.g., `char` and `int`) and loops (e.g., `for`-statements and `while`-statements)
- *Standard-library components*, such as containers (e.g., `vector` and `map`) and I/O operations (e.g., `<<` and `getline()`)

The standard-library components are perfectly ordinary C++ code provided by every C++ implementation. That is, the C++ standard library can be implemented in C++ itself and is (with very minor uses of machine code for things such as thread context switching). This implies that C++ is sufficiently expressive and efficient for the most demanding systems programming tasks.

C++ is a statically typed language. That is, the type of every entity (e.g., object, value, name, and expression) must be known to the compiler at its point of use. The type of an object determines the set of operations applicable to it.

1.2.1 Hello, World!

The minimal C++ program is

```
int main() { }          // the minimal C++ program
```

This defines a function called `main`, which takes no arguments and does nothing.

Curly braces, `{ }`, express grouping in C++. Here, they indicate the start and end of the function body. The double slash, `//`, begins a comment that extends to the end of the line. A comment is for the human reader; the compiler ignores comments.

Every C++ program must have exactly one global function named `main()`. The program starts by executing that function. The `int` integer value returned by `main()`, if any, is the program's return value to "the system." If no value is returned, the system will receive a value indicating successful completion. A nonzero value from `main()` indicates failure. Not every operating system and execution environment make use of that return value: Linux/Unix-based environments do, but Windows-based environments rarely do.

Typically, a program produces some output. Here is a program that writes **Hello, World!**:

```
#include <iostream>

int main()
{
     std::cout << "Hello, World!\n";
}
```

The line **#include <iostream>** instructs the compiler to *include* the declarations of the standard stream I/O facilities as found in **iostream**. Without these declarations, the expression

```
std::cout << "Hello, World!\n"
```

would make no sense. The operator << ("put to") writes its second argument onto its first. In this case, the string literal **"Hello, World!\n"** is written onto the standard output stream **std::cout**. A string literal is a sequence of characters surrounded by double quotes. In a string literal, the backslash character \ followed by another character denotes a single "special character." In this case, **\n** is the newline character, so that the characters written are **Hello, World!** followed by a newline.

The **std::** specifies that the name **cout** is to be found in the standard-library namespace (§3.4). I usually leave out the **std::** when discussing standard features; §3.4 shows how to make names from a namespace visible without explicit qualification.

Essentially all executable code is placed in functions and called directly or indirectly from **main()**. For example:

```
#include <iostream>           // include ("import") the declarations for the I/O stream library

using namespace std;          // make names from std visible without std:: (§3.4)

double square(double x)       // square a double precision floating-point number
{
     return x*x;
}

void print_square(double x)
{
     cout << "the square of " << x << " is " << square(x) << "\n";
}

int main()
{
     print_square(1.234);     // print: the square of 1.234 is 1.52276
}
```

A "return type" **void** indicates that a function does not return a value.

1.3 Functions

The main way of getting something done in a C++ program is to call a function to do it. Defining a function is the way you specify how an operation is to be done. A function cannot be called unless it has been previously declared.

A function declaration gives the name of the function, the type of the value returned (if any), and the number and types of the arguments that must be supplied in a call. For example:

```
Elem* next_elem();          // no argument; return a pointer to Elem (an Elem*)
void exit(int);             // int argument; return nothing
double sqrt(double);        // double argument; return a double
```

In a function declaration, the return type comes before the name of the function and the argument types come after the name enclosed in parentheses.

The semantics of argument passing are identical to the semantics of initialization (§3.6.1). That is, argument types are checked and implicit argument type conversion takes place when necessary (§1.4). For example:

```
double s2 = sqrt(2);            // call sqrt() with the argument double{2}
double s3 = sqrt("three");      // error: sqrt() requires an argument of type double
```

The value of such compile-time checking and type conversion should not be underestimated.

A function declaration may contain argument names. This can be a help to the reader of a program, but unless the declaration is also a function definition, the compiler simply ignores such names. For example:

```
double sqrt(double d);    // return the square root of d
double square(double);    // return the square of the argument
```

The type of a function consists of its return type and the sequence of its argument types. For example:

```
double get(const vector<double>& vec, int index);      // type: double(const vector<double>&,int)
```

A function can be a member of a class (§2.3, §4.2.1). For such a *member function*, the name of its class is also part of the function type. For example:

```
char& String::operator[](int index);                   // type: char& String::(int)
```

We want our code to be comprehensible, because that is the first step on the way to maintainability. The first step to comprehensibility is to break computational tasks into meaningful chunks (represented as functions and classes) and name those. Such functions then provide the basic vocabulary of computation, just as the types (built-in and user-defined) provide the basic vocabulary of data. The C++ standard algorithms (e.g., **find**, **sort**, and **iota**) provide a good start (Chapter 12). Next, we can compose functions representing common or specialized tasks into larger computations.

The number of errors in code correlates strongly with the amount of code and the complexity of the code. Both problems can be addressed by using more and shorter functions. Using a function to do a specific task often saves us from writing a specific piece of code in the middle of other code; making it a function forces us to name the activity and document its dependencies.

If two functions are defined with the same name, but with different argument types, the compiler will choose the most appropriate function to invoke for each call. For example:

```
void print(int);        // takes an integer argument
void print(double);     // takes a floating-point argument
void print(string);     // takes a string argument

void user()
{
        print(42);              // calls print(int)
        print(9.65);            // calls print(double)
        print("Barcelona");     // calls print(string)
}
```

If two alternative functions could be called, but neither is better than the other, the call is deemed ambiguous and the compiler gives an error. For example:

```
void print(int,double);
void print(double,int);

void user2()
{
        print(0,0);     // error: ambiguous
}
```

Defining multiple functions with the same name is known as *function overloading* and is one of the essential parts of generic programming (§7.2). When a function is overloaded, each function of the same name should implement the same semantics. The `print()` functions are an example of this; each `print()` prints its argument.

1.4 Types, Variables, and Arithmetic

Every name and every expression has a type that determines the operations that may be performed on it. For example, the declaration

```
int inch;
```

specifies that `inch` is of type `int`; that is, `inch` is an integer variable.

A *declaration* is a statement that introduces an entity into the program. It specifies a type for the entity:

- A *type* defines a set of possible values and a set of operations (for an object).
- An *object* is some memory that holds a value of some type.
- A *value* is a set of bits interpreted according to a type.
- A *variable* is a named object.

C++ offers a small zoo of fundamental types, but since I'm not a zoologist, I will not list them all. You can find them all in reference sources, such as [Stroustrup,2013] or the [Cppreference] on the Web. Examples are:

```
bool        // Boolean, possible values are true and false
char        // character, for example, 'a', 'z', and '9'
int         // integer, for example, -273, 42, and 1066
double      // double-precision floating-point number, for example, -273.15, 3.14, and 6.626e-34
unsigned    // non-negative integer, for example, 0, 1, and 999 (use for bitwise logical operations)
```

Each fundamental type corresponds directly to hardware facilities and has a fixed size that determines the range of values that can be stored in it:

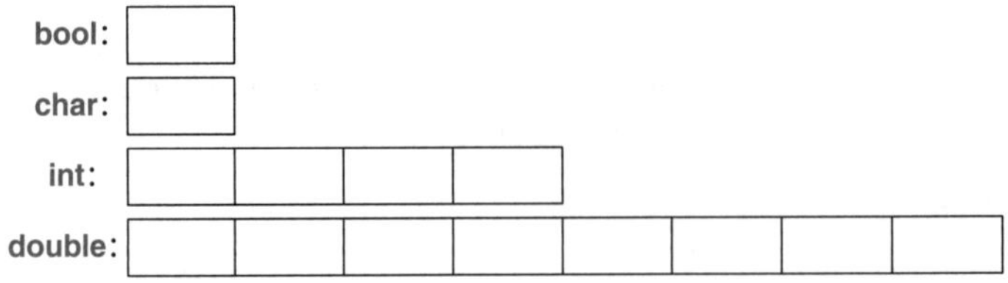

bool:

char:

int:

double:

A char variable is of the natural size to hold a character on a given machine (typically an 8-bit byte), and the sizes of other types are multiples of the size of a char. The size of a type is implementation-defined (i.e., it can vary among different machines) and can be obtained by the sizeof operator; for example, sizeof(char) equals 1 and sizeof(int) is often 4.

Numbers can be floating-point or integers.

- Floating-point numbers are recognized by a decimal point (e.g., 3.14) or by an exponent (e.g., 3e−2).
- Integer literals are by default decimal (e.g., 42 means forty-two). A 0b prefix indicates a binary (base 2) integer literal (e.g., 0b10101010). A 0x prefix indicates a hexadecimal (base 16) integer literal (e.g., 0xBAD1234). A 0 prefix indicates an octal (base 8) integer literal (e.g., 0334).

To make long literals more readable for humans, we can use a single quote (') as a digit separator. For example, π is about 3.14159'26535'89793'23846'26433'83279'50288 or if you prefer hexadecimal 0x3.243F'6A88'85A3'08D3.

1.4.1 Arithmetic

The arithmetic operators can be used for appropriate combinations of the fundamental types:

```
x+y     // plus
+x      // unary plus
x−y     // minus
−x      // unary minus
x∗y     // multiply
x/y     // divide
x%y     // remainder (modulus) for integers
```

So can the comparison operators:

```
x==y     // equal
x!=y     // not equal
x<y      // less than
x>y      // greater than
x<=y     // less than or equal
x>=y     // greater than or equal
```

Furthermore, logical operators are provided:

```
x&y      // bitwise and
x|y      // bitwise or
x^y      // bitwise exclusive or
~x       // bitwise complement
x&&y     // logical and
x||y     // logical or
!x       // logical not (negation)
```

A bitwise logical operator yields a result of the operand type for which the operation has been performed on each bit. The logical operators **&&** and || simply return **true** or **false** depending on the values of their operands.

In assignments and in arithmetic operations, C++ performs all meaningful conversions between the basic types so that they can be mixed freely:

```
void some_function()     // function that doesn't return a value
{
      double d = 2.2;    // initialize floating-point number
      int i = 7;         // initialize integer
      d = d+i;           // assign sum to d
      i = d*i;           // assign product to i; beware: truncating the double d*i to an int
}
```

The conversions used in expressions are called *the usual arithmetic conversions* and aim to ensure that expressions are computed at the highest precision of its operands. For example, an addition of a **double** and an **int** is calculated using double-precision floating-point arithmetic.

Note that = is the assignment operator and == tests equality.

In addition to the conventional arithmetic and logical operators, C++ offers more specific operations for modifying a variable:

```
x+=y     // x = x+y
++x      // increment: x = x+1
x-=y     // x = x-y
--x      // decrement: x = x-1
x*=y     // scaling: x = x*y
x/=y     // scaling: x = x/y
x%=y     // x = x%y
```

These operators are concise, convenient, and very frequently used.

The order of evaluation of expressions is left to right, except for assignments, which are right-to-left. The order of evaluation of function arguments is unfortunately unspecified.

1.4.2 Initialization

Before an object can be used, it must be given a value. C++ offers a variety of notations for expressing initialization, such as the = used above, and a universal form based on curly-brace-delimited initializer lists:

```
double d1 = 2.3;                    // initialize d1 to 2.3
double d2 {2.3};                    // initialize d2 to 2.3
double d3 = {2.3};                  // initialize d3 to 2.3 (the = is optional with { ... })
complex<double> z = 1;              // a complex number with double-precision floating-point scalars
complex<double> z2 {d1,d2};
complex<double> z3 = {d1,d2};       // the = is optional with { ... }

vector<int> v {1,2,3,4,5,6};        // a vector of ints
```

The = form is traditional and dates back to C, but if in doubt, use the general {}-list form. If nothing else, it saves you from conversions that lose information:

```
int i1 = 7.8;        // i1 becomes 7 (surprise?)
int i2 {7.8};        // error: floating-point to integer conversion
```

Unfortunately, conversions that lose information, *narrowing conversions*, such as **double** to **int** and **int** to **char**, are allowed and implicitly applied when you use = (but not when you use {}). The problems caused by implicit narrowing conversions are a price paid for C compatibility (§16.3).

A constant (§1.6) cannot be left uninitialized and a variable should only be left uninitialized in extremely rare circumstances. Don't introduce a name until you have a suitable value for it. User-defined types (such as **string**, **vector**, **Matrix**, **Motor_controller**, and **Orc_warrior**) can be defined to be implicitly initialized (§4.2.1).

When defining a variable, you don't need to state its type explicitly when it can be deduced from the initializer:

```
auto b = true;        // a bool
auto ch = 'x';        // a char
auto i = 123;         // an int
auto d = 1.2;         // a double
auto z = sqrt(y);     // z has the type of whatever sqrt(y) returns
auto bb {true};       // bb is a bool
```

With **auto**, we tend to use the = because there is no potentially troublesome type conversion involved, but if you prefer to use {} initialization consistently, you can do that instead.

We use **auto** where we don't have a specific reason to mention the type explicitly. "Specific reasons" include:

- The definition is in a large scope where we want to make the type clearly visible to readers of our code.
- We want to be explicit about a variable's range or precision (e.g., **double** rather than **float**).

Using **auto**, we avoid redundancy and writing long type names. This is especially important in generic programming where the exact type of an object can be hard for the programmer to know and the type names can be quite long (§12.2).

1.5 Scope and Lifetime

A declaration introduces its name into a scope:

- *Local scope*: A name declared in a function (§1.3) or lambda (§6.3.2) is called a *local name*. Its scope extends from its point of declaration to the end of the block in which its declaration occurs. A *block* is delimited by a { } pair. Function argument names are considered local names.
- *Class scope*: A name is called a *member name* (or a *class member name*) if it is defined in a class (§2.2, §2.3, Chapter 4), outside any function (§1.3), lambda (§6.3.2), or **enum class** (§2.5). Its scope extends from the opening { of its enclosing declaration to the end of that declaration.
- *Namespace scope*: A name is called a *namespace member name* if it is defined in a namespace (§3.4) outside any function, lambda (§6.3.2), class (§2.2, §2.3, Chapter 4), or **enum class** (§2.5). Its scope extends from the point of declaration to the end of its namespace.

A name not declared inside any other construct is called a *global name* and is said to be in the *global namespace*.

In addition, we can have objects without names, such as temporaries and objects created using **new** (§4.2.2). For example:

```
vector<int> vec;      // vec is global (a global vector of integers)

struct Record {
     string name;     // name is a member or Record (a string member)
     // ...
};

void fct(int arg)     // fct is global (a global function)
                      // arg is local (an integer argument)
{
     string motto {"Who dares wins"};   // motto is local
     auto p = new Record{"Hume"};       // p points to an unnamed Record (created by new)
     // ...
}
```

An object must be constructed (initialized) before it is used and will be destroyed at the end of its scope. For a namespace object the point of destruction is the end of the program. For a member, the point of destruction is determined by the point of destruction of the object of which it is a member. An object created by **new** "lives" until destroyed by **delete** (§4.2.2).

1.6 Constants

C++ supports two notions of immutability:

- **const**: meaning roughly "I promise not to change this value." This is used primarily to specify interfaces so that data can be passed to functions using pointers and references without fear of it being modified. The compiler enforces the promise made by **const**. The value of a **const** can be calculated at run time.

- constexpr: meaning roughly "to be evaluated at compile time." This is used primarily to specify constants, to allow placement of data in read-only memory (where it is unlikely to be corrupted), and for performance. The value of a constexpr must be calculated by the compiler.

For example:

```
constexpr int dmv = 17;              // dmv is a named constant
int var = 17;                        // var is not a constant
const double sqv = sqrt(var);        // sqv is a named constant, possibly computed at run time

double sum(const vector<double>&);          // sum will not modify its argument (§1.7)

vector<double> v {1.2, 3.4, 4.5};           // v is not a constant
const double s1 = sum(v);                   // OK: sum(v) is evaluated at run time
constexpr double s2 = sum(v);               // error: sum(v) is not a constant expression
```

For a function to be usable in a *constant expression*, that is, in an expression that will be evaluated by the compiler, it must be defined constexpr. For example:

```
constexpr double square(double x) { return x*x; }

constexpr double max1 = 1.4*square(17);     // OK 1.4*square(17) is a constant expression
constexpr double max2 = 1.4*square(var);    // error: var is not a constant expression
const double max3 = 1.4*square(var);        // OK, may be evaluated at run time
```

A constexpr function can be used for non-constant arguments, but when that is done the result is not a constant expression. We allow a constexpr function to be called with non-constant-expression arguments in contexts that do not require constant expressions. That way, we don't have to define essentially the same function twice: once for constant expressions and once for variables.

To be constexpr, a function must be rather simple and cannot have side effects and can only use information passed to it as arguments. In particular, it cannot modify non-local variables, but it can have loops and use its own local variables. For example:

```
constexpr double nth(double x, int n)    // assume 0<=n
{
     double res = 1;
     int i = 0;
     while (i<n) {      // while-loop: do while the condition is true (§1.7.1)
          res*=x;
          ++i;
     }
     return res;
}
```

In a few places, constant expressions are required by language rules (e.g., array bounds (§1.7), case labels (§1.8), template value arguments (§6.2), and constants declared using constexpr). In other cases, compile-time evaluation is important for performance. Independently of performance issues, the notion of immutability (an object with an unchangeable state) is an important design concern.

1.7 Pointers, Arrays, and References

The most fundamental collection of data is a contiguously allocated sequence of elements of the same type, called an *array*. This is basically what the hardware offers. An array of elements of type char can be declared like this:

```
char v[6];            // array of 6 characters
```

Similarly, a pointer can be declared like this:

```
char* p;              // pointer to character
```

In declarations, [ ] means "array of" and * means "pointer to." All arrays have 0 as their lower bound, so v has six elements, v[0] to v[5]. The size of an array must be a constant expression (§1.6). A pointer variable can hold the address of an object of the appropriate type:

```
char* p = &v[3];          // p points to v's fourth element
char x = *p;              // *p is the object that p points to
```

In an expression, prefix unary * means "contents of" and prefix unary & means "address of." We can represent the result of that initialized definition graphically:

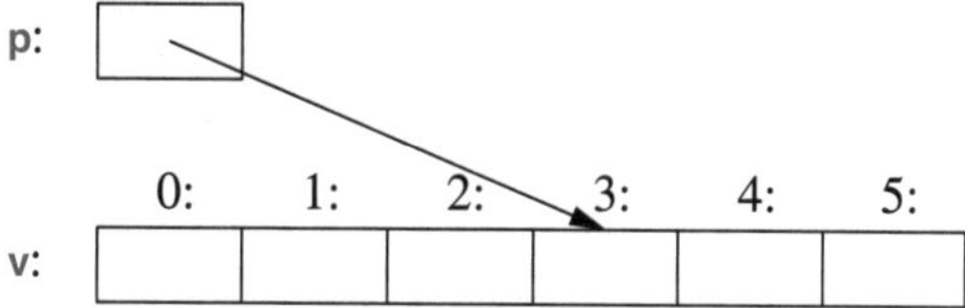

Consider copying ten elements from one array to another:

```
void copy_fct()
{
     int v1[10] = {0,1,2,3,4,5,6,7,8,9};
     int v2[10];                     // to become a copy of v1

     for (auto i=0; i!=10; ++i)  // copy elements
          v2[i]=v1[i];
     // ...
}
```

This for-statement can be read as "set i to zero; while i is not 10, copy the ith element and increment i." When applied to an integer or floating-point variable, the increment operator, ++, simply adds 1. C++ also offers a simpler for-statement, called a range-for-statement, for loops that traverse a sequence in the simplest way:

```
void print()
{
      int v[] = {0,1,2,3,4,5,6,7,8,9};

      for (auto x : v)              // for each x in v
            cout << x << '\n';

      for (auto x : {10,21,32,43,54,65})
            cout << x << '\n';
      // ...
}
```

The first range-for-statement can be read as "for every element of v, from the first to the last, place a copy in x and print it." Note that we don't have to specify an array bound when we initialize it with a list. The range-for-statement can be used for any sequence of elements (§12.1).

If we didn't want to copy the values from v into the variable x, but rather just have x refer to an element, we could write:

```
void increment()
{
      int v[] = {0,1,2,3,4,5,6,7,8,9};

      for (auto& x : v)       // add 1 to each x in v
            ++x;
      // ...
}
```

In a declaration, the unary suffix & means "reference to." A reference is similar to a pointer, except that you don't need to use a prefix ∗ to access the value referred to by the reference. Also, a reference cannot be made to refer to a different object after its initialization.

References are particularly useful for specifying function arguments. For example:

```
void sort(vector<double>& v);       // sort v (v is a vector of doubles)
```

By using a reference, we ensure that for a call sort(my_vec), we do not copy my_vec and that it really is my_vec that is sorted and not a copy of it.

When we don't want to modify an argument but still don't want the cost of copying, we use a const reference (§1.6). For example:

```
double sum(const vector<double>&)
```

Functions taking const references are very common.

When used in declarations, operators (such as &, ∗, and [ ]) are called *declarator operators*:

```
T a[n]     // T[n]: a is an array of n Ts
T∗ p       // T*: p is a pointer to T
T& r       // T&: r is a reference to T
T f(A)     // T(A): f is a function taking an argument of type A returning a result of type T
```

1.7.1 The Null Pointer

We try to ensure that a pointer always points to an object so that dereferencing it is valid. When we don't have an object to point to or if we need to represent the notion of "no object available" (e.g., for an end of a list), we give the pointer the value nullptr ("the null pointer"). There is only one nullptr shared by all pointer types:

```
double* pd = nullptr;
Link<Record>* lst = nullptr;    // pointer to a Link to a Record
int x = nullptr;                // error: nullptr is a pointer not an integer
```

It is often wise to check that a pointer argument actually points to something:

```
int count_x(const char* p, char x)
     // count the number of occurrences of x in p[]
     // p is assumed to point to a zero-terminated array of char (or to nothing)
{
     if (p==nullptr)
          return 0;
     int count = 0;
     for (; *p!=0; ++p)
          if (*p==x)
               ++count;
     return count;
}
```

Note how we can advance a pointer to point to the next element of an array using ++ and that we can leave out the initializer in a for-statement if we don't need it.

The definition of count_x() assumes that the char* is a *C-style string*, that is, that the pointer points to a zero-terminated array of char. The characters in a string literal are immutable, so to handle count_x("Hello!"), I declared count_x() a const char* argument.

In older code, 0 or NULL is typically used instead of nullptr. However, using nullptr eliminates potential confusion between integers (such as 0 or NULL) and pointers (such as nullptr).

In the count_x() example, we are not using the initializer part of the for-statement, so we can use the simpler while-statement:

```
int count_x(const char* p, char x)
     // count the number of occurrences of x in p[]
     // p is assumed to point to a zero-terminated array of char (or to nothing)
{
     if (p==nullptr)
          return 0;
     int count = 0;
     while (*p) {
          if (*p==x)
               ++count;
          ++p;
     }
     return count;
}
```

The while-statement executes until its condition becomes false.

A test of a numeric value (e.g., while (*p) in count_x()) is equivalent to comparing the value to 0 (e.g., while (*p!=0)). A test of a pointer value (e.g., if (p)) is equivalent to comparing the value to nullptr (e.g., if (p!=nullptr)).

There is no "null reference." A reference must refer to a valid object (and implementations assume that it does). There are obscure and clever ways to violate that rule; don't do that.

1.8 Tests

C++ provides a conventional set of statements for expressing selection and looping, such as if-statements, switch-statements, while-loops, and for-loops. For example, here is a simple function that prompts the user and returns a Boolean indicating the response:

```
bool accept()
{
     cout << "Do you want to proceed (y or n)?\n";       // write question
     char answer = 0;                                     // initialize to a value that will not appear on input
     cin >> answer;                                       // read answer

     if (answer == 'y')
          return true;
     return false;
}
```

To match the << output operator ("put to"), the >> operator ("get from") is used for input; cin is the standard input stream (Chapter 10). The type of the right-hand operand of >> determines what input is accepted, and its right-hand operand is the target of the input operation. The \n character at the end of the output string represents a newline (§1.2.1).

Note that the definition of answer appears where it is needed (and not before that). A declaration can appear anywhere a statement can.

The example could be improved by taking an n (for "no") answer into account:

```
bool accept2()
{
     cout << "Do you want to proceed (y or n)?\n";       // write question
     char answer = 0;                                     // initialize to a value that will not appear on input
     cin >> answer;                                       // read answer

     switch (answer) {
     case 'y':
          return true;
     case 'n':
          return false;
     default:
          cout << "I'll take that for a no.\n";
          return false;
     }
}
```

A switch-statement tests a value against a set of constants. Those constants, called case-labels, must be distinct, and if the value tested does not match any of them, the default is chosen. If the value doesn't match any case-label and no default is provided, no action is taken .

We don't have to exit a case by returning from the function that contains its switch-statement. Often, we just want to continue execution with the statement following the switch-statement. We can do that using a break statement. As an example, consider an overly clever, yet primitive, parser for a trivial command video game:

```
void action()
{
    while (true) {
        cout << "enter action:\n";          // request action
        string act;
        cin >> act;             // read characters into a string
        Point delta {0,0};      // Point holds an {x,y} pair

        for (char ch : act) {
            switch (ch) {
            case 'u':   // up
            case 'n':   // north
                ++delta.y;
                break;
            case 'r':   // right
            case 'e':   // east
                ++delta.x;
                break;
            // ... more actions ...
            default:
                cout << "I freeze!\n";
            }
            move(current+delta*scale);
            update_display();
        }
    }
}
```

Like a for-statement (§1.7), an if-statement can introduce a variable and test it. For example:

```
void do_something(vector<int>& v)
{
    if (auto n = v.size(); n!=0) {
        // ... we get here if n!=0 ...
    }
    // ...
}
```

Here, the integer n is defined for use within the if-statement , initialized with v.size(), and immediately tested by the n!=0 condition after the semicolon. A name declared in a condition is in scope on both branches of the if-statement.

As with the for-statement, the purpose of declaring a name in the condition of an if-statement is to keep the scope of the variable limited to improve readability and minimize errors.

The most common case is testing a variable against 0 (or the nullptr). To do that, simply leave out the explicit mention of the condition. For example:

```
void do_something(vector<int>& v)
{
        if (auto n = v.size()) {
                // ... we get here if n!=0 ...
        }
        // ...
}
```

Prefer to use this terser and simpler form when you can.

1.9 Mapping to Hardware

C++ offers a direct mapping to hardware. When you use one of the fundamental operations, the implementation is what the hardware offers, typically a single machine operation. For example, adding two ints, x+y executes an integer add machine instruction.

A C++ implementation sees a machine's memory as a sequence of memory locations into which it can place (typed) objects and address them using pointers:

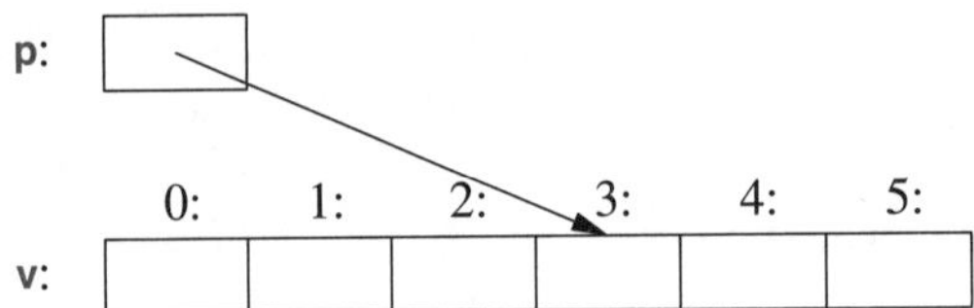

A pointer is represented in memory as a machine address, so the numeric value of p in this figure would be 3. If this looks much like an array (§1.7), that's because an array is C++'s basic abstraction of "a contiguous sequence of objects in memory."

The simple mapping of fundamental language constructs to hardware is crucial for the raw low-level performance for which C and C++ have been famous for decades. The basic machine model of C and C++ is based on computer hardware, rather than some form of mathematics.

1.9.1 Assignment

An assignment of a built-in type is a simple machine copy operation. Consider:

```
int x = 2;
int y = 3;
x = y;          // x becomes 3
// Note: x==y
```

This is obvious. We can graphically represent that like this:

x: 2 y: 3 x = y; x: 3 y: 3

Note that the two objects are independent. We can change the value of y without affecting the value of x. For example x=99 will not change the value of y. Unlike Java, C#, and other languages, but like C, that is true for all types, not just for ints.

If we want different objects to refer to the same (shared) value, we must say so. We could use pointers:

```
int x = 2;
int y = 3;
int* p = &x;
int* q = &y;      // now p!=q and *p!=*q
p = q;            // p becomes &y; now p==q, so (obviously)*p == *q
```

We can represent that graphically like this:

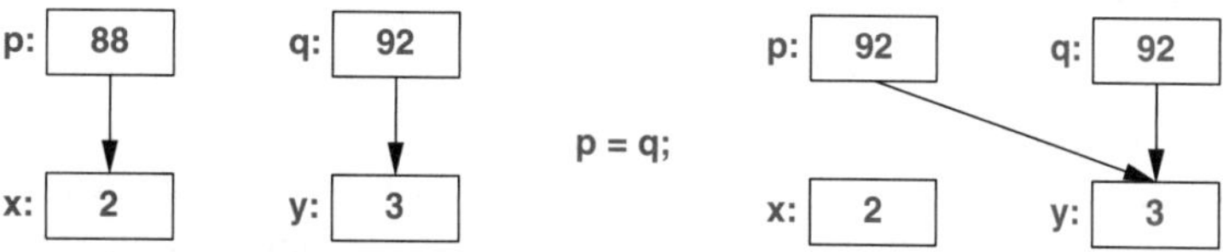

I arbitrarily chose 88 and 92 as the addresses of the ints. Again, we can see that the assigned-to object gets the value from the assigned object, yielding two independent objects (here, pointers), with the same value. That is, p=q gives p==q. After p=q, both pointers point to y.

A reference and a pointer both refer/point to an object and both are represented in memory as a machine address. However, the language rules for using them differ. Assignment to a reference does not change what the reference refers to but assigns to the referenced object:

```
int x = 2;
int y = 3;
int& r = x;       // r refers to x
int& r2 = y;      // now r2 refers to y
r = r2;           // read through r2, write through r: x becomes 3
```

We can represent that graphically like this:

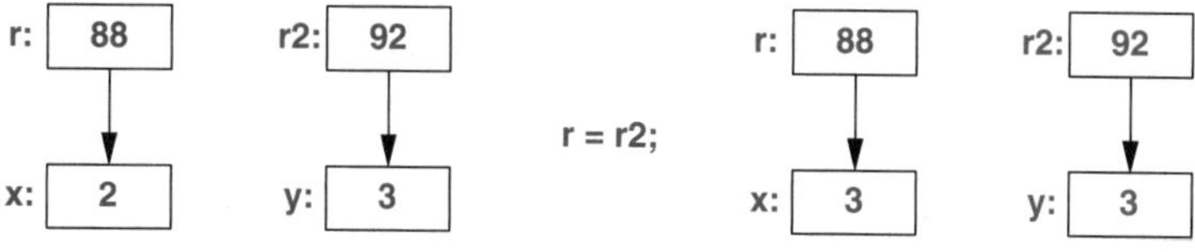

To access the value pointed to by a pointer, you use *; that is automatically (implicitly) done for a reference.

After x=y, we have x==y for every built-in type and well-designed user-defined type (Chapter 2) that offers = (assignment) and == (equality comparison).

1.9.2 Initialization

Initialization differs from assignment. In general, for an assignment to work correctly, the assigned-to object must have a value. On the other hand, the task of initialization is to make an uninitialized piece of memory into a valid object. For almost all types, the effect of reading from or writing to an uninitialized variable is undefined. For built-in types, that's most obvious for references:

```
int x = 7;
int& r {x};        // bind r to x (r refers to x)
r = 7;             // assign to whatever r refers to

int& r2;           // error: uninitialized reference
r2 = 99;           // assign to whatever r2 refers to
```

Fortunately, we cannot have an uninitialized reference; if we could, then that `r2=99` would assign `99` to some unspecified memory location; the result would eventually lead to bad results or a crash.

You can use `=` to initialize a reference but please don't let that confuse you. For example:

```
int& r = x;        // bind r to x (r refers to x)
```

This is still initialization and binds `r` to `x`, rather than any form of value copy.

The distinction between initialization and assignment is also crucial to many user-defined types, such as `string` and `vector`, where an assigned-to object owns a resource that needs to eventually be released (§5.3).

The basic semantics of argument passing and function value return are that of initialization (§3.6). For example, that's how we get pass-by-reference.

1.10 Advice

The advice here is a subset of the C++ Core Guidelines [Stroustrup,2015]. References to guidelines look like this [CG: ES.23], meaning the 23rd rule in the Expressions and Statement section. Generally, a core guideline offers further rationale and examples.

[1] Don't panic! All will become clear in time; §1.1; [CG: In.0].
[2] Don't use the built-in features exclusively or on their own. On the contrary, the fundamental (built-in) features are usually best used indirectly through libraries, such as the ISO C++ standard library (Chapters 8–15); [CG: P.10].
[3] You don't have to know every detail of C++ to write good programs.
[4] Focus on programming techniques, not on language features.
[5] For the final word on language definition issues, see the ISO C++ standard; §16.1.3; [CG: P.2].
[6] "Package" meaningful operations as carefully named functions; §1.3; [CG: F.1].
[7] A function should perform a single logical operation; §1.3 [CG: F.2].
[8] Keep functions short; §1.3; [CG: F.3].
[9] Use overloading when functions perform conceptually the same task on different types; §1.3.
[10] If a function may have to be evaluated at compile time, declare it `constexpr`; §1.6; [CG: F.4].

[11] Understand how language primitives map to hardware; §1.4, §1.7, §1.9, §2.3, §4.2.2, §4.4.
[12] Use digit separators to make large literals readable; §1.4; [CG: NL.11].
[13] Avoid complicated expressions; [CG: ES.40].
[14] Avoid narrowing conversions; §1.4.2; [CG: ES.46].
[15] Minimize the scope of a variable; §1.5.
[16] Avoid "magic constants"; use symbolic constants; §1.6; [CG: ES.45].
[17] Prefer immutable data; §1.6; [CG: P.10].
[18] Declare one name (only) per declaration; [CG: ES.10].
[19] Keep common and local names short, and keep uncommon and nonlocal names longer; [CG: ES.7].
[20] Avoid similar-looking names; [CG: ES.8].
[21] Avoid ALL_CAPS names; [CG: ES.9].
[22] Prefer the {}-initializer syntax for declarations with a named type; §1.4; [CG: ES.23].
[23] Use auto to avoid repeating type names; §1.4.2; [CG: ES.11].
[24] Avoid uninitialized variables; §1.4; [CG: ES.20].
[25] Keep scopes small; §1.5; [CG: ES.5].
[26] When declaring a variable in the condition of an if-statement, prefer the version with the implicit test against 0; §1.8.
[27] Use unsigned for bit manipulation only; §1.4; [CG: ES.101] [CG: ES.106].
[28] Keep use of pointers simple and straightforward; §1.7; [CG: ES.42].
[29] Use nullptr rather than 0 or NULL; §1.7; [CG: ES.47].
[30] Don't declare a variable until you have a value to initialize it with; §1.7, §1.8; [CG: ES.21].
[31] Don't say in comments what can be clearly stated in code; [CG: NL.1].
[32] State intent in comments; [CG: NL.2].
[33] Maintain a consistent indentation style; [CG: NL.4].

2

User-Defined Types

Don't Panic!
– Douglas Adams

- Introduction
- Structures
- Classes
- Unions
- Enumerations
- Advice

2.1 Introduction

We call the types that can be built from the fundamental types (§1.4), the `const` modifier (§1.6), and the declarator operators (§1.7) *built-in types*. C++'s set of built-in types and operations is rich, but deliberately low-level. They directly and efficiently reflect the capabilities of conventional computer hardware. However, they don't provide the programmer with high-level facilities to conveniently write advanced applications. Instead, C++ augments the built-in types and operations with a sophisticated set of *abstraction mechanisms* out of which programmers can build such high-level facilities.

The C++ abstraction mechanisms are primarily designed to let programmers design and implement their own types, with suitable representations and operations, and for programmers to simply and elegantly use such types. Types built out of other types using C++'s abstraction mechanisms are called *user-defined types*. They are referred to as *classes* and *enumerations*. User defined types can be built out of both built-in types and other user-defined types. Most of this book is devoted to the design, implementation, and use of user-defined types. User-defined types are often preferred over built-in types because they are easier to use, less error-prone, and typically as efficient for what they do as direct use of built-in types, or even faster.

The rest of this chapter presents the simplest and most fundamental facilities for defining and using types. Chapters 4–7 are a more complete description of the abstraction mechanisms and the programming styles they support. Chapters 8–15 present an overview of the standard library, and since the standard library mainly consists of user-defined types, they provide examples of what can be built using the language facilities and programming techniques presented in Chapters 1–7.

2.2 Structures

The first step in building a new type is often to organize the elements it needs into a data structure, a **struct**:

```
struct Vector {
        int sz;            // number of elements
        double* elem;  // pointer to elements
};
```

This first version of **Vector** consists of an **int** and a **double***.

A variable of type **Vector** can be defined like this:

```
Vector v;
```

However, by itself that is not of much use because **v**'s **elem** pointer doesn't point to anything. For it to be useful, we must give **v** some elements to point to. For example, we can construct a **Vector** like this:

```
void vector_init(Vector& v, int s)
{
        v.elem = new double[s];  // allocate an array of s doubles
        v.sz = s;
}
```

That is, **v**'s **elem** member gets a pointer produced by the **new** operator and **v**'s **sz** member gets the number of elements. The **&** in **Vector&** indicates that we pass **v** by non-**const** reference (§1.7); that way, **vector_init()** can modify the vector passed to it.

The **new** operator allocates memory from an area called the *free store* (also known as *dynamic memory* and *heap*). Objects allocated on the free store are independent of the scope from which they are created and "live" until they are destroyed using the **delete** operator (§4.2.2).

A simple use of **Vector** looks like this:

```
double read_and_sum(int s)
        // read s integers from cin and return their sum; s is assumed to be positive
{
        Vector v;
        vector_init(v,s);                // allocate s elements for v

        for (int i=0; i!=s; ++i)
                cin>>v.elem[i];          // read into elements
```

```
        double sum = 0;
        for (int i=0; i!=s; ++i)
                sum+=v.elem[i];                 // compute the sum of the elements
        return sum;
}
```

There is a long way to go before our Vector is as elegant and flexible as the standard-library vector. In particular, a user of Vector has to know every detail of Vector's representation. The rest of this chapter and the next two gradually improve Vector as an example of language features and techniques. Chapter 11 presents the standard-library vector, which contains many nice improvements.

I use vector and other standard-library components as examples

- to illustrate language features and design techniques, and
- to help you learn and use the standard-library components.

Don't reinvent standard-library components such as vector and string; use them.

We use . (dot) to access struct members through a name (and through a reference) and -> to access struct members through a pointer. For example:

```
void f(Vector v, Vector& rv, Vector* pv)
{
        int i1 = v.sz;          // access through name
        int i2 = rv.sz;         // access through reference
        int i3 = pv->sz;        // access through pointer
}
```

2.3 Classes

Having the data specified separately from the operations on it has advantages, such as the ability to use the data in arbitrary ways. However, a tighter connection between the representation and the operations is needed for a user-defined type to have all the properties expected of a "real type." In particular, we often want to keep the representation inaccessible to users so as to ease use, guarantee consistent use of the data, and allow us to later improve the representation. To do that we have to distinguish between the interface to a type (to be used by all) and its implementation (which has access to the otherwise inaccessible data). The language mechanism for that is called a *class*. A class has a set of *members*, which can be data, function, or type members. The interface is defined by the public members of a class, and private members are accessible only through that interface. For example:

```
class Vector {
public:
        Vector(int s) :elem{new double[s]}, sz{s} { }   // construct a Vector
        double& operator[](int i) { return elem[i]; }    // element access: subscripting
        int size() { return sz; }
private:
        double* elem;   // pointer to the elements
        int sz;         // the number of elements
};
```

Given that, we can define a variable of our new type **Vector**:

```
Vector v(6);     // a Vector with 6 elements
```

We can illustrate a **Vector** object graphically:

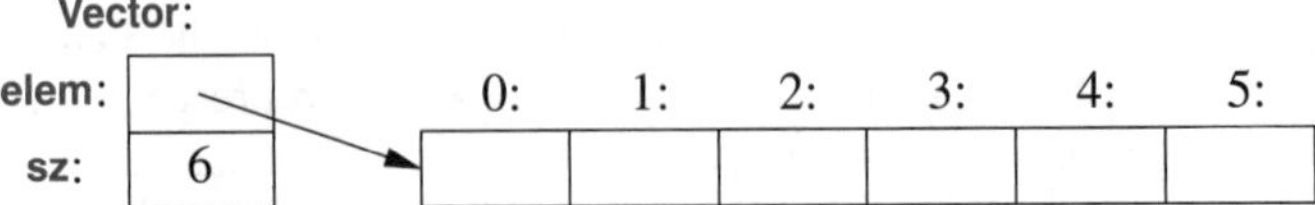

Basically, the **Vector** object is a "handle" containing a pointer to the elements (**elem**) and the number of elements (**sz**). The number of elements (6 in the example) can vary from **Vector** object to **Vector** object, and a **Vector** object can have a different number of elements at different times (§4.2.3). However, the **Vector** object itself is always the same size. This is the basic technique for handling varying amounts of information in C++: a fixed-size handle referring to a variable amount of data "elsewhere" (e.g., on the free store allocated by **new**; §4.2.2). How to design and use such objects is the main topic of Chapter 4.

Here, the representation of a **Vector** (the members **elem** and **sz**) is accessible only through the interface provided by the **public** members: **Vector()**, **operator[]()**, and **size()**. The **read_and_sum()** example from §2.2 simplifies to:

```
double read_and_sum(int s)
{
        Vector v(s);                          // make a vector of s elements
        for (int i=0; i!=v.size(); ++i)
                cin>>v[i];                    // read into elements

        double sum = 0;
        for (int i=0; i!=v.size(); ++i)
                sum+=v[i];                    // take the sum of the elements
        return sum;
}
```

A member "function" with the same name as its class is called a *constructor*, that is, a function used to construct objects of a class. So, the constructor, **Vector()**, replaces **vector_init()** from §2.2. Unlike an ordinary function, a constructor is guaranteed to be used to initialize objects of its class. Thus, defining a constructor eliminates the problem of uninitialized variables for a class.

Vector(int) defines how objects of type **Vector** are constructed. In particular, it states that it needs an integer to do that. That integer is used as the number of elements. The constructor initializes the **Vector** members using a member initializer list:

```
:elem{new double[s]}, sz{s}
```

That is, we first initialize **elem** with a pointer to **s** elements of type **double** obtained from the free store. Then, we initialize **sz** to **s**.

Access to elements is provided by a subscript function, called **operator[]**. It returns a reference to the appropriate element (a **double&** allowing both reading and writing).

The **size()** function is supplied to give users the number of elements.

Obviously, error handling is completely missing, but we'll return to that in §3.5. Similarly, we did not provide a mechanism to "give back" the array of **doubles** acquired by **new**; §4.2.2 shows how to use a destructor to elegantly do that.

There is no fundamental difference between a **struct** and a **class**; a **struct** is simply a **class** with members **public** by default. For example, you can define constructors and other member functions for a **struct**.

2.4 Unions

A **union** is a **struct** in which all members are allocated at the same address so that the **union** occupies only as much space as its largest member. Naturally, a **union** can hold a value for only one member at a time. For example, consider a symbol table entry that holds a name and a value. The value can either be a **Node*** or an **int**:

```
enum Type { ptr, num };   // a Type can hold values ptr and num (§2.5)

struct Entry {
      string name;    // string is a standard-library type
      Type t;
      Node* p;  // use p if t==ptr
      int i;        // use i if t==num
};

void f(Entry* pe)
{
      if (pe->t == num)
            cout << pe->i;
      // ...
}
```

The members **p** and **i** are never used at the same time, so space is wasted. It can be easily recovered by specifying that both should be members of a **union**, like this:

```
union Value {
      Node* p;
      int i;
};
```

The language doesn't keep track of which kind of value is held by a **union**, so the programmer must do that:

```
struct Entry {
      string name;
      Type t;
      Value v;   // use v.p if t==ptr; use v.i if t==num
};
```

```
void f(Entry* pe)
{
      if (pe->t == num)
            cout << pe->v.i;
      // ...
}
```

Maintaining the correspondence between a *type field* (here, t) and the type held in a union is error-prone. To avoid errors, we can enforce that correspondence by encapsulating the union and the type field in a class and offer access only through member functions that use the union correctly. At the application level, abstractions relying on such *tagged unions* are common and useful. The use of "naked" unions is best minimized.

The standard library type, variant, can be used to eliminate most direct uses of unions. A variant stores a value of one of a set of alternative types (§13.5.1). For example, a variant<Node*,int> can hold either a Node* or an int.

Using variant, the Entry example could be written as:

```
struct Entry {
      string name;
      variant<Node*,int> v;
};

void f(Entry* pe)
{
      if (holds_alternative<int>(pe->v))     // does *pe hold an int? (see §13.5.1)
            cout << get<int>(pe->v);         // get the int
      // ...
}
```

For many uses, a variant is simpler and safer to use than a union.

2.5 Enumerations

In addition to classes, C++ supports a simple form of user-defined type for which we can enumerate the values:

```
enum class Color { red, blue, green };
enum class Traffic_light { green, yellow, red };

Color col = Color::red;
Traffic_light light = Traffic_light::red;
```

Note that enumerators (e.g., red) are in the scope of their enum class, so that they can be used repeatedly in different enum classes without confusion. For example, Color::red is Color's red which is different from Traffic_light::red.

Enumerations are used to represent small sets of integer values. They are used to make code more readable and less error-prone than it would have been had the symbolic (and mnemonic) enumerator names not been used.

The class after the enum specifies that an enumeration is strongly typed and that its enumerators are scoped. Being separate types, enum classes help prevent accidental misuses of constants. In particular, we cannot mix Traffic_light and Color values:

```
Color x = red;                  // error: which red?
Color y = Traffic_light::red;   // error: that red is not a Color
Color z = Color::red;           // OK
```

Similarly, we cannot implicitly mix Color and integer values:

```
int i = Color::red;        // error: Color::red is not an int

Color c = 2;               // initialization error: 2 is not a Color
```

Catching attempted conversions to an enum is a good defense against errors, but often we want to initialize an enum with a value from its underlying type (by default, that's int), so that's allowed, as is explicit conversion from the underlying type:

```
Color x = Color{5};  // OK, but verbose
Color y {6};         // also OK
```

By default, an enum class has only assignment, initialization, and comparisons (e.g., == and <; §1.4) defined. However, an enumeration is a user-defined type, so we can define operators for it:

```
Traffic_light& operator++(Traffic_light& t)          // prefix increment: ++
{
     switch (t) {
     case Traffic_light::green:       return t=Traffic_light::yellow;
     case Traffic_light::yellow:      return t=Traffic_light::red;
     case Traffic_light::red:         return t=Traffic_light::green;
     }
}

Traffic_light next = ++light;          // next becomes Traffic_light::green
```

If you don't want to explicitly qualify enumerator names and want enumerator values to be ints (without the need for an explicit conversion), you can remove the class from enum class to get a "plain" enum. The enumerators from a "plain" enum are entered into the same scope as the name of their enum and implicitly converts to their integer value. For example:

```
enum Color { red, green, blue };
int col = green;
```

Here col gets the value 1. By default, the integer values of enumerators start with 0 and increase by one for each additional enumerator. The "plain" enums have been in C++ (and C) since the earliest days, so even though they are less well behaved, they are common in current code.

2.6 Advice

[1] Prefer well-defined user-defined types over built-in types when the built-in types are too low-level; §2.1.

[2] Organize related data into structures (structs or classes); §2.2; [CG: C.1].
[3] Represent the distinction between an interface and an implementation using a class; §2.3; [CG: C.3].
[4] A struct is simply a class with its members public by default; §2.3.
[5] Define constructors to guarantee and simplify initialization of classes; §2.3; [CG: C.2].
[6] Avoid "naked" unions; wrap them in a class together with a type field; §2.4; [CG: C.181].
[7] Use enumerations to represent sets of named constants; §2.5; [CG: Enum.2].
[8] Prefer class enums over "plain" enums to minimize surprises; §2.5; [CG: Enum.3].
[9] Define operations on enumerations for safe and simple use; §2.5; [CG: Enum.4].

3

Modularity

Don't interrupt me while I'm interrupting.
– Winston S. Churchill

- Introduction
- Separate Compilation
- Modules
- Namespaces
- Error Handling
  Exceptions; Invariants; Error-Handling Alternatives; Contracts; Static Assertions
- Function Arguments and Return Values
  Argument Passing; Value Return; Structured Binding
- Advice

3.1 Introduction

A C++ program consists of many separately developed parts, such as functions (§1.2.1), user-defined types (Chapter 2), class hierarchies (§4.5), and templates (Chapter 6). The key to managing this is to clearly define the interactions among those parts. The first and most important step is to distinguish between the interface to a part and its implementation. At the language level, C++ represents interfaces by declarations. A *declaration* specifies all that's needed to use a function or a type. For example:

```
double sqrt(double);      // the square root function takes a double and returns a double

class Vector {
public:
     Vector(int s);
     double& operator[](int i);
     int size();
```

```
private:
     double∗ elem; // elem points to an array of sz doubles
     int sz;
};
```

The key point here is that the function bodies, the function *definitions*, are "elsewhere." For this example, we might like for the representation of Vector to be "elsewhere" also, but we will deal with that later (abstract types; §4.3). The definition of sqrt() will look like this:

```
double sqrt(double d)          // definition of sqrt()
{
     // ... algorithm as found in math textbook ...
}
```

For Vector, we need to define all three member functions:

```
Vector::Vector(int s)                    // definition of the constructor
     :elem{new double[s]}, sz{s}         // initialize members
{
}

double& Vector::operator[](int i)        // definition of subscripting
{
     return elem[i];
}

int Vector::size()                       // definition of size()
{
     return sz;
}
```

We must define Vector's functions, but not sqrt() because it is part of the standard library. However, that makes no real difference: a library is simply "some other code we happen to use" written with the same language facilities we use.

There can be many declarations for an entity, such as a function, but only one definition.

3.2 Separate Compilation

C++ supports a notion of separate compilation where user code sees only declarations of the types and functions used. The definitions of those types and functions are in separate source files and are compiled separately. This can be used to organize a program into a set of semi-independent code fragments. Such separation can be used to minimize compilation times and to strictly enforce separation of logically distinct parts of a program (thus minimizing the chance of errors). A library is often a collection of separately compiled code fragments (e.g., functions).

Typically, we place the declarations that specify the interface to a module in a file with a name indicating its intended use. For example:

```
// Vector.h:

class Vector {
public:
        Vector(int s);
        double& operator[](int i);
        int size();
private:
        double* elem;          // elem points to an array of sz doubles
        int sz;
};
```

This declaration would be placed in a file `Vector.h`. Users then *include* that file, called a *header file*, to access that interface. For example:

```
// user.cpp:

#include "Vector.h"          // get Vector's interface
#include <cmath>             // get the standard-library math function interface including sqrt()

double sqrt_sum(Vector& v)
{
        double sum = 0;
        for (int i=0; i!=v.size(); ++i)
                sum+=std::sqrt(v[i]);                    // sum of square roots
        return sum;
}
```

To help the compiler ensure consistency, the `.cpp` file providing the implementation of `Vector` will also include the `.h` file providing its interface:

```
// Vector.cpp:

#include "Vector.h" // get Vector's interface

Vector::Vector(int s)
        :elem{new double[s]}, sz{s}            // initialize members
{
}

double& Vector::operator[](int i)
{
        return elem[i];
}

int Vector::size()
{
        return sz;
}
```

The code in `user.cpp` and `Vector.cpp` shares the `Vector` interface information presented in `Vector.h`, but the two files are otherwise independent and can be separately compiled. Graphically, the program fragments can be represented like this:

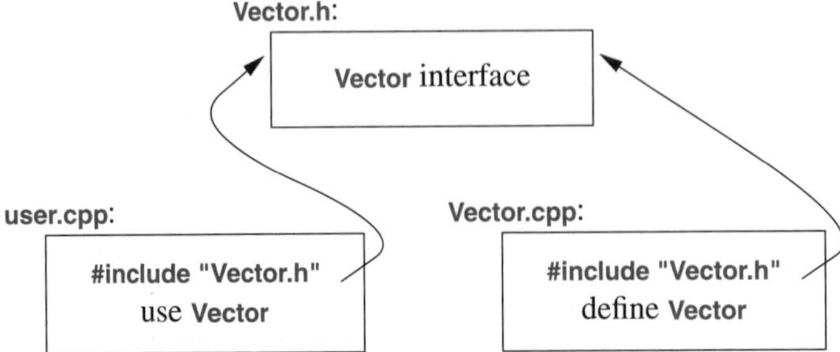

Strictly speaking, using separate compilation isn't a language issue; it is an issue of how best to take advantage of a particular language implementation. However, it is of great practical importance. The best approach to program organization is to think of the program as a set of modules with well-defined dependencies, represent that modularity logically through language features, and then exploit the modularity physically through files for effective separate compilation.

A **.cpp** file that is compiled by itself (including the **h** files it **#includes**) is called a *translation unit*. A program can consist of many thousand translation units.

3.3 Modules (C++20)

The use of **#includes** is a very old, error-prone, and rather expensive way of composing programs out of parts. If you **#include header.h** in 101 translation units, the text of **header.h** will be processed by the compiler 101 times. If you **#include header1.h** before **header2.h** the declarations and macros in **header1.h** might affect the meaning of the code in **header2.h**. If instead you **#include header2.h** before **header1.h**, it is **header2.h** that might affect the code in **header1.h**. Obviously, this is not ideal, and in fact it has been a major source of cost and bugs since 1972 when this mechanism was first introduced into C.

We are finally about to get a better way of expressing physical modules in C++. The language feature, called **modules** is not yet ISO C++, but it is an ISO Technical Specification [ModulesTS] and will be part of C++20. Implementations are in use, so I risk recommending it here even though details are likely to change and it may be years before everybody can use it in production code. Old code, in this case code using **#include**, can "live" for a very long time because it can be costly and time consuming to update.

Consider how to express the **Vector** and **sqrt_sum()** example from §3.2 using **modules**:

```
// file Vector.cpp:

module;    // this compilation will define a module

// ... here we put stuff that Vector might need for its implementation ...
```

```
export module Vector;    // defining the module called "Vector"

export class Vector {
public:
      Vector(int s);
      double& operator[](int i);
      int size();
private:
      double* elem;      // elem points to an array of sz doubles
      int sz;
};

Vector::Vector(int s)
      :elem{new double[s]}, sz{s}        // initialize members
{
}

double& Vector::operator[](int i)
{
      return elem[i];
}

int Vector::size()
{
      return sz;
}

export int size(const Vector& v) { return v.size(); }
```

This defines a **module** called **Vector**, which exports the class **Vector**, all its member functions, and the non-member function **size()**.

The way we use this **module** is to **import** it where we need it. For example:

```
// file user.cpp:

import Vector;           // get Vector's interface
#include <cmath>         // get the standard-library math function interface including sqrt()

double sqrt_sum(Vector& v)
{
      double sum = 0;
      for (int i=0; i!=v.size(); ++i)
            sum+=std::sqrt(v[i]);           // sum of square roots
      return sum;
}
```

I could have **import**ed the standard library mathematical functions also, but I used the old-fashioned **#include** just to show that you can mix old and new. Such mixing is essential for gradually upgrading older code from using **#include** to **import**.

The differences between headers and modules are not just syntactic.

- A module is compiled once only (rather than in each translation unit in which it is used).
- Two modules can be imported in either order without changing their meaning.
- If you import something into a module, users of your module do not implicitly gain access to (and are not bothered by) what you imported: import is not transitive.

The effects on maintainability and compile-time performance can be spectacular.

3.4 Namespaces

In addition to functions (§1.3), classes (§2.3), and enumerations (§2.5), C++ offers *namespaces* as a mechanism for expressing that some declarations belong together and that their names shouldn't clash with other names. For example, I might want to experiment with my own complex number type (§4.2.1, §14.4):

```
namespace My_code {
      class complex {
            // ...
      };

      complex sqrt(complex);
      // ...

      int main();
}

int My_code::main()
{
      complex z {1,2};
      auto z2 = sqrt(z);
      std::cout << '{' << z2.real() << ',' << z2.imag() << "}\n";
      // ...
}

int main()
{
      return My_code::main();
}
```

By putting my code into the namespace My_code, I make sure that my names do not conflict with the standard-library names in namespace std (§3.4). That precaution is wise, because the standard library does provide support for complex arithmetic (§4.2.1, §14.4).

The simplest way to access a name in another namespace is to qualify it with the namespace name (e.g., std::cout and My_code::main). The "real main()" is defined in the global namespace, that is, not local to a defined namespace, class, or function.

If repeatedly qualifying a name becomes tedious or distracting, we can bring the name into a scope with a using-declaration:

```
void my_code(vector<int>& x, vector<int>& y)
{
        using std::swap;            // use the standard-library swap
        // ...
        swap(x,y);                  // std::swap()
        other::swap(x,y);           // some other swap()
        // ...
}
```

A using-declaration makes a name from a namespace usable as if it was declared in the scope in which it appears. After using std::swap, it is exactly as if swap had been declared in my_code().

To gain access to all names in the standard-library namespace, we can use a using-directive:

```
using namespace std;
```

A using-directive makes unqualified names from the named namespace accessible from the scope in which we placed the directive. So after the using-directive for std, we can simply write cout rather than std::cout. By using a using-directive, we lose the ability to selectively use names from that namespace, so this facility should be used carefully, usually for a library that's pervasive in an application (e.g., std) or during a transition for an application that didn't use namespaces.

Namespaces are primarily used to organize larger program components, such as libraries. They simplify the composition of a program out of separately developed parts.

3.5 Error Handling

Error handling is a large and complex topic with concerns and ramifications that go far beyond language facilities into programming techniques and tools. However, C++ provides a few features to help. The major tool is the type system itself. Instead of painstakingly building up our applications from the built-in types (e.g., char, int, and double) and statements (e.g., if, while, and for), we build types (e.g., string, map, and regex) and algorithms (e.g., sort(), find_if(), and draw_all()) that are appropriate for our applications. Such higher-level constructs simplify our programming, limit our opportunities for mistakes (e.g., you are unlikely to try to apply a tree traversal to a dialog box), and increase the compiler's chances of catching errors. The majority of C++ language constructs are dedicated to the design and implementation of elegant and efficient abstractions (e.g., user-defined types and algorithms using them). One effect of such abstraction is that the point where a run-time error can be detected is separated from the point where it can be handled. As programs grow, and especially when libraries are used extensively, standards for handling errors become important. It is a good idea to articulate a strategy for error handling early on in the development of a program.

3.5.1 Exceptions

Consider again the Vector example. What *ought* to be done when we try to access an element that is out of range for the vector from §2.3?

- The writer of Vector doesn't know what the user would like to have done in this case (the writer of Vector typically doesn't even know in which program the vector will be running).

- The user of Vector cannot consistently detect the problem (if the user could, the out-of-range access wouldn't happen in the first place).

Assuming that out-of-range access is a kind of error that we want to recover from, the solution is for the Vector implementer to detect the attempted out-of-range access and tell the user about it. The user can then take appropriate action. For example, Vector::operator[]() can detect an attempted out-of-range access and throw an out_of_range exception:

```
double& Vector::operator[](int i)
{
        if (i<0 || size()<=i)
                throw out_of_range{"Vector::operator[]"};
        return elem[i];
}
```

The throw transfers control to a handler for exceptions of type out_of_range in some function that directly or indirectly called Vector::operator[](). To do that, the implementation will *unwind* the function call stack as needed to get back to the context of that caller. That is, the exception handling mechanism will exit scopes and functions as needed to get back to a caller that has expressed interest in handling that kind of exception, invoking destructors (§4.2.2) along the way as needed. For example:

```
void f(Vector& v)
{
        // ...
        try { // exceptions here are handled by the handler defined below

                v[v.size()] = 7; // try to access beyond the end of v
        }
        catch (out_of_range& err) {    // oops: out_of_range error
                // ... handle range error ...
                cerr << err.what() << '\n';
        }
        // ...
}
```

We put code for which we are interested in handling exceptions into a try-block. The attempted assignment to v[v.size()] will fail. Therefore, the catch-clause providing a handler for exceptions of type out_of_range will be entered. The out_of_range type is defined in the standard library (in <stdexcept>) and is in fact used by some standard-library container access functions.

I caught the exception by reference to avoid copying and used the what() function to print the error message put into it at the throw-point.

Use of the exception-handling mechanisms can make error handling simpler, more systematic, and more readable. To achieve that, don't overuse try-statements. The main technique for making error handling simple and systematic (called *Resource Acquisition Is Initialization; RAII*) is explained in §4.2.2. The basic idea behind RAII is for a constructor to acquire all resources necessary for a class to operate and have the destructor release all resources, thus making resource release guaranteed and implicit.

A function that should never throw an exception can be declared **noexcept**. For example:

```
void user(int sz) noexcept
{
    Vector v(sz);
    iota(&v[0],&v[sz],1);        // fill v with 1,2,3,4... (see §14.3)
    // ...
}
```

If all good intent and planning fails, so that **user()** still throws, **std::terminate()** is called to immediately terminate the program.

3.5.2 Invariants

The use of exceptions to signal out-of-range access is an example of a function checking its argument and refusing to act because a basic assumption, a *precondition*, didn't hold. Had we formally specified **Vector**'s subscript operator, we would have said something like "the index must be in the [**0**:**size()**) range," and that was in fact what we tested in our **operator[]()**. The [**a**:**b**) notation specifies a half-open range, meaning that **a** is part of the range, but **b** is not. Whenever we define a function, we should consider what its preconditions are and consider whether to test them (§3.5.3). For most applications it is a good idea to test simple invariants; see also §3.5.4.

However, **operator[]()** operates on objects of type **Vector** and nothing it does makes any sense unless the members of **Vector** have "reasonable" values. In particular, we did say "**elem** points to an array of **sz** doubles" but we only said that in a comment. Such a statement of what is assumed to be true for a class is called a *class invariant*, or simply an *invariant*. It is the job of a constructor to establish the invariant for its class (so that the member functions can rely on it) and for the member functions to make sure that the invariant holds when they exit. Unfortunately, our **Vector** constructor only partially did its job. It properly initialized the **Vector** members, but it failed to check that the arguments passed to it made sense. Consider:

```
Vector v(-27);
```

This is likely to cause chaos.

Here is a more appropriate definition:

```
Vector::Vector(int s)
{
    if (s<0)
        throw length_error{"Vector constructor: negative size"};
    elem = new double[s];
    sz = s;
}
```

I use the standard-library exception **length_error** to report a non-positive number of elements because some standard-library operations use that exception to report problems of this kind. If operator **new** can't find memory to allocate, it throws a **std::bad_alloc**. We can now write:

```
void test()
{
    try {
        Vector v(−27);
    }
    catch (std::length_error& err) {
        // handle negative size
    }
    catch (std::bad_alloc& err) {
        // handle memory exhaustion
    }
}
```

You can define your own classes to be used as exceptions and have them carry arbitrary information from a point where an error is detected to a point where it can be handled (§3.5.1).

Often, a function has no way of completing its assigned task after an exception is thrown. Then, "handling" an exception means doing some minimal local cleanup and rethrowing the exception. For example:

```
void test()
{
    try {
        Vector v(−27);
    }
    catch (std::length_error&) {    // do something and rethrow
        cerr << "test failed: length error\n";
        throw;      // rethrow
    }
    catch (std::bad_alloc&) {       // Ouch! this program is not designed to handle memory exhaustion
        std::terminate();      // terminate the program
    }
}
```

In well-designed code try-blocks are rare. Avoid overuse by systematically using the RAII technique (§4.2.2, §5.3).

The notion of invariants is central to the design of classes, and preconditions serve a similar role in the design of functions. Invariants

- help us to understand precisely what we want
- force us to be specific; that gives us a better chance of getting our code correct (after debugging and testing).

The notion of invariants underlies C++'s notions of resource management supported by constructors (Chapter 4) and destructors (§4.2.2, §13.2).

3.5.3 Error-Handling Alternatives

Error handling is a major issue in all real-world software, so naturally there are a variety of approaches. If an error is detected and it cannot be handled locally in a function, the function must somehow communicate the problem to some caller. Throwing an exception is C++'s most general mechanism for that.

There are languages where exceptions are designed simply to provide an alternate mechanism for returning values. C++ is not such a language: exceptions are designed to be used to report failure to complete a given task. Exceptions are integrated with constructors and destructors to provide a coherent framework for error handling and resource management (§4.2.2, §5.3). Compilers are optimized to make returning a value much cheaper than throwing the same value as an exception.

Throwing an exception is not the only way of reporting an error that cannot be handled locally. A function can indicate that it cannot perform its allotted task by:

- throwing an exception
- somehow return a value indicating failure
- terminating the program (by invoking a function like `terminate()`, `exit()`, or `abort()`).

We return an error indicator (an "error code") when:

- A failure is normal and expected. For example, it is quite normal for a request to open a file to fail (maybe there is no file of that name or maybe the file cannot be opened with the permissions requested).
- An immediate caller can reasonably be expected to handle the failure.

We throw an exception when:

- An error is so rare that a programmer is likely to forget to check for it. For example, when did you last check the return value of `printf()`?
- An error cannot be handled by an immediate caller. Instead, the error has to percolate back to an ultimate caller. For example, it is infeasible to have every function in an application reliably handle every allocation failure or network outage.
- New kinds of errors can be added in lower-modules of an application so that higher-level modules are not written to cope with such errors. For example, when a previously single-threaded application is modified to use multiple threads or resources are placed remotely to be accessed over a network.
- No suitable return path for errors codes are available. For example, a constructor does not have a return value for a "caller" to check. In particular, constructors may be invoked for several local variables or in a partially constructed complex object so that clean-up based on error codes would be quite complicated.
- The return path of a function is made more complicated or expensive by a need to pass both a value and an error indicator back (e.g., a `pair`; §13.4.3), possibly leading to the use of out-parameters, non-local error-status indicators, or other workarounds.
- The error has to be transmitted up a call chain to an "ultimate caller." Repeatedly checking an error-code would be tedious, expensive, and error-prone.
- The recovery from errors depends on the results of several function calls, leading to the need to maintain local state between calls and complicated control structures.
- The function that found the error was a callback (a function argument), so the immediate caller may not even know what function was called.
- An error implies that some "undo action" is needed.

We terminate when

- An error is of a kind from which we cannot recover. For example, for many – but not all – systems there is no reasonable way to recover from memory exhaustion.
- The system is one where error-handling is based on restarting a thread, process, or computer whenever a non-trivial error is detected.

One way to ensure termination is to add noexcept to a function so that a throw from anywhere in the function's implementation will turn into a terminate(). Note that there are applications that can't accept unconditional terminations, so alternatives must be used.

Unfortunately, these conditions are not always logically disjoint and easy to apply. The size and complexity of a program matters. Sometimes the tradeoffs change as an application evolves. Experience is required. When in doubt, prefer exceptions because their use scales better, and don't require external tools to check that all errors are handled.

Don't believe that all error codes or all exceptions are bad; there are clear uses for both. Furthermore, do not believe the myth that exception handling is slow; it is often faster than correct handling of complex or rare error conditions, and of repeated tests of error codes.

RAII (§4.2.2, §5.3) is essential for simple and efficient error-handling using exceptions. Code littered with try-blocks often simply reflects the worst aspects of error-handling strategies conceived for error codes.

3.5.4 Contracts

There is currently no general and standard way of writing optional run-time tests of invariants, preconditions, etc. A contract mechanism is proposed for C++20 [Garcia,2016] [Garcia,2018]. The aim is to support users who want to rely on testing to get programs right – running with extensive run-time checks – but then deploy code with minimal checks. This is popular in high-performance applications in organizations that rely on systematic and extensive checking.

For now, we have to rely on ad hoc mechanisms. For example, we could use a command-line macro to control a run-time check:

```
double& Vector::operator[](int i)
{
	if (RANGE_CHECK && (i<0 || size()<=i))
		throw out_of_range{"Vector::operator[]"};
	return elem[i];
}
```

The standard library offers the debug macro, assert(), to assert that a condition must hold at run time. For example:

```
void f(const char* p)
{
	assert(p!=nullptr);	// p must not be the nullptr
	// ...
}
```

If the condition of an assert() fails in "debug mode," the program terminates. If we are not in debug mode, the assert() is not checked. That's pretty crude and inflexible, but often sufficient.

3.5.5 Static Assertions

Exceptions report errors found at run time. If an error can be found at compile time, it is usually preferable to do so. That's what much of the type system and the facilities for specifying the interfaces to user-defined types are for. However, we can also perform simple checks on most properties that are known at compile time and report failures to meet our expectations as compiler error messages. For example:

```
static_assert(4<=sizeof(int), "integers are too small"); // check integer size
```

This will write **integers are too small** if **4<=sizeof(int)** does not hold; that is, if an **int** on this system does not have at least 4 bytes. We call such statements of expectations *assertions*.

The **static_assert** mechanism can be used for anything that can be expressed in terms of constant expressions (§1.6). For example:

```
constexpr double C = 299792.458;                    // km/s

void f(double speed)
{
      constexpr double local_max = 160.0/(60*60);         // 160 km/h == 160.0/(60*60) km/s

      static_assert(speed<C,"can't go that fast");        // error: speed must be a constant
      static_assert(local_max<C,"can't go that fast");    // OK

      // ...
}
```

In general, **static_assert(A,S)** prints **S** as a compiler error message if **A** is not **true**. If you don't want a specific message printed, leave out the **S** and the compiler will supply a default message:

```
static_assert(4<=sizeof(int));         // use default message
```

The default message is typically the source location of the **static_assert** plus a character representation of the asserted predicate.

The most important uses of **static_assert** come when we make assertions about types used as parameters in generic programming (§7.2, §13.9).

3.6 Function Arguments and Return Values

The primary and recommended way of passing information from one part of a program to another is through a function call. Information needed to perform a task is passed as arguments to a function and the results produced are passed back as return values. For example:

```
int sum(const vector<int>& v)
{
      int s = 0;
      for (const int i : v)
            s += i;
      return s;
}

vector fib = {1,2,3,5,8,13,21};

int x = sum(fib);          // x becomes 53
```

There are other paths through which information can be passed between functions, such as global variables (§1.5), pointer and reference parameters (§3.6.1), and shared state in a class object (Chapter 4). Global variables are strongly discouraged as a known source of errors, and state should typically be shared only between functions jointly implementing a well-defined abstraction (e.g., member functions of a class; §2.3).

Given the importance of passing information to and from functions, it is not surprising that there are a variety of ways of doing it. Key concerns are:

- Is an object copied or shared?
- If an object is shared, is it mutable?
- Is an object moved, leaving an "empty object" behind (§5.2.2)?

The default behavior for both argument passing and value return is "copy" (§1.9), but some copies can implicitly be optimized to moves.

In the sum() example, the resulting int is copied out of sum() but it would be inefficient and pointless to copy the potentially very large vector into sum(), so the argument is passed by reference (indicated by the &; §1.7).

The sum() has no reason to modify its argument. This immutability is indicated by declaring the vector argument const (§1.6), so the vector is passed by const-reference.

3.6.1 Argument Passing

First consider how to get values into a function. By default we copy ("pass-by-value") and if we want to refer to an object in the caller's environment, we use a reference ("pass-by-reference"). For example:

```
void test(vector<int> v, vector<int>& rv)          // v is passed by value; rv is passed by reference
{
     v[1] = 99;          // modify v (a local variable)
     rv[2] = 66;         // modify whatever rv refers to
}

int main()
{
     vector fib = {1,2,3,5,8,13,21};
     test(fib,fib);
     cout << fib[1] << ' ' << fib[2] << '\n';          // prints 2 66
}
```

When we care about performance, we usually pass small values by-value and larger ones by-reference. Here "small" means "something that's really cheap to copy." Exactly what "small" means depends on machine architecture, but "the size of two or three pointers or less" is a good rule of thumb.

If we want to pass by reference for performance reasons but don't need to modify the argument, we pass-by-const-reference as in the sum() example. This is by far the most common case in ordinary good code: it is fast and not error-prone.

It is not uncommon for a function argument to have a default value; that is, a value that is considered preferred or just the most common. We can specify such a default by a *default function argument*. For example:

```
void print(int value, int base =10);  // print value in base "base"

print(x,16);      // hexadecimal
print(x,60);      // sexagesimal (Sumerian)
print(x);         // use the dafault: decimal
```

This is a notationally simpler alternative to overloading:

```
void print(int value, int base);          // print value in base "base"

void print(int value)                     // print value in base 10
{
      print(value,10);
}
```

3.6.2 Value Return

Once we have computed a result, we need to get it out of the function and back to the caller. Again, the default for value return is to copy and for small objects that's ideal. We return "by reference" only when we want to grant a caller access to something that is not local to the function. For example:

```
class Vector {
public:
      // ...
      double& operator[](int i) { return elem[i]; }      // return reference to ith element
private:
      double* elem;          // elem points to an array of sz
      // ...
};
```

The ith element of a Vector exists independently of the call of the subscript operator, so we can return a reference to it.

On the other hand, a local variable disappears when the function returns, so we should not return a pointer or reference to it:

```
int& bad()
{
      int x;
      // ...
      return x;  // bad: return a reference to the local variable x
}
```

Fortunately, all major C++ compilers will catch the obvious error in bad().

Returning a reference or a value of a "small" type is efficient, but how do we pass large amounts of information out of a function? Consider:

```
Matrix operator+(const Matrix& x, const Matrix& y)
{
      Matrix res;
      // ... for all res[i,j], res[i,j] = x[i,j]+y[i,j] ...
      return res;
}

Matrix m1, m2;
// ...
Matrix m3 = m1+m2;        // no copy
```

A Matrix may be *very* large and expensive to copy even on modern hardware. So we don't copy, we give Matrix a move constructor (§5.2.2) and very cheaply move the Matrix out of operator+(). We do *not* need to regress to using manual memory management:

```
Matrix* add(const Matrix& x, const Matrix& y)        // complicated and error-prone 20th century style
{
      Matrix* p = new Matrix;
      // ... for all *p[i,j], *p[i,j] = x[i,j]+y[i,j] ...
      return p;
}

Matrix m1, m2;
// ...
Matrix* m3 = add(m1,m2);        // just copy a pointer
// ...
delete m3;                      // easily forgotten
```

Unfortunately, returning large objects by returning a pointer to it is common in older code and a major source of hard-to-find errors. Don't write such code. Note that operator+() is as efficient as add(), but far easier to define, easier to use, and less error-prone.

If a function cannot perform its required task, it can throw an exception (§3.5.1). This can help avoid code from being littered with error-code tests for "exceptional problems."

The return type of a function can be deduced from its return value. For example:

```
auto mul(int i, double d) { return i*d; }        // here, "auto" means "deduce the return type"
```

This can be convenient, especially for generic functions (function templates; §6.3.1) and lambdas (§6.3.3), but should be used carefully because a deduced type does not offer a stable interface: a change to the implementation of the function (or lambda) can change the type.

3.6.3 Structured Binding

A function can return only a single value, but that value can be a class object with many members. This allows us to efficiently return many values. For example:

```
struct Entry {
      string name;
      int value;
};
```

```
Entry read_entry(istream& is)          // naive read function (for a better version, see §10.5)
{
        string s;
        int i;
        is >> s >> i;
        return {s,i};
}

auto e = read_entry(cin);

cout << "{ " << e.name << " , " << e.value << " }\n";
```

Here, {s,i} is used to construct the Entry return value. Similarly, we can "unpack" an Entry's members into local variables:

```
auto [n,v] = read_entry(is);
cout << "{ " << n << " , " << v << " }\n";
```

The auto [n,v] declares two local variables n and v with their types deduced from read_entry()'s return type. This mechanism for giving local names to members of a class object is called *structured binding*.

Consider another example:

```
map<string,int> m;
// ... fill m ...
for (const auto [key,value] : m)
        cout << "{" << key "," << value << "}\n";
```

As usual, we can decorate auto with const and &. For example:

```
void incr(map<string,int>& m)          // increment the value of each element of m
{
        for (auto& [key,value] : m)
                ++value;
}
```

When structured binding is used for a class with no private data, it is easy to see how the binding is done: there must be the same number of names defined for the binding as there are nonstatic data members of the class, and each name introduced in the binding names the corresponding member. There will not be any difference in the object code quality compared to explicitly using a composite object; the use of structured binding is all about how best to express an idea.

It is also possible to handle classes where access is through member functions. For example:

```
complex<double> z = {1,2};
auto [re,im] = z+2;                    // re=3; im=2
```

A complex has two data members, but its interface consists of access functions, such as real() and imag(). Mapping a complex<double> to two local variables, such as re and im is feasible and efficient, but the technique for doing so is beyond the scope of this book.

3.7 Advice

[1] Distinguish between declarations (used as interfaces) and definitions (used as implementations); §3.1.
[2] Use header files to represent interfaces and to emphasize logical structure; §3.2; [CG: SF.3].
[3] #include a header in the source file that implements its functions; §3.2; [CG: SF.5].
[4] Avoid non-inline function definitions in headers; §3.2; [CG: SF.2].
[5] Prefer modules over headers (where modules are supported); §3.3.
[6] Use namespaces to express logical structure; §3.4; [CG: SF.20].
[7] Use using-directives for transition, for foundational libraries (such as std), or within a local scope; §3.4; [CG: SF.6] [CG: SF.7].
[8] Don't put a using-directive in a header file; §3.4; [CG: SF.7].
[9] Throw an exception to indicate that you cannot perform an assigned task; §3.5; [CG: E.2].
[10] Use exceptions for error handling only; §3.5.3; [CG: E.3].
[11] Use error codes when an immediate caller is expected to handle the error; §3.5.3.
[12] Throw an exception if the error is expected to percolate up through many function calls; §3.5.3.
[13] If in doubt whether to use an exception or an error code, prefer exceptions; §3.5.3.
[14] Develop an error-handling strategy early in a design; §3.5; [CG: E.12].
[15] Use purpose-designed user-defined types as exceptions (not built-in types); §3.5.1.
[16] Don't try to catch every exception in every function; §3.5; [CG: E.7].
[17] Prefer RAII to explicit try-blocks; §3.5.1, §3.5.2; [CG: E.6].
[18] If your function may not throw, declare it noexcept; §3.5; [CG: E.12].
[19] Let a constructor establish an invariant, and throw if it cannot; §3.5.2; [CG: E.5].
[20] Design your error-handling strategy around invariants; §3.5.2; [CG: E.4].
[21] What can be checked at compile time is usually best checked at compile time; §3.5.5 [CG: P.4] [CG: P.5].
[22] Pass "small" values by value and "large" values by references; §3.6.1; [CG: F.16].
[23] Prefer pass-by-const-reference over plain pass-by-reference; §3.6.1; [CG: F.17].
[24] Return values as function-return values (rather than by out-parameters); §3.6.2; [CG: F.20] [CG: F.21].
[25] Don't overuse return-type deduction; §3.6.2.
[26] Don't overuse structured binding; using a named return type is often clearer documentation; §3.6.3.

4

Classes

Those types are not "abstract";
they are as real as int *and* float.
– Doug McIlroy

- Introduction
- Concrete Types
  An Arithmetic Type; A Container; Initializing Containers
- Abstract Types
- Virtual Functions
- Class Hierarchies
  Benefits from Hierarchies; Hierarchy Navigation; Avoiding Resource Leaks
- Advice

4.1 Introduction

This chapter and the next three aim to give you an idea of C++'s support for abstraction and resource management without going into a lot of detail:

- This chapter informally presents ways of defining and using new types (*user-defined types*). In particular, it presents the basic properties, implementation techniques, and language facilities used for *concrete classes*, *abstract classes*, and *class hierarchies*.
- Chapter 5 presents the operations that have defined meaning in C++, such as constructors, destructors, and assignments. It outlines the rules for using those in combination to control the life cycle of objects and to support simple, efficient, and complete resource management.
- Chapter 6 introduces templates as a mechanism for parameterizing types and algorithms with (other) types and algorithms. Computations on user-defined and built-in types are represented as functions, sometimes generalized to *template functions* and *function objects*.
- Chapter 7 gives an overview of the concepts, techniques, and language features that underlie generic programming. The focus is on the definition and use of *concepts* for precisely

specifying interfaces to templates and guide design. *Variadic templates* are introduced for specifying the most general and most flexible interfaces.

These are the language facilities supporting the programming styles known as *object-oriented programming* and *generic programming*. Chapters 8–15 follow up by presenting examples of standard-library facilities and their use.

The central language feature of C++ is the *class*. A class is a user-defined type provided to represent a concept in the code of a program. Whenever our design for a program has a useful concept, idea, entity, etc., we try to represent it as a class in the program so that the idea is there in the code, rather than just in our heads, in a design document, or in some comments. A program built out of a well-chosen set of classes is far easier to understand and get right than one that builds everything directly in terms of the built-in types. In particular, classes are often what libraries offer.

Essentially all language facilities beyond the fundamental types, operators, and statements exist to help define better classes or to use them more conveniently. By "better," I mean more correct, easier to maintain, more efficient, more elegant, easier to use, easier to read, and easier to reason about. Most programming techniques rely on the design and implementation of specific kinds of classes. The needs and tastes of programmers vary immensely. Consequently, the support for classes is extensive. Here, we will just consider the basic support for three important kinds of classes:

- Concrete classes (§4.2)
- Abstract classes (§4.3)
- Classes in class hierarchies (§4.5)

An astounding number of useful classes turn out to be of one of these three kinds. Even more classes can be seen as simple variants of these kinds or are implemented using combinations of the techniques used for these.

4.2 Concrete Types

The basic idea of *concrete classes* is that they behave "just like built-in types." For example, a complex number type and an infinite-precision integer are much like built-in `int`, except of course that they have their own semantics and sets of operations. Similarly, a `vector` and a `string` are much like built-in arrays, except that they are better behaved (§9.2, §10.3, §11.2).

The defining characteristic of a concrete type is that its representation is part of its definition. In many important cases, such as a `vector`, that representation is only one or more pointers to data stored elsewhere, but that representation is present in each object of a concrete class. That allows implementations to be optimally efficient in time and space. In particular, it allows us to

- place objects of concrete types on the stack, in statically allocated memory, and in other objects (§1.5);
- refer to objects directly (and not just through pointers or references);
- initialize objects immediately and completely (e.g., using constructors; §2.3); and
- copy and move objects (§5.2).

The representation can be private (as it is for `Vector`; §2.3) and accessible only through the member functions, but it is present. Therefore, if the representation changes in any significant way, a user must recompile. This is the price to pay for having concrete types behave exactly like built-in types. For types that don't change often, and where local variables provide much-needed clarity and efficiency, this is acceptable and often ideal. To increase flexibility, a concrete type can keep major parts of its representation on the free store (dynamic memory, heap) and access them through the part stored in the class object itself. That's the way vector and string are implemented; they can be considered resource handles with carefully crafted interfaces.

4.2.1 An Arithmetic Type

The "classical user-defined arithmetic type" is complex:

```
class complex {
     double re, im; // representation: two doubles
public:
     complex(double r, double i) :re{r}, im{i} {}          // construct complex from two scalars
     complex(double r) :re{r}, im{0} {}                    // construct complex from one scalar
     complex() :re{0}, im{0} {}                            // default complex: {0,0}

     double real() const { return re; }
     void real(double d) { re=d; }
     double imag() const { return im; }
     void imag(double d) { im=d; }

     complex& operator+=(complex z)
     {
          re+=z.re;             // add to re and im
          im+=z.im;
          return *this;         // and return the result
     }

     complex& operator-=(complex z)
     {
          re-=z.re;
          im-=z.im;
          return *this;
     }

     complex& operator*=(complex);     // defined out-of-class somewhere
     complex& operator/=(complex);     // defined out-of-class somewhere
};
```

This is a slightly simplified version of the standard-library complex (§14.4). The class definition itself contains only the operations requiring access to the representation. The representation is simple and conventional. For practical reasons, it has to be compatible with what Fortran provided 60 years ago, and we need a conventional set of operators. In addition to the logical demands, complex must be efficient or it will remain unused. This implies that simple operations must be inlined. That is, simple operations (such as constructors, +=, and imag()) must be implemented without function calls in the generated machine code. Functions defined in a class are inlined by default. It is possible to explicitly request inlining by preceding a function declaration with the keyword inline.

An industrial-strength complex (like the standard-library one) is carefully implemented to do appropriate inlining.

A constructor that can be invoked without an argument is called a *default constructor*. Thus, complex() is complex's default constructor. By defining a default constructor you eliminate the possibility of uninitialized variables of that type.

The const specifiers on the functions returning the real and imaginary parts indicate that these functions do not modify the object for which they are called. A const member function can be invoked for both const and non-const objects, but a non-const member function can only be invoked for non-const objects. For example:

```
complex z = {1,0};
const complex cz {1,3};
z = cz;                  // OK: assigning to a non-const variable
cz = z;                  // error: complex::operator=() is a non-const member function
double x = z.real();     // OK: complex::real() is a const member function
```

Many useful operations do not require direct access to the representation of complex, so they can be defined separately from the class definition:

```
complex operator+(complex a, complex b) { return a+=b; }
complex operator–(complex a, complex b) { return a–=b; }
complex operator–(complex a) { return {–a.real(), –a.imag()}; }      // unary minus
complex operator*(complex a, complex b) { return a*=b; }
complex operator/(complex a, complex b) { return a/=b; }
```

Here, I use the fact that an argument passed by value is copied so that I can modify an argument without affecting the caller's copy and use the result as the return value.

The definitions of == and != are straightforward:

```
bool operator==(complex a, complex b)      // equal
{
      return a.real()==b.real() && a.imag()==b.imag();
}

bool operator!=(complex a, complex b)      // not equal
{
      return !(a==b);
}

complex sqrt(complex);          // the definition is elsewhere

// ...
```

Class complex can be used like this:

```
void f(complex z)
{
      complex a {2.3};          // construct {2.3,0.0} from 2.3
      complex b {1/a};
      complex c {a+z*complex{1,2.3}};
```

```
    // ...
    if (c != b)
        c = -(b/a)+2*b;
}
```

The compiler converts operators involving complex numbers into appropriate function calls. For example, c!=b means operator!=(c,b) and 1/a means operator/(complex{1},a).

User-defined operators ("overloaded operators") should be used cautiously and conventionally. The syntax is fixed by the language, so you can't define a unary /. Also, it is not possible to change the meaning of an operator for built-in types, so you can't redefine + to subtract ints.

4.2.2 A Container

A *container* is an object holding a collection of elements. We call class Vector a container because objects of type Vector are containers. As defined in §2.3, Vector isn't an unreasonable container of doubles: it is simple to understand, establishes a useful invariant (§3.5.2), provides range-checked access (§3.5.1), and provides size() to allow us to iterate over its elements. However, it does have a fatal flaw: it allocates elements using new but never deallocates them. That's not a good idea because although C++ defines an interface for a garbage collector (§5.3), it is not guaranteed that one is available to make unused memory available for new objects. In some environments you can't use a collector, and often you prefer more precise control of destruction for logical or performance reasons. We need a mechanism to ensure that the memory allocated by the constructor is deallocated; that mechanism is a *destructor*:

```
class Vector {
public:
    Vector(int s) :elem{new double[s]}, sz{s}     // constructor: acquire resources
    {
        for (int i=0; i!=s; ++i)          // initialize elements
            elem[i]=0;
    }

    ~Vector() { delete[] elem; }                 // destructor: release resources

    double& operator[](int i);
    int size() const;
private:
    double* elem;        // elem points to an array of sz doubles
    int sz;
};
```

The name of a destructor is the complement operator, ~, followed by the name of the class; it is the complement of a constructor. Vector's constructor allocates some memory on the free store (also called the *heap* or *dynamic store*) using the new operator. The destructor cleans up by freeing that memory using the delete[] operator. Plain delete deletes an individual object, delete[] deletes an array.

This is all done without intervention by users of Vector. The users simply create and use Vectors much as they would variables of built-in types. For example:

```
void fct(int n)
{
    Vector v(n);
    // ... use v ...
    {
        Vector v2(2*n);
        // ... use v and v2 ...
    } // v2 is destroyed here
    // ... use v ..
} // v is destroyed here
```

Vector obeys the same rules for naming, scope, allocation, lifetime, etc. (§1.5), as does a built-in type, such as int and char. This Vector has been simplified by leaving out error handling; see §3.5.

The constructor/destructor combination is the basis of many elegant techniques. In particular, it is the basis for most C++ general resource management techniques (§5.3, §13.2). Consider a graphical illustration of a Vector:

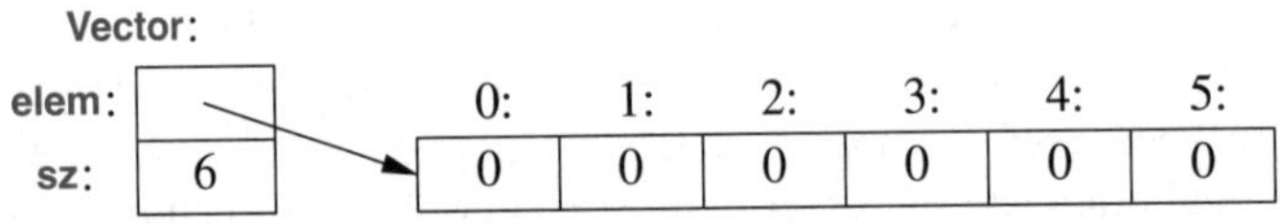

Vector:

elem:

sz: 6

0:	1:	2:	3:	4:	5:
0	0	0	0	0	0

The constructor allocates the elements and initializes the Vector members appropriately. The destructor deallocates the elements. This *handle-to-data model* is very commonly used to manage data that can vary in size during the lifetime of an object. The technique of acquiring resources in a constructor and releasing them in a destructor, known as *Resource Acquisition Is Initialization* or *RAII*, allows us to eliminate "naked new operations," that is, to avoid allocations in general code and keep them buried inside the implementation of well-behaved abstractions. Similarly, "naked delete operations" should be avoided. Avoiding naked new and naked delete makes code far less error-prone and far easier to keep free of resource leaks (§13.2).

4.2.3 Initializing Containers

A container exists to hold elements, so obviously we need convenient ways of getting elements into a container. We can create a Vector with an appropriate number of elements and then assign to them, but typically other ways are more elegant. Here, I just mention two favorites:

- *Initializer-list constructor*: Initialize with a list of elements.
- push_back(): Add a new element at the end of (at the back of) the sequence.

These can be declared like this:

```
class Vector {
public:
    Vector(std::initializer_list<double>);    // initialize with a list of doubles
    // ...
    void push_back(double);                   // add element at end, increasing the size by one
    // ...
};
```

The push_back() is useful for input of arbitrary numbers of elements. For example:

```
Vector read(istream& is)
{
      Vector v;
      for (double d; is>>d; )          // read floating-point values into d
            v.push_back(d);            // add d to v
      return v;
}
```

The input loop is terminated by an end-of-file or a formatting error. Until that happens, each number read is added to the Vector so that at the end, v's size is the number of elements read. I used a for-statement rather than the more conventional while-statement to keep the scope of d limited to the loop. The way to provide Vector with a move constructor, so that returning a potentially huge amount of data from read() is cheap, is explained in §5.2.2:

```
Vector v = read(cin);      // no copy of Vector elements here
```

The way that std::vector is represented to make push_back() and other operations that change a vector's size efficient is presented in §11.2.

The std::initializer_list used to define the initializer-list constructor is a standard-library type known to the compiler: when we use a {}-list, such as {1,2,3,4}, the compiler will create an object of type initializer_list to give to the program. So, we can write:

```
Vector v1 = {1,2,3,4,5};                // v1 has 5 elements
Vector v2 = {1.23, 3.45, 6.7, 8};       // v2 has 4 elements
```

Vector's initializer-list constructor might be defined like this:

```
Vector::Vector(std::initializer_list<double> lst)      // initialize with a list
     :elem{new double[lst.size()]}, sz{static_cast<int>(lst.size())}
{
     copy(lst.begin(),lst.end(),elem);                 // copy from lst into elem (§12.6)
}
```

Unfortunately, the standard-library uses unsigned integers for sizes and subscripts, so I need to use the ugly static_cast to explicitly convert the size of the initializer list to an int. This is pedantic because the chance that the number of elements in a handwritten list is larger than the largest integer (32,767 for 16-bit integers and 2,147,483,647 for 32-bit integers) is rather low. However, the type system has no common sense. It knows about the possible values of variables, rather than actual values, so it might complain where there is no actual violation. Such warnings can occasionally save the programmer from a bad error.

A static_cast does not check the value it is converting; the programmer is trusted to use it correctly. This is not always a good assumption, so if in doubt, check the value. Explicit type conversions (often called *casts* to remind you that they are used to prop up something broken) are best avoided. Try to use unchecked casts only for the lowest level of a system. They are error-prone.

Other casts are reinterpret_cast for treating an object as simply a sequence of bytes and const_cast for "casting away const." Judicious use of the type system and well-designed libraries allow us to eliminate unchecked casts in higher-level software.

4.3 Abstract Types

Types such as complex and Vector are called *concrete types* because their representation is part of their definition. In that, they resemble built-in types. In contrast, an *abstract type* is a type that completely insulates a user from implementation details. To do that, we decouple the interface from the representation and give up genuine local variables. Since we don't know anything about the representation of an abstract type (not even its size), we must allocate objects on the free store (§4.2.2) and access them through references or pointers (§1.7, §13.2.1).

First, we define the interface of a class Container, which we will design as a more abstract version of our Vector:

```
class Container {
public:
      virtual double& operator[](int) = 0;      // pure virtual function
      virtual int size() const = 0;             // const member function (§4.2.1)
      virtual ~Container() {}                   // destructor (§4.2.2)
};
```

This class is a pure interface to specific containers defined later. The word virtual means "may be redefined later in a class derived from this one." Unsurprisingly, a function declared virtual is called a *virtual function*. A class derived from Container provides an implementation for the Container interface. The curious =0 syntax says the function is *pure virtual*; that is, some class derived from Container *must* define the function. Thus, it is not possible to define an object that is just a Container. For example:

```
Container c;                                // error: there can be no objects of an abstract class
Container* p = new Vector_container(10);    // OK: Container is an interface
```

A Container can only serve as the interface to a class that implements its operator[]() and size() functions. A class with a pure virtual function is called an *abstract class*.

This Container can be used like this:

```
void use(Container& c)
{
      const int sz = c.size();

      for (int i=0; i!=sz; ++i)
            cout << c[i] << '\n';
}
```

Note how use() uses the Container interface in complete ignorance of implementation details. It uses size() and [ ] without any idea of exactly which type provides their implementation. A class that provides the interface to a variety of other classes is often called a *polymorphic type*.

As is common for abstract classes, Container does not have a constructor. After all, it does not have any data to initialize. On the other hand, Container does have a destructor and that destructor is virtual, so that classes derived from Container can provide implementations. Again, that is common for abstract classes because they tend to be manipulated through references or pointers, and someone destroying a Container through a pointer has no idea what resources are owned by its implementation; see also §4.5.

The abstract class Container defines only an interface and no implementation. For Container to be useful, we have to implement a container that implements the functions required by its interface. For that, we could use the concrete class Vector:

```
class Vector_container : public Container {   // Vector_container implements Container
public:
      Vector_container(int s) : v(s) { }     // Vector of s elements
      ~Vector_container() {}

      double& operator[](int i) override { return v[i]; }
      int size() const override { return v.size(); }
private:
      Vector v;
};
```

The :public can be read as "is derived from" or "is a subtype of." Class Vector_container is said to be *derived* from class Container, and class Container is said to be a *base* of class Vector_container. An alternative terminology calls Vector_container and Container *subclass* and *superclass*, respectively. The derived class is said to inherit members from its base class, so the use of base and derived classes is commonly referred to as *inheritance*.

The members operator[]() and size() are said to *override* the corresponding members in the base class Container. I used the explicit override to make clear what's intended. The use of override is optional, but being explicit allows the compiler to catch mistakes, such as misspellings of function names or slight differences between the type of a virtual function and its intended overrider. The explicit use of override is particularly useful in larger class hiearchies where it can otherwise be hard to know what is supposed to override what.

The destructor (~Vector_container()) overrides the base class destructor (~Container()). Note that the member destructor (~Vector()) is implicitly invoked by its class's destructor (~Vector_container()).

For a function like use(Container&) to use a Container in complete ignorance of implementation details, some other function will have to make an object on which it can operate. For example:

```
void g()
{
      Vector_container vc(10);       // Vector of ten elements
      // ... fill vc ...
      use(vc);
}
```

Since use() doesn't know about Vector_containers but only knows the Container interface, it will work just as well for a different implementation of a Container. For example:

```
class List_container : public Container {     // List_container implements Container
public:
      List_container() { }         // empty List
      List_container(initializer_list<double> il) : ld{il} { }
      ~List_container() {}
```

```
        double& operator[](int i) override;
        int size() const override { return ld.size(); }
private:
        std::list<double> ld;      // (standard-library) list of doubles (§11.3)
};

double& List_container::operator[](int i)
{
        for (auto& x : ld) {
                if (i==0)
                        return x;
                --i;
        }
        throw out_of_range{"List container"};
}
```

Here, the representation is a standard-library list<double>. Usually, I would not implement a container with a subscript operation using a list, because performance of list subscripting is atrocious compared to vector subscripting. However, here I just wanted to show an implementation that is radically different from the usual one.

A function can create a List_container and have use() use it:

```
void h()
{
        List_container lc = { 1, 2, 3, 4, 5, 6, 7, 8, 9 };
        use(lc);
}
```

The point is that use(Container&) has no idea if its argument is a Vector_container, a List_container, or some other kind of container; it doesn't need to know. It can use any kind of Container. It knows only the interface defined by Container. Consequently, use(Container&) needn't be recompiled if the implementation of List_container changes or a brand-new class derived from Container is used.

The flip side of this flexibility is that objects must be manipulated through pointers or references (§5.2, §13.2.1).

4.4 Virtual Functions

Consider again the use of Container:

```
void use(Container& c)
{
        const int sz = c.size();

        for (int i=0; i!=sz; ++i)
                cout << c[i] << '\n';
}
```

How is the call c[i] in use() resolved to the right operator[]()? When h() calls use(), List_container's operator[]() must be called. When g() calls use(), Vector_container's operator[]() must be called. To achieve this resolution, a **Container** object must contain information to allow it to select the right function to call at run time. The usual implementation technique is for the compiler to convert the name of a virtual function into an index into a table of pointers to functions. That table is usually called the *virtual function table* or simply the **vtbl**. Each class with virtual functions has its own **vtbl** identifying its virtual functions. This can be represented graphically like this:

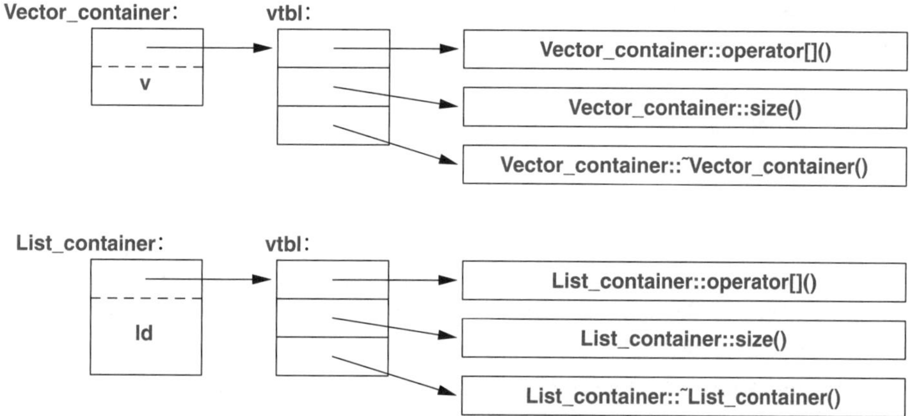

The functions in the **vtbl** allow the object to be used correctly even when the size of the object and the layout of its data are unknown to the caller. The implementation of the caller needs only to know the location of the pointer to the **vtbl** in a **Container** and the index used for each virtual function. This virtual call mechanism can be made almost as efficient as the "normal function call" mechanism (within 25%). Its space overhead is one pointer in each object of a class with virtual functions plus one **vtbl** for each such class.

4.5 Class Hierarchies

The **Container** example is a very simple example of a class hierarchy. A *class hierarchy* is a set of classes ordered in a lattice created by derivation (e.g., **: public**). We use class hierarchies to represent concepts that have hierarchical relationships, such as "A fire engine is a kind of a truck which is a kind of a vehicle" and "A smiley face is a kind of a circle which is a kind of a shape." Huge hierarchies, with hundreds of classes, that are both deep and wide are common. As a semi-realistic classic example, let's consider shapes on a screen:

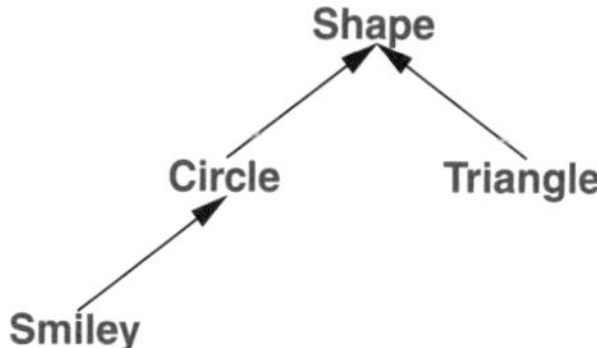

The arrows represent inheritance relationships. For example, class **Circle** is derived from class

Shape. A class hierachy is conventionally drawn growing down from the most basic class, the root, towards the (later defined) derived classes. To represent that simple diagram in code, we must first specify a class that defines the general properties of all shapes:

```
class Shape {
public:
      virtual Point center() const =0;         // pure virtual
      virtual void move(Point to) =0;

      virtual void draw() const = 0;           // draw on current "Canvas"
      virtual void rotate(int angle) = 0;

      virtual ~Shape() {}                      // destructor
      // ...
};
```

Naturally, this interface is an abstract class: as far as representation is concerned, *nothing* (except the location of the pointer to the vtbl) is common for every Shape. Given this definition, we can write general functions manipulating vectors of pointers to shapes:

```
void rotate_all(vector<Shape*>& v, int angle) // rotate v's elements by angle degrees
{
      for (auto p : v)
            p->rotate(angle);
}
```

To define a particular shape, we must say that it is a Shape and specify its particular properties (including its virtual functions):

```
class Circle : public Shape {
public:
      Circle(Point p, int rad);          // constructor

      Point center() const override
      {
            return x;
      }
      void move(Point to) override
      {
            x = to;
      }

      void draw() const override;
      void rotate(int) override {}             // nice simple algorithm
private:
      Point x;    // center
      int r;      // radius
};
```

So far, the Shape and Circle example provides nothing new compared to the Container and Vector_container example, but we can build further:

```
class Smiley : public Circle {  // use the circle as the base for a face
public:
     Smiley(Point p, int rad) : Circle{p,rad}, mouth{nullptr} { }

     ~Smiley()
     {
          delete mouth;
          for (auto p : eyes)
               delete p;
     }

     void move(Point to) override;

     void draw() const override;
     void rotate(int) override;

     void add_eye(Shape* s)
     {
          eyes.push_back(s);
     }
     void set_mouth(Shape* s);
     virtual void wink(int i);          // wink eye number i

     // ...

private:
     vector<Shape*> eyes;               // usually two eyes
     Shape* mouth;
};
```

The push_back() member of vector copies its argument into the vector (here, eyes) as the last element, increasing that vector's size by one.

We can now define Smiley::draw() using calls to Smiley's base and member draw()s:

```
void Smiley::draw() const
{
     Circle::draw();
     for (auto p : eyes)
          p->draw();
     mouth->draw();
}
```

Note the way that Smiley keeps its eyes in a standard-library vector and deletes them in its destructor. Shape's destructor is virtual and Smiley's destructor overrides it. A virtual destructor is essential for an abstract class because an object of a derived class is usually manipulated through the interface provided by its abstract base class. In particular, it may be deleted through a pointer to a base class. Then, the virtual function call mechanism ensures that the proper destructor is called. That destructor then implicitly invokes the destructors of its bases and members.

In this simplified example, it is the programmer's task to place the eyes and mouth appropriately within the circle representing the face.

We can add data members, operations, or both as we define a new class by derivation. This gives great flexibility with corresponding opportunities for confusion and poor design.

4.5.1 Benefits from Hierarchies

A class hierarchy offers two kinds of benefits:

- *Interface inheritance*: An object of a derived class can be used wherever an object of a base class is required. That is, the base class acts as an interface for the derived class. The Container and Shape classes are examples. Such classes are often abstract classes.
- *Implementation inheritance*: A base class provides functions or data that simplifies the implementation of derived classes. Smiley's uses of Circle's constructor and of Circle::draw() are examples. Such base classes often have data members and constructors.

Concrete classes – especially classes with small representations – are much like built-in types: we define them as local variables, access them using their names, copy them around, etc. Classes in class hierarchies are different: we tend to allocate them on the free store using new, and we access them through pointers or references. For example, consider a function that reads data describing shapes from an input stream and constructs the appropriate Shape objects:

```
enum class Kind { circle, triangle, smiley };

Shape* read_shape(istream& is)    // read shape descriptions from input stream is
{
    // ... read shape header from is and find its Kind k ...

    switch (k) {
    case Kind::circle:
        // read circle data {Point,int} into p and r
        return new Circle{p,r};
    case Kind::triangle:
        // read triangle data {Point,Point,Point} into p1, p2, and p3
        return new Triangle{p1,p2,p3};
    case Kind::smiley:
        // read smiley data {Point,int,Shape,Shape,Shape} into p, r, e1, e2, and m
        Smiley* ps = new Smiley{p,r};
        ps->add_eye(e1);
        ps->add_eye(e2);
        ps->set_mouth(m);
        return ps;
    }
}
```

A program may use that shape reader like this:

```
void user()
{
      std::vector<Shape*> v;
      while (cin)
            v.push_back(read_shape(cin));
      draw_all(v);                          // call draw() for each element
      rotate_all(v,45);                     // call rotate(45) for each element
      for (auto p : v)                      // remember to delete elements
            delete p;
}
```

Obviously, the example is simplified – especially with respect to error handling – but it vividly illustrates that user() has absolutely no idea of which kinds of shapes it manipulates. The user() code can be compiled once and later used for new Shapes added to the program. Note that there are no pointers to the shapes outside user(), so user() is responsible for deallocating them. This is done with the delete operator and relies critically on Shape's virtual destructor. Because that destructor is virtual, delete invokes the destructor for the most derived class. This is crucial because a derived class may have acquired all kinds of resources (such as file handles, locks, and output streams) that need to be released. In this case, a Smiley deletes its eyes and mouth objects. Once it has done that, it calls Circle's destructor. Objects are constructed "bottom up" (base first) by constructors and destroyed "top down" (derived first) by destructors.

4.5.2 Hierarchy Navigation

The read_shape() function returns Shape* so that we can treat all Shapes alike. However, what can we do if we want to use a member function that is only provided by a particular derived class, such as Smiley's wink()? We can ask "is this Shape a kind of Smiley?" using the dynamic_cast operator:

```
Shape* ps {read_shape(cin)};

if (Smiley* p = dynamic_cast<Smiley*>(ps)) { // ... does ps point to a Smiley? ...
      // ... a Smiley; use it
}
else {
      // ... not a Smiley, try something else ...
}
```

If at run time the object pointed to by the argument of dynamic_cast (here, ps) is not of the expected type (here, Smiley) or a class derived from the expected type, dynamic_cast returns nullptr.

We use dynamic_cast to a pointer type when a pointer to an object of a different derived class is a valid argument. We then test whether the result is nullptr. This test can often conveniently be placed in the initialization of a variable in a condition.

When a different type is unacceptable, we can simply dynamic_cast to a reference type. If the object is not of the expected type, dynamic_cast throws a bad_cast exception:

```
Shape* ps {read_shape(cin)};
Smiley& r {dynamic_cast<Smiley&>(*ps)};     // somewhere, catch std::bad_cast
```

Code is cleaner when dynamic_cast is used with restraint. If we can avoid using type information, we can write simpler and more efficient code, but occasionally type information is lost and must be recovered. This typically happens when we pass an object to some system that accepts an interface specified by a base class. When that system later passes the object back to us, we might have to recover the original type. Operations similar to dynamic_cast are known as "is kind of" and "is instance of" operations.

4.5.3 Avoiding Resource Leaks

Experienced programmers will have noticed that I left open three opportunities for mistakes:

- The implementer of Smiley may fail to delete the pointer to mouth.
- A user of read_shape() might fail to delete the pointer returned.
- The owner of a container of Shape pointers might fail to delete the objects pointed to.

In that sense, pointers to objects allocated on the free store is dangerous: a "plain old pointer" should not be used to represent ownership. For example:

```
void user(int x)
{
        Shape* p = new Circle{Point{0,0},10};
        // ...
        if (x<0) throw Bad_x{};     // potential leak
        if (x==0) return;           // potential leak
        // ...
        delete p;
}
```

This will leak unless x is positive. Assigning the result of new to a "naked pointer" is asking for trouble.

One simple solution to such problems is to use a standard-library unique_ptr (§13.2.1) rather than a "naked pointer" when deletion is required:

```
class Smiley : public Circle {
        // ...
private:
        vector<unique_ptr<Shape>> eyes; // usually two eyes
        unique_ptr<Shape> mouth;
};
```

This is an example of a simple, general, and efficient technique for resource management (§5.3).

As a pleasant side effect of this change, we no longer need to define a destructor for Smiley. The compiler will implicitly generate one that does the required destruction of the unique_ptrs (§5.3) in the vector. The code using unique_ptr will be exactly as efficient as code using the raw pointers correctly.

Now consider users of read_shape():

```
unique_ptr<Shape> read_shape(istream& is) // read shape descriptions from input stream is
{
        // read shape header from is and find its Kind k
```

```
        switch (k) {
        case Kind::circle:
                // read circle data {Point,int} into p and r
                return unique_ptr<Shape>{new Circle{p,r}};          // §13.2.1
        // ...
}

void user()
{
        vector<unique_ptr<Shape>> v;
        while (cin)
                v.push_back(read_shape(cin));
        draw_all(v);                        // call draw() for each element
        rotate_all(v,45);                   // call rotate(45) for each element
} // all Shapes implicitly destroyed
```

Now each object is owned by a unique_ptr that will delete the object when it is no longer needed, that is, when its unique_ptr goes out of scope.

For the unique_ptr version of user() to work, we need versions of draw_all() and rotate_all() that accept vector<unique_ptr<Shape>>s. Writing many such _all() functions could become tedious, so §6.3.2 shows an alternative.

4.6 Advice

[1] Express ideas directly in code; §4.1; [CG: P.1].
[2] A concrete type is the simplest kind of class. Where applicable, prefer a concrete type over more complicated classes and over plain data structures; §4.2; [CG: C.10].
[3] Use concrete classes to represent simple concepts; §4.2.
[4] Prefer concrete classes over class hierarchies for performance-critical components; §4.2.
[5] Define constructors to handle initialization of objects; §4.2.1, §5.1.1; [CG: C.40] [CG: C.41].
[6] Make a function a member only if it needs direct access to the representation of a class; §4.2.1; [CG: C.4].
[7] Define operators primarily to mimic conventional usage; §4.2.1; [CG: C.160].
[8] Use nonmember functions for symmetric operators; §4.2.1; [CG: C.161].
[9] Declare a member function that does not modify the state of its object const; §4.2.1.
[10] If a constructor acquires a resource, its class needs a destructor to release the resource; §4.2.2; [CG: C.20].
[11] Avoid "naked" new and delete operations; §4.2.2; [CG: R.11].
[12] Use resource handles and RAII to manage resources; §4.2.2; [CG: R.1].
[13] If a class is a container, give it an initializer-list constructor; §4.2.3; [CG: C.103].
[14] Use abstract classes as interfaces when complete separation of interface and implementation is needed; §4.3; [CG: C.122].
[15] Access polymorphic objects through pointers and references; §4.3.
[16] An abstract class typically doesn't need a constructor; §4.3; [CG: C.126].
[17] Use class hierarchies to represent concepts with inherent hierarchical structure; §4.5.

[18] A class with a virtual function should have a virtual destructor; §4.5; [CG: C.127].
[19] Use override to make overriding explicit in large class hierarchies; §4.5.1; [CG: C.128].
[20] When designing a class hierarchy, distinguish between implementation inheritance and interface inheritance; §4.5.1; [CG: C.129].
[21] Use dynamic_cast where class hierarchy navigation is unavoidable; §4.5.2; [CG: C.146].
[22] Use dynamic_cast to a reference type when failure to find the required class is considered a failure; §4.5.2; [CG: C.147].
[23] Use dynamic_cast to a pointer type when failure to find the required class is considered a valid alternative; §4.5.2; [CG: C.148].
[24] Use unique_ptr or shared_ptr to avoid forgetting to delete objects created using new; §4.5.3; [CG: C.149].

5

Essential Operations

When someone says
I want a programming language in which
I need only say what I wish done,
give him a lollipop.
– Alan Perlis

- Introduction
  Essential Operations; Conversions; Member Initializers
- Copy and Move
  Copying Containers; Moving Containers
- Resource Management
- Conventional Operations
  Comparisons; Container Operations; Input and Output Operators; User-Defined Literals; **swap()**; **hash<>**
- Advice

5.1 Introduction

Some operations, such as initialization, assignment, copy, and move, are fundamental in the sense that language rules make assumptions about them. Other operations, such as == and <<, have conventional meanings that are perilous to ignore.

5.1.1 Essential Operations

Construction of objects plays a key role in many designs. This wide variety of uses is reflected in the range and flexibility of the language features supporting initialization.

Constructors, destructors, and copy and move operations for a type are not logically separate. We must define them as a matched set or suffer logical or performance problems. If a class **X** has a destructor that performs a nontrivial task, such as free-store deallocation or lock release, the class is likely to need the full complement of functions:

```
class X {
public:
      X(Sometype);                  // "ordinary constructor": create an object
      X();                          // default constructor
      X(const X&);                  // copy constructor
      X(X&&);                       // move constructor
      X& operator=(const X&);  // copy assignment: clean up target and copy
      X& operator=(X&&);            // move assignment: clean up target and move
      ~X();                         // destructor: clean up
      // ...
};
```

There are five situations in which an object can be copied or moved:

- As the source of an assignment
- As an object initializer
- As a function argument
- As a function return value
- As an exception

An assignment uses a copy or move assignment operator. In principle, the other cases use a copy or move constructor. However, a copy or move constructor invocation is often optimized away by constructing the object used to initialize right in the target object. For example:

```
X make(Sometype);
X x = make(value);
```

Here, a compiler will typically construct the X from make() directly in x; thus eliminating ("eliding") a copy.

In addition to the initialization of named objects and of objects on the free store, constructors are used to initialize temporary objects and to implement explicit type conversion.

Except for the "ordinary constructor," these special member functions will be generated by the compiler as needed. If you want to be explicit about generating default implementations, you can:

```
class Y {
public:
      Y(Sometype);
      Y(const Y&) = default;     // I really do want the default copy constructor
      Y(Y&&) = default;          // and the default move constructor
      // ...
};
```

If you are explicit about some defaults, other default definitions will not be generated.

When a class has a pointer member, it is usually a good idea to be explicit about copy and move operations. The reason is that a pointer may point to something that the class needs to delete, in which case the default memberwise copy would be wrong. Alternatively, it might point to something that the class must *not* delete. In either case, a reader of the code would like to know. For an example, see §5.2.1.

A good rule of thumb (sometimes called *the rule of zero*) is to either define all of the essential operations or none (using the default for all). For example:

```
struct Z {
      Vector v;
      string s;
};

Z z1;             // default initialize z1.v and z1.s
Z z2 = z1;        // default copy z1.v and z1.s
```

Here, the compiler will synthesize memberwise default construction, copy, move, and destructor as needed, and all with the correct semantics.
To complement =default, we have =delete to indicate that an operation is not to be generated. A base class in a class hierarchy is the classical example where we don't want to allow a memberwise copy. For example:

```
class Shape {
public:
      Shape(const Shape&) =delete;                  // no copy operations
      Shape& operator=(const Shape&) =delete;
      // ...
};

void copy(Shape& s1, const Shape& s2)
{
      s1 = s2;    // error: Shape copy is deleted
}
```

A =delete makes an attempted use of the deleted function a compile-time error; =delete can be used to suppress any function, not just essential member functions.

5.1.2 Conversions

A constructor taking a single argument defines a conversion from its argument type. For example, complex (§4.2.1) provides a constructor from a double:

```
complex z1 = 3.14;  // z1 becomes {3.14,0.0}
complex z2 = z1*2;  // z2 becomes z1*{2.0,0} == {6.28,0.0}
```

This implicit conversion is sometimes ideal, but not always. For example, Vector (§4.2.2) provides a constructor from an int:

```
Vector v1 = 7;  // OK: v1 has 7 elements
```

This is typically considered unfortunate, and the standard-library vector does not allow this int-to-vector "conversion."

The way to avoid this problem is to say that only explicit "conversion" is allowed; that is, we can define the constructor like this:

```
class Vector {
public:
      explicit Vector(int s);        // no implicit conversion from int to Vector
      // ...
};
```

That gives us:

```
Vector v1(7);    // OK: v1 has 7 elements
Vector v2 = 7;   // error: no implicit conversion from int to Vector
```

When it comes to conversions, more types are like **Vector** than are like **complex**, so use **explicit** for constructors that take a single argument unless there is a good reason not to.

5.1.3 Member Initializers

When a data member of a class is defined, we can supply a default initializer called a *default member initializer*. Consider a revision of **complex** (§4.2.1):

```
class complex {
      double re = 0;
      double im = 0; // representation: two doubles with default value 0.0
public:
      complex(double r, double i) :re{r}, im{i} {}      // construct complex from two scalars: {r,i}
      complex(double r) :re{r} {}                        // construct complex from one scalar: {r,0}
      complex() {}                                       // default complex: {0,0}
      // ...
}
```

The default value is used whenever a constructor doesn't provide a value. This simplifies code and helps us to avoid accidentally leaving a member uninitialized.

5.2 Copy and Move

By default, objects can be copied. This is true for objects of user-defined types as well as for built-in types. The default meaning of copy is memberwise copy: copy each member. For example, using **complex** from §4.2.1:

```
void test(complex z1)
{
      complex z2 {z1};     // copy initialization
      complex z3;
      z3 = z2;             // copy assignment
      // ...
}
```

Now **z1**, **z2**, and **z3** have the same value because both the assignment and the initialization copied both members.

When we design a class, we must always consider if and how an object might be copied. For simple concrete types, memberwise copy is often exactly the right semantics for copy. For some sophisticated concrete types, such as Vector, memberwise copy is not the right semantics for copy; for abstract types it almost never is.

5.2.1 Copying Containers

When a class is a *resource handle* – that is, when the class is responsible for an object accessed through a pointer – the default memberwise copy is typically a disaster. Memberwise copy would violate the resource handle's invariant (§3.5.2). For example, the default copy would leave a copy of a Vector referring to the same elements as the original:

```
void bad_copy(Vector v1)
{
      Vector v2 = v1;         // copy v1's representation into v2
      v1[0] = 2;              // v2[0] is now also 2!
      v2[1] = 3;              // v1[1] is now also 3!
}
```

Assuming that v1 has four elements, the result can be represented graphically like this:

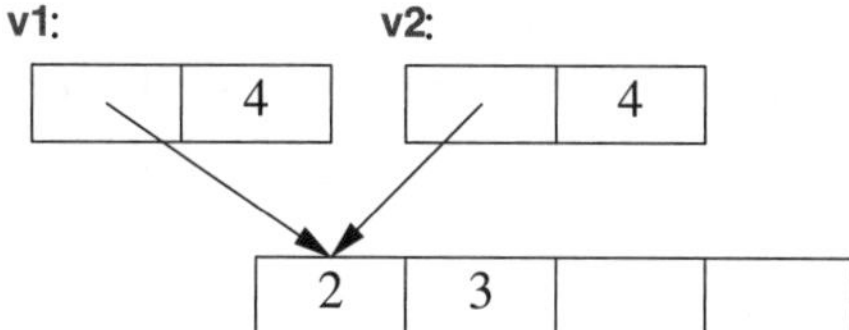

Fortunately, the fact that Vector has a destructor is a strong hint that the default (memberwise) copy semantics is wrong and the compiler should at least warn against this example. We need to define better copy semantics.

Copying of an object of a class is defined by two members: a *copy constructor* and a *copy assignment*:

```
class Vector {
private:
      double* elem; // elem points to an array of sz doubles
      int sz;
public:
      Vector(int s);                          // constructor: establish invariant, acquire resources
      ~Vector() { delete[] elem; }            // destructor: release resources

      Vector(const Vector& a);                // copy constructor
      Vector& operator=(const Vector& a);     // copy assignment

      double& operator[](int i);
      const double& operator[](int i) const;

      int size() const;
};
```

A suitable definition of a copy constructor for Vector allocates the space for the required number of elements and then copies the elements into it so that after a copy each Vector has its own copy of the elements:

```
Vector::Vector(const Vector& a)     // copy constructor
        :elem{new double[a.sz]},    // allocate space for elements
         sz{a.sz}
{
        for (int i=0; i!=sz; ++i)   // copy elements
                elem[i] = a.elem[i];
}
```

The result of the v2=v1 example can now be presented as:

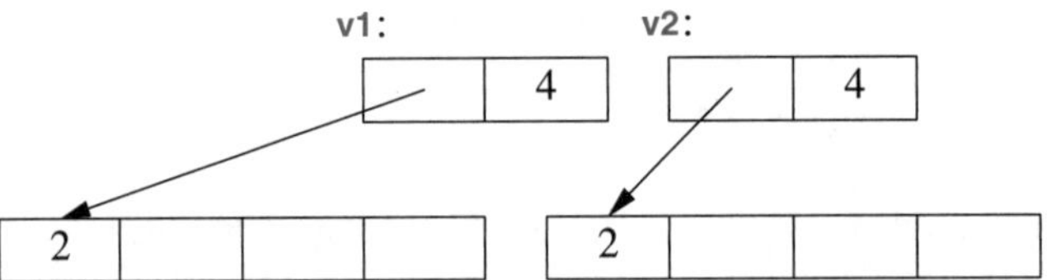

Of course, we need a copy assignment in addition to the copy constructor:

```
Vector& Vector::operator=(const Vector& a)        // copy assignment
{
        double* p = new double[a.sz];
        for (int i=0; i!=a.sz; ++i)
                p[i] = a.elem[i];
        delete[] elem;          // delete old elements
        elem = p;
        sz = a.sz;
        return *this;
}
```

The name this is predefined in a member function and points to the object for which the member function is called.

5.2.2 Moving Containers

We can control copying by defining a copy constructor and a copy assignment, but copying can be costly for large containers. We avoid the cost of copying when we pass objects to a function by using references, but we can't return a reference to a local object as the result (the local object would be destroyed by the time the caller got a chance to look at it). Consider:

```
Vector operator+(const Vector& a, const Vector& b)
{
        if (a.size()!=b.size())
                throw Vector_size_mismatch{};

        Vector res(a.size());
```

```
        for (int i=0; i!=a.size(); ++i)
              res[i]=a[i]+b[i];
        return res;
}
```

Returning from a + involves copying the result out of the local variable res and into some place where the caller can access it. We might use this + like this:

```
void f(const Vector& x, const Vector& y, const Vector& z)
{
        Vector r;
        // ...
        r = x+y+z;
        // ...
}
```

That would be copying a Vector at least twice (one for each use of the + operator). If a Vector is large, say, 10,000 doubles, that could be embarrassing. The most embarrassing part is that res in operator+() is never used again after the copy. We didn't really want a copy; we just wanted to get the result out of a function: we wanted to *move* a Vector rather than *copy* it. Fortunately, we can state that intent:

```
class Vector {
        // ...

        Vector(const Vector& a);                    // copy constructor
        Vector& operator=(const Vector& a);         // copy assignment

        Vector(Vector&& a);                         // move constructor
        Vector& operator=(Vector&& a);              // move assignment
};
```

Given that definition, the compiler will choose the *move constructor* to implement the transfer of the return value out of the function. This means that r=x+y+z will involve no copying of Vectors. Instead, Vectors are just moved.

As is typical, Vector's move constructor is trivial to define:

```
Vector::Vector(Vector&& a)
        :elem{a.elem},              // "grab the elements" from a
         sz{a.sz}
{
        a.elem = nullptr;           // now a has no elements
        a.sz = 0;
}
```

The && means "rvalue reference" and is a reference to which we can bind an rvalue. The word "rvalue" is intended to complement "lvalue," which roughly means "something that can appear on the left-hand side of an assignment." So an rvalue is – to a first approximation – a value that you can't assign to, such as an integer returned by a function call. Thus, an rvalue reference is a reference to something that *nobody else* can assign to, so we can safely "steal" its value. The res local variable in operator+() for Vectors is an example.

A move constructor does *not* take a **const** argument: after all, a move constructor is supposed to remove the value from its argument. A *move assignment* is defined similarly.

A move operation is applied when an rvalue reference is used as an initializer or as the right-hand side of an assignment.

After a move, a moved-from object should be in a state that allows a destructor to be run. Typically, we also allow assignment to a moved-from object. The standard-library algorithms (Chapter 12) assumes that. Our **Vector** does that.

Where the programmer knows that a value will not be used again, but the compiler can't be expected to be smart enough to figure that out, the programmer can be specific:

```
Vector f()
{
        Vector x(1000);
        Vector y(2000);
        Vector z(3000);
        z = x;                  // we get a copy (x might be used later in f())
        y = std::move(x);       // we get a move (move assignment)
        // ... better not use x here ...
        return z;               // we get a move
}
```

The standard-library function **move()** doesn't actually move anything. Instead, it returns a reference to its argument from which we may move – an *rvalue reference*; it is a kind of cast (§4.2.3).

Just before the **return** we have:

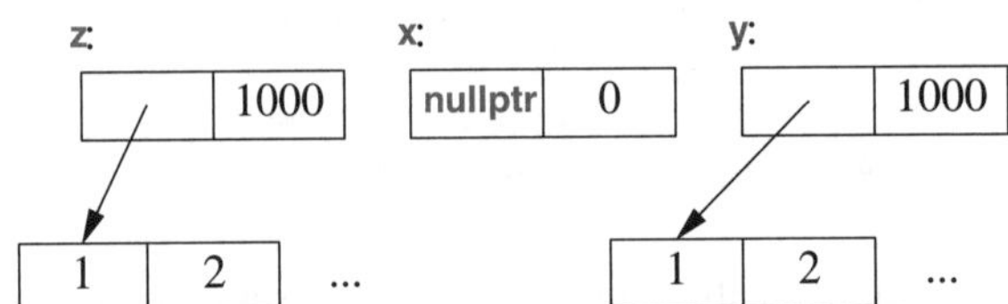

When we return from **f()**, **z** is destroyed after its elements has been moved out of **f()** by the **return**. However, **y**'s destructor will **delete[]** its elements.

The compiler is obliged (by the C++ standard) to eliminate most copies associated with initialization, so move constructors are not invoked as often as you might imagine. This *copy elision* eliminates even the very minor overhead of a move. On the other hand, it is typically not possible to implicitly eliminate copy or move operations from assignments, so move assignments can be critical for performance.

5.3 Resource Management

By defining constructors, copy operations, move operations, and a destructor, a programmer can provide complete control of the lifetime of a contained resource (such as the elements of a container). Furthermore, a move constructor allows an object to move simply and cheaply from one scope to another. That way, objects that we cannot or would not want to copy out of a scope can be simply and cheaply moved out instead. Consider a standard-library **thread** representing a concurrent activity (§15.2) and a **Vector** of a million **doubles**. We can't copy the former and don't want to copy the latter.

```
std::vector<thread> my_threads;

Vector init(int n)
{
     thread t {heartbeat};                    // run heartbeat concurrently (in a separate thread)
     my_threads.push_back(std::move(t));      // move t into my_threads (§13.2.2)
     // ... more initialization ...

     Vector vec(n);
     for (int i=0; i!=vec.size(); ++i)
          vec[i] = 777;
     return vec;                              // move vec out of init()
}

auto v = init(1'000'000);            // start heartbeat and initialize v
```

Resource handles, such as **Vector** and **thread**, are superior alternatives to direct use of built-in pointers in many cases. In fact, the standard-library "smart pointers," such as **unique_ptr**, are themselves resource handles (§13.2.1).

I used the standard-library **vector** to hold the **threads** because we don't get to parameterize our simple **Vector** with an element type until §6.2.

In very much the same way that **new** and **delete** disappear from application code, we can make pointers disappear into resource handles. In both cases, the result is simpler and more maintainable code, without added overhead. In particular, we can achieve *strong resource safety*; that is, we can eliminate resource leaks for a general notion of a resource. Examples are **vectors** holding memory, **threads** holding system threads, and **fstreams** holding file handles.

In many languages, resource management is primarily delegated to a garbage collector. C++ also offers a garbage collection interface so that you can plug in a garbage collector. However, I consider garbage collection the last choice after cleaner, more general, and better localized alternatives to resource management have been exhausted. My ideal is not to create any garbage, thus eliminating the need for a garbage collector: Do not litter!

Garbage collection is fundamentally a global memory management scheme. Clever implementations can compensate, but as systems are getting more distributed (think caches, multicores, and clusters), locality is more important than ever.

Also, memory is not the only resource. A resource is anything that has to be acquired and (explicitly or implicitly) released after use. Examples are memory, locks, sockets, file handles, and thread handles. Unsurprisingly, a resource that is not just memory is called a *non-memory resource*. A good resource management system handles all kinds of resources. Leaks must be avoided in any long-running system, but excessive resource retention can be almost as bad as a leak. For example, if a system holds on to memory, locks, files, etc. for twice as long, the system needs to be provisioned with potentially twice as many resources.

Before resorting to garbage collection, systematically use resource handles: let each resource have an owner in some scope and by default be released at the end of its owners scope. In C++, this is known as *RAII* (*Resource Acquisition Is Initialization*) and is integrated with error handling in the form of exceptions. Resources can be moved from scope to scope using move semantics or "smart pointers," and shared ownership can be represented by "shared pointers" (§13.2.1).

In the C++ standard library, RAII is pervasive: for example, memory (`string`, `vector`, `map`, `unordered_map`, etc.), files (`ifstream`, `ofstream`, etc.), threads (`thread`), locks (`lock_guard`, `unique_lock`, etc.), and general objects (through `unique_ptr` and `shared_ptr`). The result is implicit resource management that is invisible in common use and leads to low resource retention durations.

5.4 Conventional Operations

Some operations have conventional meanings when defined for a type. These conventional meanings are often assumed by programmers and libraries (notably, the standard library), so it is wise to conform to them when designing new types for which the operations make sense.

- Comparisons: `==`, `!=`, `<`, `<=`, `>`, and `>=` (§5.4.1)
- Container operations: `size()`, `begin()`, and `end()` (§5.4.2)
- Input and output operations: `>>` and `<<` (§5.4.3)
- User-defined literals (§5.4.4)
- `swap()` (§5.4.5)
- Hash functions: `hash<>` (§5.4.6)

5.4.1 Comparisons

The meaning of the equality comparisons (`==` and `!=`) is closely related to copying. After a copy, the copies should compare equal:

```
X a = something;
X b = a;
assert(a==b);   // if a!=b here, something is very odd (§3.5.4).
```

When defining `==`, also define `!=` and make sure that `a!=b` means `!(a==b)`.

Similarly, if you define `<`, also define `<=`, `>` , `>=`, and make sure that the usual equivalences hold:

- `a<=b` means `(a<b)||(a==b)` and `!(b<a)`.
- `a>b` means `b<a`.
- `a>=b` means `(a>b)||(a==b)` and `!(a<b)`.

To give identical treatment to both operands of a binary operator, such as `==`, it is best defined as a free-standing function in the namespace of its class. For example:

```
namespace NX {
        class X {
                // ...
        };
        bool operator==(const X&, const X&);
        // ...
};
```

5.4.2 Container Operations

Unless there is a really good reason not to, design containers in the style of the standard-library containers (Chapter 11). In particular, make the container resource safe by implementing it as a handle with appropriate essential operations (§5.1.1, §5.2).

The standard-library containers all know their number of elements and we can obtain it by calling size(). For example:

```
for (size_t i = 0; i<c.size(); ++i)        // size_t is the name of the type returned by a standard-library size()
      c[i] = 0;
```

However, rather than traversing containers using indices from 0 to size(), the standard algorithms (Chapter 12) rely on the notion of *sequences* delimited by pairs of *iterators*:

```
for (auto p = c.begin(); p!=c.end(); ++p)
      *p = 0;
```

Here, c.begin() is an iterator pointing to the first element of c and c.end() points one-beyond-the-last element of c. Like pointers, iterators support ++ to move to the next element and * to access the value of the element pointed to. This *iterator model* (§12.3) allows for great generality and efficiency. Iterators are used to pass sequences to standard-library algorithms. For example:

```
sort(v.begin(),v.end());
```

For details and more container operations, see Chapter 11 and Chapter 12.

Another way of using the number of elements implicitly is a range-for loop:

```
for (auto& x : c)
      x = 0;
```

This uses c.begin() and c.end() implicitly and is roughly equivalent to the more explicit loop.

5.4.3 Input and Output Operations

For pairs of integers, << means left-shift and >> means right-shift. However, for iostreams, they are the output and input operator, respectively (§1.8, Chapter 10). For details and more I/O operations, see Chapter 10.

5.4.4 User-Defined Literals

One purpose of classes was to enable the programmer to design and implement types to closely mimic built-in types. Constructors provide initialization that equals or exceeds the flexibility and efficiency of built-in type initialization, but for built-in types, we have literals:

- 123 is an int.
- 0xFF00u is an unsigned int.
- 123.456 is a double.
- "Surprise!" is a const char[10].

It can be useful to provide such literals for a user-defined type also. This is done by defining the meaning of a suitable suffix to a literal, so we can get

- "Surprise!"s is a std::string.
- 123s is seconds.
- 12.7i is imaginary so that 12.7i+47 is a complex number (i.e., {47,12.7}).

In particular, we can get these examples from the standard library by using suitable headers and namespaces:

Standard-Library Suffixes for Literals		
<chrono>	std::literals::chrono_literals	h, min, s, ms, us, ns
<string>	std::literals::string_literals	s
<string_view>	std::literals::string_literals	sv
<complex>	std::literals::complex_literals	i, il, if

Unsurprisingly, literals with user-defined suffixes are called *user-defined literals* or *UDLs*. Such literals are defined using *literal operators*. A literal operator converts a literal of its argument type, followed by a subscript, into its return type. For example, the i for imaginary suffix might be implemented like this:

```
constexpr complex<double> operator""i(long double arg)      // imaginary literal
{
     return {0,arg};
}
```

Here

- The operator"" indicates that we are defining a literal operator.
- The i after the "literal indicator" "" is the suffix to which the operator gives a meaning.
- The argument type, long double, indicates that the suffix (i) is being defined for a floating-point literal.
- The return type, complex<double>, specifies the type of the resulting literal.

Given that, we can write

```
complex<double> z = 2.7182818+6.283185i;
```

5.4.5 swap()

Many algorithms, most notably sort(), use a swap() function that exchanges the values of two objects. Such algorithms generally assume that swap() is very fast and doesn't throw an exception. The standard-library provides a std::swap(a,b) implemented as three move operations: (tmp=a, a=b, b=tmp). If you design a type that is expensive to copy and could plausibly be swapped (e.g., by a sort function), then give it move operations or a swap() or both. Note that the standard-library containers (Chapter 11) and string (§9.2.1) have fast move operations.

5.4.6 hash<>

The standard-library unordered_map<K,V> is a hash table with K as the key type and V as the value type (§11.5). To use a type X as a key, we must define hash<X>. The standard library does that for us for common types, such as std::string.

5.5 Advice

[1] Control construction, copy, move, and destruction of objects; §5.1.1; [CG: R.1].
[2] Design constructors, assignments, and the destructor as a matched set of operations; §5.1.1; [CG: C.22].
[3] Define all essential operations or none; §5.1.1; [CG: C.21].
[4] If a default constructor, assignment, or destructor is appropriate, let the compiler generate it (don't rewrite it yourself); §5.1.1; [CG: C.20].
[5] If a class has a pointer member, consider if it needs a user-defined or deleted destructor, copy and move; §5.1.1; [CG: C.32] [CG: C.33].
[6] If a class has a user-defined destructor, it probably needs user-defined or deleted copy and move; §5.2.1.
[7] By default, declare single-argument constructors `explicit`; §5.1.1; [CG: C.46].
[8] If a class member has a reasonable default value, provide it as a data member initializer; §5.1.3; [CG: C.48].
[9] Redefine or prohibit copying if the default is not appropriate for a type; §5.2.1, §4.6.5; [CG: C.61].
[10] Return containers by value (relying on move for efficiency); §5.2.2; [CG: F.20].
[11] For large operands, use `const` reference argument types; §5.2.2; [CG: F.16].
[12] Provide strong resource safety; that is, never leak anything that you think of as a resource; §5.3; [CG: R.1].
[13] If a class is a resource handle, it needs a user-defined constructor, a destructor, and non-default copy operations; §5.3; [CG: R.1].
[14] Overload operations to mimic conventional usage; §5.4; [CG: C.160].
[15] Follow the standard-library container design; §5.4.2; [CG: C.100].

6

Templates

Your quote here.
– B. Stroustrup

- Introduction
- Parameterized Types
  Constrained Template Arguments; Value Template Arguments; Template Argument Deduction
- Parameterized Operations
  Function Templates; Function Objects; Lambda Expressions
- Template Mechanisms
  Variable Templates; Aliases; Compile-Time if
- Advice

6.1 Introduction

Someone who wants a vector is unlikely always to want a vector of doubles. A vector is a general concept, independent of the notion of a floating-point number. Consequently, the element type of a vector ought to be represented independently. A *template* is a class or a function that we parameterize with a set of types or values. We use templates to represent ideas that are best understood as something general from which we can generate specific types and functions by specifying arguments, such as the vector's element type double.

6.2 Parameterized Types

We can generalize our vector-of-doubles type to a vector-of-anything type by making it a template and replacing the specific type double with a type parameter. For example:

```
template<typename T>
class Vector {
private:
      T* elem;  // elem points to an array of sz elements of type T
      int sz;
public:
      explicit Vector(int s);           // constructor: establish invariant, acquire resources
      ~Vector() { delete[] elem; }      // destructor: release resources

      // ... copy and move operations ...

      T& operator[](int i);                   // for non-const Vectors
      const T& operator[](int i) const;       // for const Vectors (§4.2.1)
      int size() const { return sz; }
};
```

The template<typename T> prefix makes T a parameter of the declaration it prefixes. It is C++'s version of the mathematical "for all T" or more precisely "for all types T." If you want the mathematical "for all T, such that P(T)," you need concepts (§6.2.1, §7.2). Using class to introduce a type parameter is equivalent to using typename, and in older code we often see template<class T> as the prefix.

The member functions might be defined similarly:

```
template<typename T>
Vector<T>::Vector(int s)
{
      if (s<0)
            throw Negative_size{};
      elem = new T[s];
      sz = s;
}

template<typename T>
const T& Vector<T>::operator[](int i) const
{
      if (i<0 || size()<=i)
            throw out_of_range{"Vector::operator[]"};
      return elem[i];
}
```

Given these definitions, we can define Vectors like this:

```
Vector<char> vc(200);          // vector of 200 characters
Vector<string> vs(17);         // vector of 17 strings
Vector<list<int>> vli(45);     // vector of 45 lists of integers
```

The >> in Vector<list<int>> terminates the nested template arguments; it is not a misplaced input operator.

We can use Vectors like this:

```
void write(const Vector<string>& vs)          // Vector of some strings
{
      for (int i = 0; i!=vs.size(); ++i)
            cout << vs[i] << '\n';
}
```

To support the range-for loop for our Vector, we must define suitable begin() and end() functions:

```
template<typename T>
T* begin(Vector<T>& x)
{
      return x.size() ? &x[0] : nullptr;       // pointer to first element or nullptr
}

template<typename T>
T* end(Vector<T>& x)
{
      return x.size() ? &x[0]+x.size() : nullptr;       // pointer to one-past-last element
}
```

Given those, we can write:

```
void f2(Vector<string>& vs)     // Vector of some strings
{
      for (auto& s : vs)
            cout << s << '\n';
}
```

Similarly, we can define lists, vectors, maps (that is, associative arrays), unordered maps (that is, hash tables), etc., as templates (Chapter 11).

Templates are a compile-time mechanism, so their use incurs no run-time overhead compared to hand-crafted code. In fact, the code generated for Vector<double> is identical to the code generated for the version of Vector from Chapter 4. Furthermore, the code generated for the standard-library vector<double> is likely to be better (because more effort has gone into its implementation).

A template plus a set of template arguments is called an *instantiation* or a *specialization*. Late in the compilation process, at *instantiation time*, code is generated for each instantiation used in a program (§7.5). The code generated is type checked so that the generated code is as type safe as handwritten code. Unfortunately, that type check often occurs late in the compilation process, at instantiation time.

6.2.1 Constrained Template Arguments (C++20)

Most often, a template will make sense only for template arguments that meet certain criteria. For example, a Vector typically offers a copy operation, and if it does, it must require that its elements must be copyable. That is, we must require that Vector's template argument is not just a typename but an Element where "Element" specifies the requirements of a type that can be an element:

```
template<Element T>
class Vector {
private:
      T* elem;  // elem points to an array of sz elements of type T
      int sz;
      // ...
};
```

This template<Element T> prefix is C++'s version of mathematic's "for all T such that Element(T)"; that is, Element is a predicate that checks whether T has all the properties that a Vector requires. Such a predicate is called a *concept* (§7.2). A template argument for which a concept is specified is called a *constrained argument* and a template for which an argument is constrained is called a *constrained template*.

It is a compile-time error to try to instantiate a template with a type that does not meet its requirements. For example:

```
Vector<int> v1;      // OK: we can copy an int
Vector<thread> v2;  // error: we can't copy a standard thread (§15.2)
```

Since C++ does not officially support concepts before C++20, older code uses unconstrained template arguments and leaves requirements to documentation.

6.2.2 Value Template Arguments

In addition to type arguments, a template can take value arguments. For example:

```
template<typename T, int N>
struct Buffer {
      using value_type = T;
      constexpr int size() { return N; }
      T[N];
      // ...
};
```

The alias (value_type) and the constexpr function are provided to allow users (read-only) access to the template arguments.

Value arguments are useful in many contexts. For example, Buffer allows us to create arbitrarily sized buffers with no use of the free store (dynamic memory):

```
Buffer<char,1024> glob;  // global buffer of characters (statically allocated)

void fct()
{
      Buffer<int,10> buf;  // local buffer of integers (on the stack)
      // ...
}
```

A template value argument must be a constant expression.

6.2.3 Template Argument Deduction

Consider using the standard-library template pair:

```
pair<int,double> p = {1,5.2};
```

Many have found the need to specify the template argument types tedious, so the standard library offers a function, make_pair(), that deduces the template arguments of the pair it returns from its function arguments:

```
auto p = make_pair(1,5.2);        // p is a pair<int,double>
```

This leads to the obvious question "Why can't we just deduce template parameters from constructor arguments?" So, in C++17, we can. That is:

```
pair p = {1,5.2};        // p is a pair<int,double>
```

This is not just a problem with pair; make_ functions are very common. Consider a simple example:

```
template<typename T>
class Vector {
public:
        Vector(int);
        Vector(initializer_list<T>);        // initializer-list constructor
        // ...
};

Vector v1 {1,2,3};        // deduce v1's element type from the initializer element type
Vector v2 = v1;           // deduce v2's element type from v1's element type

auto p = new Vector{1,2,3};        // p points to a Vector<int>

Vector<int> v3(1);    // here we need to be explicit about the element type (no element type is mentioned)
```

Clearly, this simplifies notation and can eliminate annoyances caused by mistyping redundant template argument types. However, it is not a panacea. Deduction can cause surprises (both for make_ functions and constructors). Consider:

```
Vector<string> vs1 {"Hello", "World"};   // Vector<string>
Vector vs {"Hello", "World"};            // deduces to Vector<const char*> (Surprise?)
Vector vs2 {"Hello"s, "World"s};         // deduces to Vector<string>
Vector vs3 {"Hello"s, "World"};          // error: the initializer list is not homogenous
```

The type of a C-style string literal is const char* (§1.7.1). If that was not what was intended, use the s suffix to make it a proper string (§9.2). If elements of an initializer list have differing types, we cannot deduce a unique element type, so we get an error.

When a template argument cannot be deduced from the constructor arguments, we can help by providing a *deduction guide*. Consider:

```
template<typename T>
class Vector2 {
public:
      using value_type = T;
      // ...
      Vector2(initializer_list<T>);      // initializer-list constructor

      template<typename Iter>
            Vector2(Iter b, Iter e);      // [b:e) range constructor
      // ...
};

Vector2 v1 {1,2,3,4,5};                  // element type is int
Vector2 v2(v1.begin(),v1.begin()+2);
```

Obviously, `v2` should be a `Vector2<int>`, but without help, the compiler cannot deduce that. The code only states that there is a constructor from a pair of values of the same type. Without language support for concepts (§7.2), the compiler cannot assume anything about that type. To allow deduction, we can add a *deduction guide* after the declaration of `Vector2`:

```
template<typename Iter>
      Vector2(Iter,Iter) -> Vector2<typename Iter::value_type>;
```

That is, if we see a `Vector2` initialized by a pair of iterators, we should deduce `Vector2::value_type` to be the iterator's value type.

The effects of deduction guides are often subtle, so it is best to design class templates so that deduction guides are not needed. However, the standard library is full of classes that don't (yet) use `concept`s (§7.2) and have such ambiguities, so it uses quite a few deduction guides.

6.3 Parameterized Operations

Templates have many more uses than simply parameterizing a container with an element type. In particular, they are extensively used for parameterization of both types and algorithms in the standard library (§11.6, §12.6).

There are three ways of expressing an operation parameterized by types or values:

- A function template
- A function object: an object that can carry data and be called like a function
- A lambda expression: a shorthand notation for a function object

6.3.1 Function Templates

We can write a function that calculates the sum of the element values of any sequence that a range-`for` can traverse (e.g., a container) like this:

```
template<typename Sequence, typename Value>
Value sum(const Sequence& s, Value v)
{
     for (auto x : s)
          v+=x;
     return v;
}
```

The Value template argument and the function argument v are there to allow the caller to specify the type and initial value of the accumulator (the variable in which to accumulate the sum):

```
void user(Vector<int>& vi, list<double>& ld, vector<complex<double>>& vc)
{
     int x = sum(vi,0);                        // the sum of a vector of ints (add ints)
     double d = sum(vi,0.0);                   // the sum of a vector of ints (add doubles)
     double dd = sum(ld,0.0);                  // the sum of a list of doubles
     auto z = sum(vc,complex{0.0,0.0});        // the sum of a vector of complex<double>s
}
```

The point of adding ints in a double would be to gracefully handle a number larger than the largest int. Note how the types of the template arguments for sum<Sequence,Value> are deduced from the function arguments. Fortunately, we do not need to explicitly specify those types.

This sum() is a simplified version of the standard-library accumulate() (§14.3).

A function template can be a member function, but not a virtual member. The compiler would not know all instantiations of such a template in a program, so it could not generate a vtbl (§4.4).

6.3.2 Function Objects

One particularly useful kind of template is the *function object* (sometimes called a *functor*), which is used to define objects that can be called like functions. For example:

```
template<typename T>
class Less_than {
     const T val;     // value to compare against
public:
     Less_than(const T& v) :val{v} { }
     bool operator()(const T& x) const { return x<val; } // call operator
};
```

The function called operator() implements the "function call," "call," or "application" operator ().

We can define named variables of type Less_than for some argument type:

```
Less_than lti {42};                  // lti(i) will compare i to 42 using < (i<42)
Less_than lts {"Backus"s};           // lts(s) will compare s to "Backus" using < (s<"Backus")
Less_than<string> lts2 {"Naur"};     // "Naur" is a C-style string, so we need <string> to get the right <
```

We can call such an object, just as we call a function:

```
void fct(int n, const string& s)
{
      bool b1 = lti(n);        // true if n<42
      bool b2 = lts(s);        // true if s<"Backus"
      // ...
}
```

Such function objects are widely used as arguments to algorithms. For example, we can count the occurrences of values for which a predicate returns `true`:

```
template<typename C, typename P>
      // requires Sequence<C> && Callable<P,Value_type<P>>
int count(const C& c, P pred)
{
      int cnt = 0;
      for (const auto& x : c)
            if (pred(x))
                  ++cnt;
      return cnt;
}
```

A *predicate* is something that we can invoke to return `true` or `false`. For example:

```
void f(const Vector<int>& vec, const list<string>& lst, int x, const string& s)
{
      cout << "number of values less than " << x << ": " << count(vec,Less_than{x}) << '\n';
      cout << "number of values less than " << s << ": " << count(lst,Less_than{s}) << '\n';
}
```

Here, `Less_than{x}` constructs an object of type `Less_than<int>`, for which the call operator compares to the `int` called `x`; `Less_than{s}` constructs an object that compares to the `string` called `s`. The beauty of these function objects is that they carry the value to be compared against with them. We don't have to write a separate function for each value (and each type), and we don't have to introduce nasty global variables to hold values. Also, for a simple function object like `Less_than`, inlining is simple, so a call of `Less_than` is far more efficient than an indirect function call. The ability to carry data plus their efficiency makes function objects particularly useful as arguments to algorithms.

Function objects used to specify the meaning of key operations of a general algorithm (such as `Less_than` for `count()`) are often referred to as *policy objects*.

6.3.3 Lambda Expressions

In §6.3.2, we defined `Less_than` separately from its use. That can be inconvenient. Consequently, there is a notation for implicitly generating function objects:

```
void f(const Vector<int>& vec, const list<string>& lst, int x, const string& s)
{
      cout << "number of values less than " << x
            << ": " << count(vec,[&](int a){ return a<x; })
            << '\n';
```

```
        cout << "number of values less than " << s
             << ": " << count(lst,[&](const string& a){ return a<s; })
             << '\n';
}
```

The notation [&](int a){ return a<x; } is called a *lambda expression*. It generates a function object exactly like Less_than<int>{x}. The [&] is a *capture list* specifying that all local names used in the lambda body (such as x) will be accessed through references. Had we wanted to "capture" only x, we could have said so: [&x]. Had we wanted to give the generated object a copy of x, we could have said so: [=x]. Capture nothing is [ ], capture all local names used by reference is [&], and capture all local names used by value is [=].

Using lambdas can be convenient and terse, but also obscure. For nontrivial actions (say, more than a simple expression), I prefer to name the operation so as to more clearly state its purpose and to make it available for use in several places in a program.

In §4.5.3, we noted the annoyance of having to write many functions to perform operations on elements of vectors of pointers and unique_ptrs, such as draw_all() and rotate_all(). Function objects (in particular, lambdas) can help by allowing us to separate the traversal of the container from the specification of what is to be done with each element.

First, we need a function that applies an operation to each object pointed to by the elements of a container of pointers:

```
template<typename C, typename Oper>
void for_all(C& c, Oper op)          // assume that C is a container of pointers
     // requires Sequence<C> && Callable<Oper,Value_type<C>> (see §7.2.1)
{
     for (auto& x : c)
          op(x);                      // pass op() a reference to each element pointed to
}
```

Now, we can write a version of user() from §4.5 without writing a set of _all functions:

```
void user2()
{
     vector<unique_ptr<Shape>> v;
     while (cin)
          v.push_back(read_shape(cin));
     for_all(v,[](unique_ptr<Shape>& ps){ ps->draw(); });            // draw_all()
     for_all(v,[](unique_ptr<Shape>& ps){ ps->rotate(45); });        // rotate_all(45)
}
```

I pass a unique_ptr<Shape>& to a lambda so that for_all() doesn't have to care exactly how the objects are stored. In particular, those for_all() calls do not affect the lifetime of the Shapes passed and the bodies of the lambdas use the argument just as if they had been a plain-old pointers.

Like a function, a lambda can be generic. For example:

```
template<class S>
void rotate_and_draw(vector<S>& v, int r)
{
     for_all(v,[](auto& s){ s->rotate(r); s->draw(); });
}
```

Here, like in variable declarations, **auto** means that any type is accepted as an initializer (an argument is considered to initialize the formal parameter in a call). This makes a lambda with an **auto** parameter a template, a *generic lambda*. For reasons lost in standards committee politics, this use of **auto** is not currently allowed for function arguments.

We can call this generic **rotate_and_draw()** with any container of objects that you can **draw()** and **rotate()**. For example:

```
void user4()
{
	vector<unique_ptr<Shape>> v1;
	vector<Shape*> v2;
	// ...
	rotate_and_draw(v1,45);
	rotate_and_draw(v2,90);
}
```

Using a lambda, we can turn any statement into an expression. This is mostly used to provide an operation to compute a value as an argument value, but the ability is general. Consider a complicated initialization:

```
enum class Init_mode { zero, seq, cpy, patrn };	// initializer alternatives

// messy code:

// int n, Init_mode m, vector<int>& arg, and iterators p and q are defined somewhere

vector<int> v;

switch (m) {
case zero:
	v = vector<int>(n);	// n elements initialized to 0
	break;
case cpy:
	v = arg;
	break;
};

// ...

if (m == seq)
	v.assign(p,q);		// copy from sequence [p:q)

// ...
```

This is a stylized example, but unfortunately not atypical. We need to select among a set of alternatives for initializing a data structure (here **v**) and we need to do different computations for different alternatives. Such code is often messy, deemed essential "for efficiency," and a source of bugs:

- The variable could be used before it gets its intended value.
- The "initialization code" could be mixed with other code, making it hard to comprehend.

- When "initialization code" is mixed with other code it is easier to forget a case.
- This isn't initialization, it's assignment.

Instead, we could convert it to a lambda used as an initializer:

```
// int n, Init_mode m, vector<int>& arg, and iterators p and q are defined somewhere

vector<int> v = [&] {
      switch (m) {
      case zero:
            return vector<int>(n);          // n elements initialized to 0
      case seq:
            return vector<int>{p,q};        // copy from sequence [p:q)
      case cpy:
            return arg;
      }
}();
// ...
```

I still "forgot" a `case`, but now that's easily spotted.

6.4 Template Mechanisms

To define good templates, we need some supporting language facilities:

- Values dependent on a type: *variable templates* (§6.4.1).
- Aliases for types and templates: *alias templates* (§6.4.2).
- A compile-time selection mechanism: `if constexpr` (§6.4.3).
- A compile-time mechanism to inquire about properties of types and expressions: `requires`-expressions (§7.2.3).

In addition, `constexpr` functions (§1.6) and `static_asserts` (§3.5.5) often take part in template design and use.

These basic mechanisms are primarily tools for building general, foundational abstractions.

6.4.1 Variable Templates

When we use a type, we often want constants and values of that type. This is of course also the case when we use a class template: when we define a `C<T>`, we often want constants and variables of type `T` and other types depending on `T`. Here is an example from a fluid dynamic simulation [Garcia,2015]:

```
template <class T>
      constexpr T viscosity = 0.4;

template <class T>
      constexpr space_vector<T> external_acceleration = { T{}, T{-9.8}, T{} };

auto vis2 = 2*viscosity<double>;
auto acc = external_acceleration<float>;
```

Here, `space_vector` is a three-dimensional vector.

Naturally, we can use arbitrary expressions of suitable type as initializers. Consider:

```
template<typename T, typename T2>
      constexpr bool Assignable = is_assignable<T&,T2>::value;    // is_assignable is a type trait (§13.9.1)

template<typename T>
void testing()
{
      static_assert(Assignable<T&,double>, "can't assign a double");
      static_assert(Assignable<T&,string>, "can't assign a string");
}
```

After some significant mutations, this idea becomes the heart of concept definitions (§7.2).

6.4.2 Aliases

Surprisingly often, it is useful to introduce a synonym for a type or a template. For example, the standard header <cstddef> contains a definition of the alias size_t, maybe:

```
using size_t = unsigned int;
```

The actual type named size_t is implementation-dependent, so in another implementation size_t may be an unsigned long. Having the alias size_t allows the programmer to write portable code.

It is very common for a parameterized type to provide an alias for types related to their template arguments. For example:

```
template<typename T>
class Vector {
public:
      using value_type = T;
      // ...
};
```

In fact, every standard-library container provides value_type as the name of its value type (Chapter 11). This allows us to write code that will work for every container that follows this convention. For example:

```
template<typename C>
using Value_type = typename C::value_type;          // the type of C's elements

template<typename Container>
void algo(Container& c)
{
      Vector<Value_type<Container>> vec;          // keep results here
      // ...
}
```

The aliasing mechanism can be used to define a new template by binding some or all template arguments. For example:

```
template<typename Key, typename Value>
class Map {
    // ...
};

template<typename Value>
using String_map = Map<string,Value>;

String_map<int> m;        // m is a Map<string,int>
```

6.4.3 Compile-Time if

Consider writing an operation that can use one of two operations slow_and_safe(T) or simple_and_fast(T). Such problems abound in foundational code where generality and optimal performance are essential. The traditional solution is to write a pair of overloaded functions and select the most appropriate based on a trait (§13.9.1), such as the standard-library is_pod. If a class hierarchy is involved, a base class can provide the slow_and_safe general operation and a derived class can override with a simple_and_fast implementation.

In C++17, we can use a compile-time if:

```
template<typename T>
void update(T& target)
{
    // ...
    if constexpr(is_pod<T>::value)
        simple_and_fast(target); // for "plain old data"
    else
        slow_and_safe(target);
    // ...
}
```

The is_pod<T> is a type trait (§13.9.1) that tells us whether a type can be trivially copied.

Only the selected branch of an if constexpr is instantiated. This solution offers optimal performance and locality of the optimization.

Importantly, an if constexpr is not a text-manipulation mechanism and cannot be used to break the usual rules of grammar, type, and scope. For example:

```
template<typename T>
void bad(T arg)
{
    if constexpr(Something<T>::value)
        try {                          // syntax error

    g(arg);

    if constexpr(Something<T>::value)
        } catch(...) { /* ... */ }     // syntax error
}
```

Allowing such text manipulation could seriously compromise readability of code and create problems for tools relying on modern program representation techniques (such as "abstract syntax trees").

6.5 Advice

[1] Use templates to express algorithms that apply to many argument types; §6.1; [CG: T.2].
[2] Use templates to express containers; §6.2; [CG: T.3].
[3] Use templates to raise the level of abstraction of code; §6.2; [CG: T.1].
[4] Templates are type safe, but checking happens too late; §6.2.
[5] Let constructors or function templates deduce class template argument types; §6.2.3.
[6] Use function objects as arguments to algorithms; §6.3.2; [CG: T.40].
[7] Use a lambda if you need a simple function object in one place only; §6.3.2.
[8] A virtual function member cannot be a template member function; §6.3.1.
[9] Use template aliases to simplify notation and hide implementation details; §6.4.2.
[10] To use a template, make sure its definition (not just its declaration) is in scope; §7.5.
[11] Templates offer compile-time "duck typing"; §7.5.
[12] There is no separate compilation of templates: #include template definitions in every translation unit that uses them.

7

Concepts and Generic Programming

Programming:
you have to start with interesting algorithms.
– Alex Stepanov

- Introduction
- Concepts
  Use of Concepts; Concept-Based Overloading; Valid Code; Definition of Concepts
- Generic Programming
  Use of Concepts; Abstraction Using Templates
- Variadic Templates
  Fold Expressions; Forwarding Arguments
- Template Compilation Model
- Advice

7.1 Introduction

What are templates for? In other words, what programming techniques are effective when you use templates? Templates offer:

- The ability to pass types (as well as values and templates) as arguments without loss of information. This implies excellent opportunities for inlining, of which current implementations take great advantage.
- Opportunities to weave together information from different contexts at instantiation time. This implies optimization opportunities.
- The ability to pass constant values as arguments. This implies the ability to do compile-time computation.

In other words, templates provide a powerful mechanism for compile-time computation and type manipulation that can lead to very compact and efficient code. Remember that types (classes) can contain both code (§6.3.2) and values (§6.2.2).

The first and most common use of templates is to support *generic programming*, that is, programming focused on the design, implementation, and use of general algorithms. Here, "general" means that an algorithm can be designed to accept a wide variety of types as long as they meet the algorithm's requirements on its arguments. Together with concepts, the template is C++'s main support for generic programming. Templates provide (compile-time) parametric polymorphism.

7.2 Concepts (C++20)

Consider the sum() from §6.3.1:

```
template<typename Seq, typename Num>
Num sum(Seq s, Num v)
{
      for (const auto& x : s)
            v+=x;
      return v;
}
```

It can be invoked for any data structure that supports begin() and end() so that the range-for will work. Such structures include the standard-library vector, list, and map. Furthermore, the element type of the data structure is limited only by its use: it must be a type that we can add to the Value argument. Examples are ints, doubles, and Matrixes (for any reasonable definition of Matrix). We could say that the sum() algorithm is generic in two dimensions: the type of the data structure used to store elements ("the sequence") and the type of elements.

So, sum() requires that its first template argument is some kind of sequence and its second template argument is some kind of number. We call such requirements *concepts*.

Language support for concepts is not yet ISO C++, but it is an ISO Technical Specification [ConceptsTS]. Implementations are in use, so I risk recommending it here even though details are likely to change and it may be years before everybody can use it in production code.

7.2.1 Use of Concepts

Most template arguments must meet specific requirements for the template to compile properly and for the generated code to work properly. That is, most templates must be constrained templates (§6.2.1). The type-name introducer typename is the least constraining, requiring only that the argument be a type. Usually, we can do better than that. Consider that sum() again:

```
template<Sequence Seq, Number Num>
Num sum(Seq s, Num v)
{
      for (const auto& x : s)
            v+=x;
      return v;
}
```

That's much clearer. Once we have defined what the concepts Sequence and Number mean, the compiler can reject bad calls by looking at sum()'s interface only, rather than looking at its implementation. This improves error reporting.

However, the specification of sum()'s interface is not complete: I "forgot" to say that we should be able to add elements of a Sequence to a Number. We can do that:

```
template<Sequence Seq, Number Num>
    requires Arithmetic<Value_type<Seq>,Num>
Num sum(Seq s, Num n);
```

The Value_type of a sequence is the type of the elements in the sequence. Arithmetic<X,Y> is a concept specifying that we can do arithmetic with numbers of types X and Y. This saves us from accidentally trying to calculate the sum() of a vector<string> or a vector<int*> while still accepting vector<int> and vector<complex<double>>.

In this example, we needed only +=, but for simplicity and flexibility, we should not constrain our template argument too tightly. In particular, we might someday want to express sum() in terms of + and = rather than +=, and then we'd be happy that we used a general concept (here, Arithmetic) rather than a narrow requirement to "have +=."

Partial specifications, as in the first sum() using concepts, can be very useful. Unless the specification is complete, some errors will not be found until instantiation time. However, partial specifications can help a lot, express intent, and are essential for smooth incremental development where we don't initially recognize all the requirements we need. With mature libraries of concepts, initial specifications will be close to perfect.

Unsurprisingly, requires Arithmetic<Value_type<Seq>,Num> is called a requirements-clause. The template<Sequence Seq> notation is simply a shorthand for an explicit use of requires Sequence<Seq>. If I liked verbosity, I could equivalently have written

```
template<typename Seq, typename Num>
    requires Sequence<Seq> && Number<Num> && Arithmetic<Value_type<Seq>,Num>
Num sum(Seq s, Num n);
```

On the other hand, we could also use the equivalence between the two notations to write:

```
template<Sequence Seq, Arithmetic<Value_type<Seq>> Num>
Num sum(Seq s, Num n);
```

Where we cannot yet use concepts, we have to make do with naming conventions and comments, such as:

```
template<typename Sequence, typename Number>
    // requires Arithmetic<Value_type<Sequence>,Number>
Numer sum(Sequence s, Number n);
```

Whatever notation we chose, it is important to design a template with semantically meaningful constraints on its arguments (§7.2.4).

7.2.2 Concept-based Overloading

Once we have properly specified templates with their interfaces, we can overload based on their properties, much as we do for functions. Consider a slightly simplified standard-library function advance() that advances an iterator (§12.3):

```
template<Forward_iterator Iter>
void advance(Iter p, int n)          // move p n elements forward
{
     while (n--)
          ++p;        // a forward iterator has ++, but not + or +=
}

template<Random_access_iterator Iter>
void advance(Iter p, int n)          // move p n elements forward
{
     p+=n;            // a random-access iterator has +=
}
```

The compiler will select the template with the strongest requirements met by the arguments. In this case, a list only supplies forward iterators, but a vector offers random-access iterators, so we get:

```
void user(vector<int>::iterator vip, list<string>::iterator lsp)
{
     advance(vip,10);     // use the fast advance()
     advance(lsp,10);     // use the slow advance()
}
```

Like other overloading, this is a compile-time mechanism implying no run-time cost, and where the compiler does not find a best choice, it gives an ambiguity error. The rules for concept-based overloading are far simpler than the rules for general overloading (§1.3). Consider first a single argument for several alternative functions:

- If the argument doesn't match the concept, that alternative cannot be chosen.
- If the argument matches the concept for just one alternative, that alternative is chosen.
- If arguments from two alternatives are equally good matches for a concept, we have an ambiguity.
- If arguments from two alternatives match a concept and one is stricter than the other (match all the requirements of the other and more), that alternative is chosen.

For an alternative to be chosen it has to be

- a match for all of its arguments, and
- at least an equally good match for all arguments as other alternatives, and
- a better match for at least one argument.

7.2.3 Valid Code

The question of whether a set of template arguments offers what a template requires of its template parameters ultimately boils down to whether some expressions are valid.

Using a requires-expression, we can check if a set of expressions is valid. For example:

```
template<Forward_iterator Iter>
void advance(Iter p, int n)          // move p n elements forward
{
     while (n--)
          ++p;        // a forward iterator has ++, but not + or +=
}
```

```
template<Forward_iterator Iter, int n>
    requires requires(Iter p, int i) { p[i]; p+i; }      // Iter has subscripting and addition
void advance(Iter p, int n)          // move p n elements forward
{
    p+=n;          // a random-access iterator has +=
}
```

No, that **requires requires** is not a typo. The first **requires** starts the **requirements**-clause and the second **requires** starts the **requires**–expression

```
requires(Iter p, int i) { p[i]; p+i; }
```

A **requires**–expression is a predicate that is **true** if the statements in it are valid code and **false** if they are not.

I consider **requires**-expressions the assembly code of generic programming. Like ordinary assembly code, **requires**-expressions are extremely flexible and impose no programming discipline. In some form or other, they are at the bottom of most interesting generic code, just as assembly code is at the bottom of most interesting ordinary code. Like assembly code, **requires**-expressions should not be seen in "ordinary code." If you see **requires requires** in your code, it is probably too low level.

The use of **requires requires** in **advance()** is deliberately inelegant and hackish. Note that I "forgot" to specify += and the required return types for the operations. You have been warned! Prefer named concepts for which the name indicates its semantic meaning.

Prefer use of properly named concepts with well-specified semantics (§7.2.4) and use **requires**-expressions in the definition of those.

7.2.4 Definition of Concepts

Eventually, we expect to find useful concepts, such as **Sequence** and **Arithmetic** in libraries, including the standard library. The Ranges Technical Specification [RangesTS] already offers a set for constraining standard-library algorithms (§12.7). However, simple concepts are not hard to define.

A concept is a compile-time predicate specifying how one or more types can be used. Consider first one of the simplest examples:

```
template<typename T>
concept Equality_comparable =
    requires (T a, T b) {
        { a == b } -> bool;    // compare Ts with ==
        { a != b } -> bool;    // compare Ts with !=
    };
```

Equality_comparable is the concept we use to ensure that we can compare values of a type equal and non-equal. We simply say that, given two values of the type, they must be comparable using == and != and the result of those operations must be convertible to **bool**. For example:

```
static_assert(Equality_comparable<int>);      // succeeds

struct S { int a; };
static_assert(Equality_comparable<S>);        // fails because structs don't automatically get == and !=
```

The definition of the concept Equality_comparable is exactly equivalent to the English description and no longer. The value of a concept is always bool.

Defining Equality_comparable to handle nonhomogeneous comparisons is almost as easy:

```
template<typename T, typename T2 =T>
concept Equality_comparable =
    requires (T a, T2 b) {
        { a == b } -> bool;   // compare a T to a T2 with ==
        { a != b } -> bool;   // compare a T to a T2 with !=
        { b == a } -> bool;   // compare a T2 to a T with ==
        { b != a } -> bool;   // compare a T2 to a T with !=
    };
```

The typename T2 =T says that if we don't specify a second template argument, T2 will be the same as T; T is a *default template argument*.

We can test Equality_comparable like this:

```
static_assert(Equality_comparable<int,double>);  // succeeds
static_assert(Equality_comparable<int>);         // succeeds (T2 is defaulted to int)
static_assert(Equality_comparable<int,string>);  // fails
```

For a more complex example, consider a sequence:

```
template<typename S>
concept Sequence = requires(S a) {
    typename Value_type<S>;              // S must have a value type.
    typename Iterator_type<S>;           // S must have an iterator type.

    { begin(a) } -> Iterator_type<S>;    // begin(a) must return an iterator
    { end(a) } -> Iterator_type<S>;      // end(a) must return an iterator

    requires Same_type<Value_type<S>,Value_type<Iterator_type<S>>>;
    requires Input_iterator<Iterator_type<S>>;
};
```

For a type S to be a Sequence, it must provide a Value_type (the type of its elements) and an Iterator_type (the type of its iterators; see §12.1). It must also ensure that there exist begin() and end() functions that return iterators, as is idiomatic for standard-library containers (§11.3). Finally, the Iterator_type really must be an input_iterator with elements of the same type as the elements of S.

The hardest concepts to define are the ones that represent fundamental language concepts. Consequently, it is best to use a set from an established library. For a useful collection, see §12.7.

7.3 Generic Programming

The form of *generic programming* supported by C++ centers around the idea of abstracting from concrete, efficient algorithms to obtain generic algorithms that can be combined with different data representations to produce a wide variety of useful software [Stepanov,2009]. The abstractions representing the fundamental operations and data structures are called *concepts*; they appear as requirements for template parameters.

7.3.1 Use of Concepts

Good, useful concepts are fundamental and are discovered more than they are designed. Examples are integer and floating-point number (as defined even in Classic C), sequence, and more general mathematical concepts, such as field and vector space. They represent the fundamental concepts of a field of application. That is why they are called "concepts." Identifying and formalizing concepts to the degree necessary for effective generic programming can be a challenge.

For basic use, consider the concept Regular (§12.7). A type is regular when it behaves much like an int or a vector. An object of a regular type

- can be default constructed.
- can be copied (with the usual semantics of copy, yielding two objects that are independent and compare equal) using a constructor or an assignment.
- can be compared using == and !=.
- doesn't suffer technical problems from overly clever programming tricks.

A string is another example of a regular type. Like int, string is also StrictTotallyOrdered (§12.7). That is, two strings can be compared using <, <=, >, and >= with the appropriate semantics.

A concept is not just a syntactic notion, it is fundamentally about semantics. For example, don't define + to divide; that would not match the requirements for any reasonable number. Unfortunately, we do not yet have any language support for expressing semantics, so we have to rely on expert knowledge and common sense to get semantically meaningful concepts. Do not define semantically meaningless concepts, such as Addable and Subtractable. Instead, rely on domain knowledge to define concepts that match fundamental concepts in an application domain.

7.3.2 Abstraction Using Templates

Good abstractions are carefully grown from concrete examples. It is not a good idea to try to "abstract" by trying to prepare for every conceivable need and technique; in that direction lies inelegance and code bloat. Instead, start with one – and preferably more – concrete examples from real use and try to eliminate inessential details. Consider:

```
double sum(const vector<int>& v)
{
    double res = 0;
    for (auto x : v)
        res += x;
    return res;
}
```

This is obviously one of many ways to compute the sum of a sequence of numbers.

Consider what makes this code less general than it needs to be:

- Why just ints?
- Why just vectors?
- Why accumulate in a double?
- Why start at 0?
- Why add?

Answering the first four questions by making the concrete types into template arguments, we get the simplest form of the standard-library accumulate algorithm:

```
template<typename Iter, typename Val>
Val accumulate(Iter first, Iter last, Val res)
{
     for (auto p = first; p!=last; ++p)
          res += *p;
     return res;
}
```

Here, we have:

- The data structure to be traversed has been abstracted into a pair of iterators representing a sequence (§12.1).
- The type of the accumulator has been made into a parameter.
- The initial value is now an input; the type of the accumulator is the type of this initial value.

A quick examination or – even better – measurement will show that the code generated for calls with a variety of data structures is identical to what you get from the hand-coded original example. For example:

```
void use(const vector<int>& vec, const list<double>& lst)
{
     auto sum = accumulate(begin(vec),end(vec),0.0);  // accumulate in a double
     auto sum2 = accumulate(begin(lst),end(lst),sum);
     //
}
```

The process of generalizing from a concrete piece of code (and preferably from several) while preserving performance is called *lifting*. Conversely, the best way to develop a template is often to

- first, write a concrete version
- then, debug, test, and measure it
- finally, replace the concrete types with template arguments.

Naturally, the repetition of begin() and end() is tedious, so we can simplify the user interface a bit:

```
template<Range R, Number Val>   // a Range is something with begin() and end()
Val accumulate(const R& r, Val res = 0)
{
     for (auto p = begin(r); p!=end(r); ++p)
          res += *p;
     return res;
}
```

For full generality, we can abstract the += operation also; see §14.3.

7.4 Variadic Templates

A template can be defined to accept an arbitrary number of arguments of arbitrary types. Such a template is called a *variadic template*. Consider a simple function to write out values of any type that has a << operator:

```
void user()
{
	print("first: ", 1, 2.2, "hello\n"s);                      // first:  1 2.2 hello

	print("\nsecond: ", 0.2, 'c', "yuck!"s, 0, 1, 2, '\n');    // second: 0.2 c yuck! 0 1 2
}
```

Traditionally, implementing a variadic template has been to separate the first argument from the rest and then recursively call the variadic template for the tail of the arguments:

```
void print()
{
	// what we do for no arguments: nothing
}

template<typename T, typename... Tail>
void print(T head, Tail... tail)
{
	// what we do for each argument, e.g.,
	cout << head << ' ';
	print(tail...);
}
```

The **typename...** indicates that **Tail** is a sequence of types. The **Tail...** indicates that **tail** is a sequence of values of the types in **Tail**. A parameter declared with a **...** is called a *parameter pack*. Here, **tail** is a (function argument) parameter pack where the elements are of the types found in the (template argument) parameter pack **Tail**. So, **print()** can take any number of arguments of any types.

A call of **print()** separates the arguments into a head (the first) and a tail (the rest). The head is printed and then **print()** is called for the tail. Eventually, of course, **tail** will become empty, so we need the no-argument version of **print()** to deal with that. If we don't want to allow the zero-argument case, we can eliminate that **print()** using a compile-time **if**:

```
template<typename T, typename... Tail>
void print(T head, Tail... tail)
{
	cout << head << ' ';
	if constexpr(sizeof...(tail)> 0)
		print(tail...);
}
```

I used a compile-time **if** (§6.4.3), rather than a plain run-time **if** to avoid a final, never called, call **print()** from being generated.

The strength of variadic templates (sometimes just called *variadics*) is that they can accept any arguments you care to give them. Weaknesses include

- The recursive implementations can be tricky to get right.
- The recursive implementations can be surprisingly expensive in compile time.
- The type checking of the interface is a possibly elaborate template program.

Because of their flexibility, variadic templates are widely used in the standard library, and occasionally wildly overused.

7.4.1 Fold Expressions

To simplify the implementation of simple variadic templates, C++17 offers a limited form of iteration over elements of a parameter pack. For example:

```
template<Number... T>
int sum(T... v)
{
    return (v + ... + 0);       // add all elements of v starting with 0
}
```

Here, sum() can take any number of arguments of any types. Assuming that sum() really adds its arguments, we get:

```
int x = sum(1, 2, 3, 4, 5); // x becomes 15
int y = sum('a', 2.4, x);    // y becomes 114 (2.4 is truncated and the value of 'a' is 97)
```

The body of sum uses a fold expression:

```
return (v + ... + 0);   // add all elements of v to 0
```

Here, (v+...+0) means add all the elements of v starting with the initial value 0. The first element to be added is the "rightmost" (the one with the highest index): (v[0]+(v[1]+(v[2]+(v[3]+(v[4]+0))))). That is, starting from the right where the 0 is. It is called a *right fold*. Alternatively, we could have used a *left fold*:

```
template<Number... T>
int sum2(T... v)
{
    return (0 + ... + v); // add all elements of v to 0
}
```

Now, the first element to be added is the "leftmost" (the one with the lowest index): (((((0+v[0])+v[1])+v[2])+v[3])+v[4]). That is, starting from the left where the 0 is.

Fold is a very powerful abstraction, clearly related to the standard-library accumulate(), with a variety of names in different languages and communities. In C++, the fold expressions are currently restricted to simplify the implementation of variadic templates. A fold does not have to perform numeric computations. Consider a famous example:

```
template<typename ...T>
void print(T&&... args)
{
    (std::cout << ... << args) << '\n';   // print all arguments
}

print("Hello!"s,' ',"World ",2017);     // (((((std::cout << "Hello!"s) << ' ') << "World ") << 2017) << '\n');
```

Many use cases simply involve a set of values that can be converted to a common type. In such cases, simply copying the arguments into a vector or the desired type often simplifies further use:

```
template<typename Res, typename... Ts>
vector<Res> to_vector(Ts&&... ts)
{
      vector<Res> res;
      (res.push_back(ts) ...);   // no initial value needed
      return res;
}
```

We can use to_vector like this:

```
auto x = to_vector<double>(1,2,4.5,'a');

template<typename... Ts>
int fct(Ts&&... ts)
{
      auto args = to_vector<string>(ts...);       // args[i] is the ith argument
      // ... use args here ...
}

int y = fct("foo", "bar", s);
```

7.4.2 Forwarding Arguments

Passing arguments unchanged through an interface is an important use of variadic templates. Consider a notion of a network input channel for which the actual method of moving values is a parameter. Different transport mechanisms have different sets of constructor parameters:

```
template<typename Transport>
  requires concepts::InputTransport<Transport>
class InputChannel {
public:
      // ...
     InputChannel(TransportArgs&&... transportArgs)
       : _transport(std::forward<TransportArgs>(transportArgs)...)
     {}
    // ...
    Transport _transport;
};
```

The standard-library function forward() (§13.2.2) is used to move the arguments unchanged from the InputChannel constructor to the Transport constructor.

The point here is that the writer of InputChannel can construct an object of type Transport without having to know what arguments are required to construct a particular Transport. The implementer of InputChannel needs only to know the common user interface for all Transport objects.

Forwarding is very common in foundational libraries where generality and low run-time overhead are necessary and very general interfaces are common.

7.5 Template Compilation Model

Assuming concepts (§7.2), the arguments for a template are checked against its concepts. Errors found here will be reported and the programmer has to fix the problems. What cannot be checked at this point, such as arguments for unconstrained template arguments, is postponed until code is generated for the template and a set of template arguments: "at template instantiation time." For pre-concept code, this is where all type checking happens. When using concepts, we get here only after concept checking succeeded.

An unfortunate side effect of instantiation-time (late) type checking is that a type error can be found uncomfortably late and can result in spectacularly bad error messages because the compiler found the problem only after combining information from several places in the program.

The instantiation-time type checking provided for templates checks the use of arguments in the template definition. This provides a compile-time variant of what is often called *duck typing* ("If it walks like a duck and it quacks like a duck, it's a duck"). Or – using more technical terminology – we operate on values, and the presence and meaning of an operation depend solely on its operand values. This differs from the alternative view that objects have types, which determine the presence and meaning of operations. Values "live" in objects. This is the way objects (e.g., variables) work in C++, and only values that meet an object's requirements can be put into it. What is done at compile time using templates mostly does not involve objects, only values. The exception is local variables in a `constexpr` function (§1.6) that are used as objects inside the compiler.

To use an unconstrained template, its definition (not just its declaration) must be in scope at its point of use. For example, the standard header `<vector>` holds the definition of `vector`. In practice, this means that template definitions are typically found in header files, rather than `.cpp` files. This changes when we start to use modules (§3.3). Using modules, the source code is organized in the same way for ordinary functions and template functions. In both cases, definitions will be protected against the problems of textual inclusion.

7.6 Advice

[1] Templates provide a general mechanism for compile-time programming; §7.1.
[2] When designing a template, carefully consider the concepts (requirements) assumed for its template arguments; §7.3.2.
[3] When designing a template, use a concrete version for initial implementation, debugging, and measurement; §7.3.2.
[4] Use concepts as a design tool; §7.2.1.
[5] Specify concepts for all template arguments; §7.2; [CG: T.10].
[6] Whenever possible use standard concepts (e.g., the Ranges concepts); §7.2.4; [CG: T.11].
[7] Use a lambda if you need a simple function object in one place only; §6.3.2.
[8] There is no separate compilation of templates: `#include` template definitions in every translation unit that uses them.
[9] Use templates to express containers and ranges; §7.3.2; [CG: T.3].
[10] Avoid "concepts" without meaningful semantics; §7.2; [CG: T.20].
[11] Require a complete set of operations for a concept; §7.2; [CG: T.21].

[12] Use variadic templates when you need a function that takes a variable number of arguments of a variety of types; §7.4.
[13] Don't use variadic templates for homogeneous argument lists (prefer initializer lists for that); §7.4.
[14] To use a template, make sure its definition (not just its declaration) is in scope; §7.5.
[15] Templates offer compile-time "duck typing"; §7.5.

8

Library Overview

Why waste time learning
when ignorance is instantaneous?
– Hobbes

- Introduction
- Standard-Library Components
- Standard-Library Headers and Namespace
- Advice

8.1 Introduction

No significant program is written in just a bare programming language. First, a set of libraries is developed. These then form the basis for further work. Most programs are tedious to write in the bare language, whereas just about any task can be rendered simple by the use of good libraries.

Continuing from Chapters 1–7, Chapters 9–15 give a quick tour of key standard-library facilities. I very briefly present useful standard-library types, such as `string`, `ostream`, `variant`, `vector`, `map`, `path`, `unique_ptr`, `thread`, `regex`, and `complex`, as well as the most common ways of using them.

As in Chapters 1–7, you are strongly encouraged not to be distracted or discouraged by an incomplete understanding of details. The purpose of this chapter is to convey a basic understanding of the most useful library facilities.

The specification of the standard library is over two thirds of the ISO C++ standard. Explore it, and prefer it to home-made alternatives. Much thought has gone into its design, more still into its implementations, and much effort will go into its maintenance and extension.

The standard-library facilities described in this book are part of every complete C++ implementation. In addition to the standard-library components, most implementations offer "graphical user interface" systems (GUIs), Web interfaces, database interfaces, etc. Similarly, most application-development environments provide "foundation libraries" for corporate or industrial "standard" development and/or execution environments. Here, I do not describe such systems and libraries.

The intent is to provide a self-contained description of C++ as defined by the standard and to keep the examples portable. Naturally, a programmer is encouraged to explore the more extensive facilities available on most systems.

8.2 Standard-Library Components

The facilities provided by the standard library can be classified like this:

- Run-time language support (e.g., for allocation and run-time type information).
- The C standard library (with very minor modifications to minimize violations of the type system).
- Strings (with support for international character sets, localization, and read-only views of substrings); see §9.2.
- Support for regular expression matching; see §9.4.
- I/O streams is an extensible framework for input and output to which users can add their own types, streams, buffering strategies, locales, and character sets (Chapter 10). There is also a library for manipulating file systems in a portable manner (§10.10).
- A framework of containers (such as `vector` and `map`) and algorithms (such as `find()`, `sort()`, and `merge()`); see Chapter 11 and Chapter 12. This framework, conventionally called the STL [Stepanov,1994], is extensible so users can add their own containers and algorithms.
- Support for numerical computation (such as standard mathematical functions, complex numbers, vectors with arithmetic operations, and random number generators); see §4.2.1 and Chapter 14.
- Support for concurrent programming, including `threads` and locks; see Chapter 15. The concurrency support is foundational so that users can add support for new models of concurrency as libraries.
- Parallel versions of most STL algorithms and some numerical algorithms (e.g., `sort()` and `reduce()`); see §12.9 and §14.3.1.
- Utilities to support template metaprogramming (e.g., type traits; §13.9), STL-style generic programming (e.g., `pair`; §13.4.3), general programming (e.g., `variant` and `optional`; §13.5.1, §13.5.2), and `clock` (§13.7).
- Support for efficient and safe management of general resources, plus an interface to optional garbage collectors (§5.3).
- "Smart pointers" for resource management (e.g., `unique_ptr` and `shared_ptr`; §13.2.1).
- Special-purpose containers, such as `array` (§13.4.1), `bitset` (§13.4.2), and `tuple` (§13.4.3).
- Suffixes for popular units, such as `ms` for milliseconds and `i` for imaginary (§5.4.4).

The main criteria for including a class in the library were that:

- it could be helpful to almost every C++ programmer (both novices and experts),
- it could be provided in a general form that did not add significant overhead compared to a simpler version of the same facility, and
- simple uses should be easy to learn (relative to the inherent complexity of their task).

Essentially, the C++ standard library provides the most common fundamental data structures together with the fundamental algorithms used on them.

8.3 Standard-Library Headers and Namespace

Every standard-library facility is provided through some standard header. For example:

```
#include<string>
#include<list>
```

This makes the standard string and list available.

The standard library is defined in a namespace (§3.4) called std. To use standard-library facilities, the std:: prefix can be used:

```
std::string sheep {"Four legs Good; two legs Baaad!"};
std::list<std::string> slogans {"War is Peace", "Freedom is Slavery", "Ignorance is Strength"};
```

For simplicity, I will rarely use the std:: prefix explicitly in examples. Neither will I always #include the necessary headers explicitly. To compile and run the program fragments here, you must #include the appropriate headers and make the names they declare accessible. For example:

```
#include<string>              // make the standard string facilities accessible
using namespace std;          // make std names available without std:: prefix

string s {"C++ is a general−purpose programming language"};      // OK: string is std::string
```

It is generally in poor taste to dump every name from a namespace into the global namespace. However, in this book, I use the standard library exclusively and it is good to know what it offers.

Here is a selection of standard-library headers, all supplying declarations in namespace std:

Selected Standard Library Headers		
<algorithm>	copy(), find(), sort()	Chapter 12
<array>	array	§13.4.1
<chrono>	duration, time_point	§13.7
<cmath>	sqrt(), pow()	§14.2
<complex>	complex, sqrt(), pow()	§14.4
<filesystem>	path	§10.10
<forward_list>	forward_list	§11.6
<fstream>	fstream, ifstream, ofstream	§10.7
<future>	future, promise	§15.7
<ios>	hex, dec, scientific, fixed, defaultfloat	§10.6
<iostream>	istream, ostream, cin, cout	Chapter 10
<map>	map, multimap	§11.5
<memory>	unique_ptr, shared_ptr, allocator	§13.2.1
<random>	default_random_engine, normal_distribution	§14.5
<regex>	regex, smatch	§9.4
<string>	string, basic_string	§9.2
<set>	set, multiset	§11.6
<sstream>	istringstream, ostringstream	§10.8

Selected Standard Library Headers (Continued)		
<stdexcept>	length_error, out_of_range, runtime_error	§3.5.1
<thread>	thread	§15.2
<unordered_map>	unordered_map, unordered_multimap	§11.5
<utility>	move(), swap(), pair	Chapter 13
<variant>	variant	§13.5.1
<vector>	vector	§11.2

This listing is far from complete.

Headers from the C standard library, such as <stdlib.h> are provided. For each such header there is also a version with its name prefixed by c and the .h removed. This version, such as <cstdlib> places its declarations in the std namespace.

8.4 Advice

[1] Don't reinvent the wheel; use libraries; §8.1; [CG: SL.1.]
[2] When you have a choice, prefer the standard library over other libraries; §8.1; [CG: SL.2].
[3] Do not think that the standard library is ideal for everything; §8.1.
[4] Remember to #include the headers for the facilities you use; §8.3.
[5] Remember that standard-library facilities are defined in namespace std; §8.3; [CG: SL.3].

9

Strings and Regular Expressions

Prefer the standard to the offbeat.
– Strunk & White

- Introduction
- Strings
  string Implementation;
- String Views
- Regular Expressions
  Searching; Regular Expression Notation; Iterators
- Advice

9.1 Introduction

Text manipulation is a major part of most programs. The C++ standard library offers a string type to save most users from C-style manipulation of arrays of characters through pointers. A string_view type allows us to manipulate sequences of characters however they may be stored (e.g., in a std::string or a char[]). In addition, regular expression matching is offered to help find patterns in text. The regular expressions are provided in a form similar to what is common in most modern languages. Both strings and regex objects can use a variety of character types (e.g., Unicode).

9.2 Strings

The standard library provides a string type to complement the string literals (§1.2.1); string is a Regular type (§7.2, §12.7) for owning and manipulating a sequence of characters of various character types. The string type provides a variety of useful string operations, such as concatenation. For example:

```
string compose(const string& name, const string& domain)
{
      return name + '@' + domain;
}

auto addr = compose("dmr","bell-labs.com");
```

Here, addr is initialized to the character sequence dmr@bell-labs.com. "Addition" of strings means concatenation. You can concatenate a string, a string literal, a C-style string, or a character to a string. The standard string has a move constructor, so returning even long strings by value is efficient (§5.2.2).

In many applications, the most common form of concatenation is adding something to the end of a string. This is directly supported by the += operation. For example:

```
void m2(string& s1, string& s2)
{
      s1 = s1 + '\n';  // append newline
      s2 += '\n';      // append newline
}
```

The two ways of adding to the end of a string are semantically equivalent, but I prefer the latter because it is more explicit about what it does, more concise, and possibly more efficient.

A string is mutable. In addition to = and +=, subscripting (using [ ]) and substring operations are supported. For example:

```
string name = "Niels Stroustrup";

void m3()
{
      string s = name.substr(6,10);          // s = "Stroustrup"
      name.replace(0,5,"nicholas");          // name becomes "nicholas Stroustrup"
      name[0] = toupper(name[0]);            // name becomes "Nicholas Stroustrup"
}
```

The substr() operation returns a string that is a copy of the substring indicated by its arguments. The first argument is an index into the string (a position), and the second is the length of the desired substring. Since indexing starts from 0, s gets the value Stroustrup.

The replace() operation replaces a substring with a value. In this case, the substring starting at 0 with length 5 is Niels; it is replaced by nicholas. Finally, I replace the initial character with its uppercase equivalent. Thus, the final value of name is Nicholas Stroustrup. Note that the replacement string need not be the same size as the substring that it is replacing.

Among the many useful string operations are assignment (using =), subscripting (using [ ] or at() as for vector; §11.2.2), comparison (using == and !=), and lexicographical ordering (using <, <=, >, and >=), iteration (using iterators as for vector; §12.2), input (§10.3), and streaming (§10.8).

Naturally, strings can be compared against each other, against C-style strings §1.7.1), and against string literals. For example:

```
string incantation;

void respond(const string& answer)
{
      if (answer == incantation) {
            // perform magic
      }
      else if (answer == "yes") {
            // ...
      }
      // ...
}
```

If you need a C-style string (a zero-terminated array of char), string offers read-only access to its contained characters. For example:

```
void print(const string& s)
{
      printf("For people who like printf: %s\n",s.c_str());      // s.c_str() returns a pointer to s' characters
      cout << "For people who like streams: " << s << '\n';
}
```

A string literal is by definition a const char*. To get a literal of type std::string use a s suffix. For example:

```
auto s = "Cat"s;      // a std::string
auto p = "Dog";       // a C-style string: a const char*
```

To use the s suffix, you need to use the namespace std::literals::string_literals (§5.4.4).

9.2.1 string Implementation

Implementing a string class is a popular and useful exercise. However, for general-purpose use, our carefully crafted first attempts rarely match the standard string in convenience or performance. These days, string is usually implemented using the *short-string optimization*. That is, short string values are kept in the string object itself and only longer strings are placed on free store. Consider:

```
string s1 {"Annemarie"};                 // short string
string s2 {"Annemarie Stroustrup"};      // long string
```

The memory layout will be something like this:

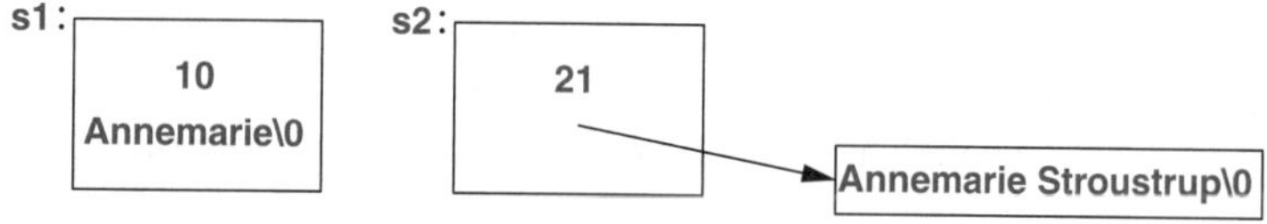

When a string's value changes from a short to a long string (and vice versa) its representation adjusts appropriately. How many characters can a "short" string have? That's implementation defined, but "about 14 characters" isn't a bad guess.

The actual performance of strings can depend critically on the run-time environment. In particular, in multi-threaded implementations, memory allocation can be relatively costly. Also, when lots of strings of differing lengths are used, memory fragmentation can result. These are the main reasons that the short-string optimization has become ubiquitous.

To handle multiple character sets, string is really an alias for a general template basic_string with the character type char:

```
template<typename Char>
class basic_string {
      // ... string of Char ...
};

using string = basic_string<char>;
```

A user can define strings of arbitrary character types. For example, assuming we have a Japanese character type Jchar, we can write:

```
using Jstring = basic_string<Jchar>;
```

Now we can do all the usual string operations on Jstring, a string of Japanese characters.

9.3 String Views

The most common use of a sequence of characters is to pass it to some function to read. This can be achieved by passing a string by value, a reference to a string, or a C-style string. In many systems there are further alternatives, such as string types not offered by the standard. In all of these cases, there are extra complexities when we want to pass a substring. To address this, the standard library offers string_view; a string_view is basically a (pointer,length) pair denoting a sequence of characters:

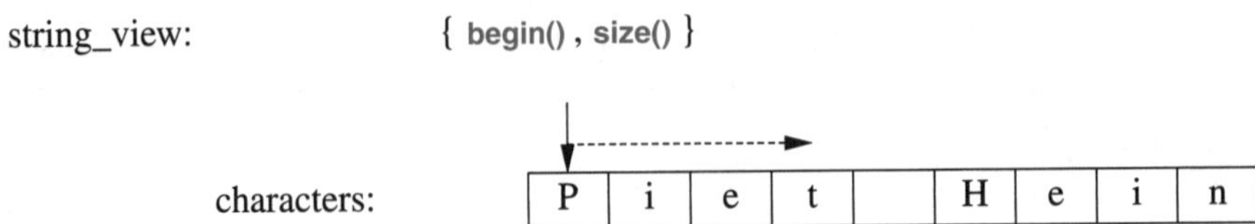

A string_view gives access to a contiguous sequence of characters. The characters can be stored in many possible ways, including in a string and in a C-style string. A string_view is like a pointer or a reference in that it does not own the characters it points to. In that, it resembles an STL pair of iterators (§12.3).

Consider a simple function concatenating two strings:

```
string cat(string_view sv1, string_view sv2)
{
      string res(sv1.length()+sv2.length());
      char* p = &res[0];
      for (char c : sv1)                    // one way to copy
            *p++ = c;
      copy(sv2.begin(),sv2.end(),p);        // another way
      return res;
}
```

We can call this cat():

```
string king = "Harold";
auto s1 = cat(king,"William");                  // string and const char*
auto s2 = cat(king,king);                       // string and string
auto s3 = cat("Edward","Stephen"sv);            // const char * and string_view
auto s4 = cat("Canute"sv,king);
auto s5 = cat({&king[0],2},"Henry"sv);          // HaHenry
auto s6 = cat({&king[0],2},{&king[2],4});       // Harold
```

This cat() has three advantages over the compose() that takes const string& arguments (§9.2):

- It can be used for character sequences managed in many different ways.
- No temporary string arguments are created for C-style string arguments.
- We can easily pass substrings.

Note the use of the sv ("string view") suffix. To use that we need to

```
using namespace std::literals::string_view_literals;       // §5.4.4
```

Why bother? The reason is that when we pass "Edward" we need to construct a string_view from a const char* and that requires counting the characters. For "Stephen"sv the length is computed at compile time.

When returning a string_view, remember that it is very much like a pointer; it needs to point to something:

```
string_view bad()
{
      string s = "Once upon a time";
      return {&s[5],4};             // bad: returning a pointer to a local
}
```

We are returning a pointer to characters of a string that will be destroyed before we can use them.

One significant restriction of string_view is that it is a read-only view of its characters. For example, you cannot use a string_view to pass characters to a function that modifies its argument to lowercase. For that, you might consider using a gsl::span or gsl::string_span (§13.3).

The behavior of out-of-range access to a string_view is unspecified. If you want guaranteed range checking, use at(), which throws out_of_range for attempted out-of-range access, use a gsl::string_span (§13.3), or "just be careful."

9.4 Regular Expressions

Regular expressions are a powerful tool for text processing. They provide a way to simply and tersely describe patterns in text (e.g., a U.S. postal code such as **TX 77845**, or an ISO-style date, such as **2009–06–07**) and to efficiently find such patterns. In **<regex>**, the standard library provides support for regular expressions in the form of the **std::regex** class and its supporting functions. To give a taste of the style of the **regex** library, let us define and print a pattern:

```
regex pat {R"(\w{2}\s*\d{5}(–\d{4})?)"};   // U.S. postal code pattern: XXddddd-dddd and variants
```

People who have used regular expressions in just about any language will find **\w{2}\s*\d{5}(–\d{4})?** familiar. It specifies a pattern starting with two letters **\w{2}** optionally followed by some space **\s*** followed by five digits **\d{5}** and optionally followed by a dash and four digits **–\d{4}**. If you are not familiar with regular expressions, this may be a good time to learn about them ([Stroustrup,2009], [Maddock,2009], [Friedl,1997]).

To express the pattern, I use a *raw string literal* starting with **R"(** and terminated by **)"**. This allows backslashes and quotes to be used directly in the string. Raw strings are particularly suitable for regular expressions because they tend to contain a lot of backslashes. Had I used a conventional string, the pattern definition would have been:

```
regex pat {"\\w{2}\\s*\\d{5}(–\\d{4})?"};   // U.S. postal code pattern
```

In **<regex>**, the standard library provides support for regular expressions:

- **regex_match()**: Match a regular expression against a string (of known size) (§9.4.2).
- **regex_search()**: Search for a string that matches a regular expression in an (arbitrarily long) stream of data (§9.4.1).
- **regex_replace()**: Search for strings that match a regular expression in an (arbitrarily long) stream of data and replace them.
- **regex_iterator**: Iterate over matches and submatches (§9.4.3).
- **regex_token_iterator**: Iterate over non-matches.

9.4.1 Searching

The simplest way of using a pattern is to search for it in a stream:

```
int lineno = 0;
for (string line; getline(cin,line); ) {          // read into line buffer
      ++lineno;
      smatch matches;                              // matched strings go here
      if (regex_search(line,matches,pat))          // search for pat in line
            cout << lineno << ": " << matches[0] << '\n';
}
```

The **regex_search(line,matches,pat)** searches the **line** for anything that matches the regular expression stored in **pat** and if it finds any matches, it stores them in **matches**. If no match was found, **regex_search(line,matches,pat)** returns **false**. The **matches** variable is of type **smatch**. The "s" stands for "sub" or "string," and an **smatch** is a **vector** of submatches of type **string**. The first element, here **matches[0]**, is the complete match. The result of a **regex_search()** is a collection of matches, typically represented as an **smatch**:

```
void use()
{
    ifstream in("file.txt");     // input file
    if (!in)                     // check that the file was opened
        cerr << "no file\n";

    regex pat {R"(\w{2}\s*\d{5}(-\d{4})?)"};   // U.S. postal code pattern

    int lineno = 0;
    for (string line; getline(in,line); ) {
        ++lineno;
        smatch matches;    // matched strings go here
        if (regex_search(line, matches, pat)) {
            cout << lineno << ": " << matches[0] << '\n';        // the complete match
            if (1<matches.size() && matches[1].matched)          // if there is a sub-pattern
                                                                 // and if it is matched
                cout << "\t: " << matches[1] << '\n';            // submatch
        }
    }
}
```

This function reads a file looking for U.S. postal codes, such as TX77845 and DC 20500−0001. An smatch type is a container of regex results. Here, matches[0] is the whole pattern and matches[1] is the optional four-digit subpattern.

The newline character, \n, can be part of a pattern, so we can search for multiline patterns. Obviously, we shouldn't read one line at a time if we want to do that.

The regular expression syntax and semantics are designed so that regular expressions can be compiled into state machines for efficient execution [Cox,2007]. The regex type performs this compilation at run time.

9.4.2 Regular Expression Notation

The regex library can recognize several variants of the notation for regular expressions. Here, I use the default notation, a variant of the ECMA standard used for ECMAScript (more commonly known as JavaScript).

The syntax of regular expressions is based on characters with special meaning:

Regular Expression Special Characters			
.	Any single character (a "wildcard")	\	Next character has a special meaning
[	Begin character class	*	Zero or more (suffix operation)
]	End character class	+	One or more (suffix operation)
{	Begin count	?	Optional (zero or one) (suffix operation)
}	End count	|	Alternative (or)
(	Begin grouping	^	Start of line; negation
)	End grouping	$	End of line

For example, we can specify a line starting with zero or more As followed by one or more Bs followed by an optional C like this:

```
^A*B+C?$
```

Examples that match:

```
AAAAAAAAAAAABBBBBBBBBC
BC
B
```

Examples that do not match:

```
AAAAA          // no B
  AAAABC       // initial space
AABBCC         // too many Cs
```

A part of a pattern is considered a subpattern (which can be extracted separately from an smatch) if it is enclosed in parentheses. For example:

```
\d+−\d+        // no subpatterns
\d+(−\d+)      // one subpattern
(\d+)(−\d+)    // two subpatterns
```

A pattern can be optional or repeated (the default is exactly once) by adding a suffix:

Repetition	
{ n }	Exactly n times
{ n, }	n or more times
{n,m}	At least n and at most m times
*	Zero or more, that is, {0,}
+	One or more, that is, {1,}
?	Optional (zero or one), that is {0,1}

For example:

```
A{3}B{2,4}C*
```

Examples that match:

```
AAABBC
AAABBB
```

Examples that do not match:

```
AABBC          // too few As
AAABC          // too few Bs
AAABBBBBCCC    // too many Bs
```

A suffix ? after any of the repetition notations (?, *, +, and { }) makes the pattern matcher "lazy" or "non-greedy." That is, when looking for a pattern, it will look for the shortest match rather than the longest. By default, the pattern matcher always looks for the longest match; this is known as the *Max Munch rule*. Consider:

```
ababab
```

The pattern (ab)+ matches all of ababab. However, (ab)+? matches only the first ab.

The most common character classifications have names:

Character Classes	
alnum	Any alphanumeric character
alpha	Any alphabetic character
blank	Any whitespace character that is not a line separator
cntrl	Any control character
d	Any decimal digit
digit	Any decimal digit
graph	Any graphical character
lower	Any lowercase character
print	Any printable character
punct	Any punctuation character
s	Any whitespace character
space	Any whitespace character
upper	Any uppercase character
w	Any word character (alphanumeric characters plus the underscore)
xdigit	Any hexadecimal digit character

In a regular expression, a character class name must be bracketed by [: :]. For example, [:digit:] matches a decimal digit. Furthermore, they must be used within a [ ] pair defining a character class.

Several character classes are supported by shorthand notation:

Character Class Abbreviations		
\d	A decimal digit	[[:digit:]]
\s	A space (space, tab, etc.)	[[:space:]]
\w	A letter (a-z) or digit (0-9) or underscore (_)	[_[:alnum:]]
\D	Not \d	[^[:digit:]]
\S	Not \s	[^[:space:]]
\W	Not \w	[^_[:alnum:]]

In addition, languages supporting regular expressions often provide:

Nonstandard (but Common) Character Class Abbreviations		
\l	A lowercase character	[[:lower:]]
\u	An uppercase character	[[:upper:]]
\L	Not \l	[^[:lower:]]
\U	Not \u	[^[:upper:]]

For full portability, use the character class names rather than these abbreviations.

As an example, consider writing a pattern that describes C++ identifiers: an underscore or a letter followed by a possibly empty sequence of letters, digits, or underscores. To illustrate the subtleties involved, I include a few false attempts:

```
[:alpha:][:alnum:]*              // wrong: characters from the set ":alpha" followed by ...
[[:alpha:]][[:alnum:]]*          // wrong: doesn't accept underscore ('_' is not alpha)
([[:alpha:]]|_)[[:alnum:]]*      // wrong: underscore is not part of alnum either

([[:alpha:]]|_)([[:alnum:]]|_)*      // OK, but clumsy
[[:alpha:]_][[:alnum:]_]*            // OK: include the underscore in the character classes
[_[:alpha:]][_[:alnum:]]*            // also OK
[_[:alpha:]]\w*                      // \w is equivalent to [_[:alnum:]]
```

Finally, here is a function that uses the simplest version of **regex_match()** (§9.4.1) to test whether a string is an identifier:

```
bool is_identifier(const string& s)
{
        regex pat {"[_[:alpha:]]\\w*"}; // underscore or letter
                                        // followed by zero or more underscores, letters, or digits
        return regex_match(s,pat);
}
```

Note the doubling of the backslash to include a backslash in an ordinary string literal. Use raw string literals to alleviate problems with special characters. For example:

```
bool is_identifier(const string& s)
{
        regex pat {R"([_[:alpha:]]\w*)"};
        return regex_match(s,pat);
}
```

Here are some examples of patterns:

```
Ax*                 // A, Ax, Axxxx
Ax+                 // Ax, Axxx          Not A
\d-?\d              // 1-2, 12           Not 1--2
\w{2}-\d{4,5}       // Ab-1234, XX-54321, 22-5432        Digits are in \w
(\d*:)?(\d+)        // 12:3, 1:23, 123, :123        Not 123:
(bs|BS)             // bs, BS            Not bS
[aeiouy]            // a, o, u           An English vowel, not x
[^aeiouy]           // x, k              Not an English vowel, not e
[a^eiouy]           // a, ^, o, u        An English vowel or ^
```

A **group** (a subpattern) potentially to be represented by a **sub_match** is delimited by parentheses. If you need parentheses that should not define a subpattern, use **(?:** rather than plain **(**. For example:

```
(\s|:|,)*(\d*)      // optional spaces, colons, and/or commas followed by an optional number
```

Assuming that we were not interested in the characters before the number (presumably separators), we could write:

```
(?:\s|:|,)*(\d*)    // optional spaces, colons, and/or commas followed by an optional number
```

This would save the regular expression engine from having to store the first characters: the **(?:** variant has only one subpattern.

Regular Expression Grouping Examples	
\d*\s\w+	No groups (subpatterns)
(\d*)\s(\w+)	Two groups
(\d*)(\s(\w+))+	Two groups (groups do not nest)
(\s*\w*)+	One group; one or more subpatterns; only the last subpattern is saved as a **sub_match**
<(.*?)>(.*?)</\1>	Three groups; the \1 means "same as group 1"

That last pattern is useful for parsing XML. It finds tag/end-of-tag markers. Note that I used a non-greedy match (a *lazy match*), .*?, for the subpattern between the tag and the end tag. Had I used plain .*, this input would have caused a problem:

```
Always look on the <b>bright</b> side of <b>life</b>.
```

A *greedy match* for the first subpattern would match the first < with the last >. That would be correct behavior, but unlikely what the programmer wanted.

For a more exhaustive presentation of regular expressions, see [Friedl,1997].

9.4.3 Iterators

We can define a **regex_iterator** for iterating over a sequence of characters finding matches for a pattern. For example, we can use a **sregex_iterator** (a **regex_iterator<string>**) to output all whitespace-separated words in a **string**:

```
void test()
{
        string input = "aa as; asd ++e^asdf asdfg";
        regex pat {R"(\s+(\w+))"};
        for (sregex_iterator p(input.begin(),input.end(),pat); p!=sregex_iterator{}; ++p)
                cout << (*p)[1] << '\n';
}
```

This outputs:

```
as
asd
asdfg
```

We missed the first word, **aa**, because it has no preceding whitespace. If we simplify the pattern to **R"((\w+))"**, we get

```
aa
as
asd
e
asdf
asdfg
```

A **regex_iterator** is a bidirectional iterator, so we cannot directly iterate over an **istream** (which offers only an input iterator). Also, we cannot write through a **regex_iterator**, and the default **regex_iterator** (**regex_iterator{}**) is the only possible end-of-sequence.

9.5 Advice

[1] Use std::string to own character sequences; §9.2; [CG: SL.str.1].
[2] Prefer string operations to C-style string functions; §9.1.
[3] Use string to declare variables and members rather than as a base class; §9.2.
[4] Return strings by value (rely on move semantics); §9.2, §9.2.1.
[5] Directly or indirectly, use substr() to read substrings and replace() to write substrings; §9.2.
[6] A string can grow and shrink, as needed; §9.2.
[7] Use at() rather than iterators or [ ] when you want range checking; §9.2.
[8] Use iterators and [ ] rather than at() when you want to optimize speed; §9.2.
[9] string input doesn't overflow; §9.2, §10.3.
[10] Use c_str() to produce a C-style string representation of a string (only) when you have to; §9.2.
[11] Use a stringstream or a generic value extraction function (such as to<X>) for numeric conversion of strings; §10.8.
[12] A basic_string can be used to make strings of characters on any type; §9.2.1.
[13] Use the s suffix for string literals meant to be standard-library strings; §9.3 [CG: SL.str.12].
[14] Use string_view as an argument of functions that needs to read character sequences stored in various ways; §9.3 [CG: SL.str.2].
[15] Use gsl::string_span as an argument of functions that needs to write character sequences stored in various ways; §9.3. [CG: SL.str.2] [CG: SL.str.11].
[16] Think of a string_view as a kind of pointer with a size attached; it does not own its characters; §9.3.
[17] Use the sv suffix for string literals meant to be standard-library string_views; §9.3.
[18] Use regex for most conventional uses of regular expressions; §9.4.
[19] Prefer raw string literals for expressing all but the simplest patterns; §9.4.
[20] Use regex_match() to match a complete input; §9.4, §9.4.2.
[21] Use regex_search() to search for a pattern in an input stream; §9.4.1.
[22] The regular expression notation can be adjusted to match various standards; §9.4.2.
[23] The default regular expression notation is that of ECMAScript; §9.4.2.
[24] Be restrained; regular expressions can easily become a write-only language; §9.4.2.
[25] Note that \i allows you to express a subpattern in terms of a previous subpattern; §9.4.2.
[26] Use ? to make patterns "lazy"; §9.4.2.
[27] Use regex_iterators for iterating over a stream looking for a pattern; §9.4.3.

10

Input and Output

What you see is all you get.
– Brian W. Kernighan

- Introduction
- Output
- Input
- I/O State
- I/O of User-Defined Types
- Formatting
- File Streams
- String Streams
- C-style I/O
- File System
- Advice

10.1 Introduction

The I/O stream library provides formatted and unformatted buffered I/O of text and numeric values.

An ostream converts typed objects to a stream of characters (bytes):

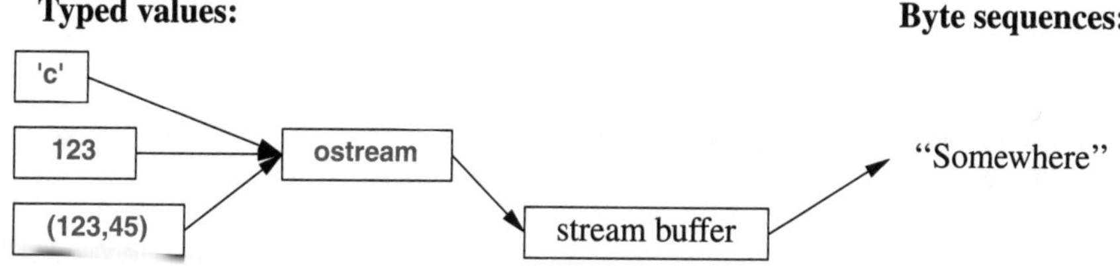

An istream converts a stream of characters (bytes) to typed objects:

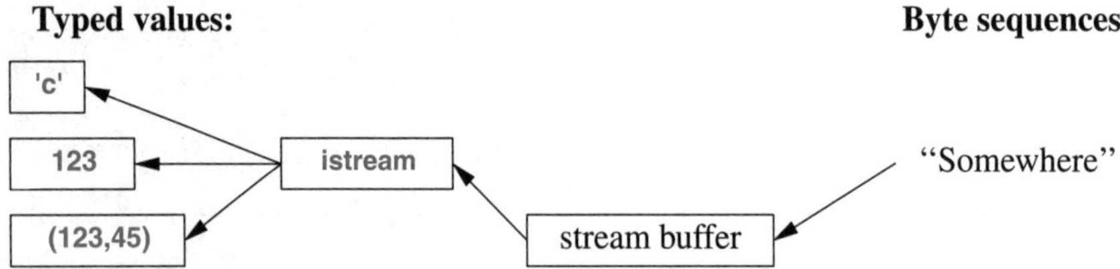

The operations on istreams and ostreams are described in §10.2 and §10.3. The operations are type-safe, type-sensitive, and extensible to handle user-defined types (§10.5).

Other forms of user interaction, such as graphical I/O, are handled through libraries that are not part of the ISO standard and therefore not described here.

These streams can be used for binary I/O, be used for a variety of character types, be locale specific, and use advanced buffering strategies, but these topics are beyond the scope of this book.

The streams can be used for input into and output from std::strings (§10.3), for formatting into string buffers (§10.8), and for file I/O (§10.10).

The I/O stream classes all have destructors that free all resources owned (such as buffers and file handles). That is, they are examples of "Resource Acquisition Is Initialization" (RAII; §5.3).

10.2 Output

In <ostream>, the I/O stream library defines output for every built-in type. Further, it is easy to define output of a user-defined type (§10.5). The operator << ("put to") is used as an output operator on objects of type ostream; cout is the standard output stream and cerr is the standard stream for reporting errors. By default, values written to cout are converted to a sequence of characters. For example, to output the decimal number 10, we can write:

```
void f()
{
      cout << 10;
}
```

This places the character 1 followed by the character 0 on the standard output stream.

Equivalently, we could write:

```
void g()
{
      int x {10};
      cout << x;
}
```

Output of different types can be combined in the obvious way:

```
void h(int i)
{
	cout << "the value of i is ";
	cout << i;
	cout << '\n';
}
```

For h(10), the output will be:

```
the value of i is 10
```

People soon tire of repeating the name of the output stream when outputting several related items. Fortunately, the result of an output expression can itself be used for further output. For example:

```
void h2(int i)
{
	cout << "the value of i is " << i << '\n';
}
```

This h2() produces the same output as h().

A character constant is a character enclosed in single quotes. Note that a character is output as a character rather than as a numerical value. For example:

```
void k()
{
	int b = 'b';		// note: char implicitly converted to int
	char c = 'c';
	cout << 'a' << b << c;
}
```

The integer value of the character 'b' is 98 (in the ASCII encoding used on the C++ implementation that I used), so this will output a98c.

10.3 Input

In <istream>, the standard library offers istreams for input. Like ostreams, istreams deal with character string representations of built-in types and can easily be extended to cope with user-defined types.

The operator >> ("get from") is used as an input operator; cin is the standard input stream. The type of the right-hand operand of >> determines what input is accepted and what is the target of the input operation. For example:

```
void f()
{
	int i;
	cin >> i;		// read an integer into i

	double d;
	cin >> d;		// read a double-precision floating-point number into d
}
```

This reads a number, such as 1234, from the standard input into the integer variable i and a floating-point number, such as 12.34e5, into the double-precision floating-point variable d.

Like output operations, input operations can be chained, so I could equivalently have written:

```
void f()
{
    int i;
    double d;
    cin >> i >> d;        // read into i and d
}
```

In both cases, the read of the integer is terminated by any character that is not a digit. By default, >> skips initial whitespace, so a suitable complete input sequence would be

```
1234
12.34e5
```

Often, we want to read a sequence of characters. A convenient way of doing that is to read into a string. For example:

```
void hello()
{
    cout << "Please enter your name\n";
    string str;
    cin >> str;
    cout << "Hello, " << str << "!\n";
}
```

If you type in Eric the response is:

```
Hello, Eric!
```

By default, a whitespace character, such as a space or a newline, terminates the read, so if you enter Eric Bloodaxe pretending to be the ill-fated king of York, the response is still:

```
Hello, Eric!
```

You can read a whole line using the getline() function. For example:

```
void hello_line()
{
    cout << "Please enter your name\n";
    string str;
    getline(cin,str);
    cout << "Hello, " << str << "!\n";
}
```

With this program, the input Eric Bloodaxe yields the desired output:

```
Hello, Eric Bloodaxe!
```

The newline that terminated the line is discarded, so cin is ready for the next input line.

Using the formatted I/O operations is usually less error-prone, more efficient, and less code than manipulating characters one by one. In particular, istreams take care of memory management and range checking. We can do formatting to and from memory using stringstreams (§10.8).

The standard strings have the nice property of expanding to hold what you put in them; you don't have to pre-calculate a maximum size. So, if you enter a couple of megabytes of semicolons, the program will echo pages of semicolons back at you.

10.4 I/O State

An iostream has a state that we can examine to determine whether an operation succeeded. The most common use is to read a sequence of values:

```
vector<int> read_ints(istream& is)
{
        vector<int> res;
        for (int i; is>>i; )
                res.push_back(i);
        return res;
}
```

This reads from is until something that is not an integer is encountered. That something will typically be the end of input. What is happening here is that the operation is>>i returns a reference to is, and testing an iostream yields true if the stream is ready for another operation.

In general, the I/O state holds all the information needed to read or write, such as formatting information (§10.6), error state (e.g., has end-of-input been reached?), and what kind of buffering is used. In particular, a user can set the state to reflect that an error has occurred (§10.5) and clear the state if an error wasn't serious. For example, we could imagine a version of read_ints() that accepted a terminating string:

```
vector<int> read_ints(istream& is, const string& terminator)
{
        vector<int> res;
        for (int i; is >> i; )
                res.push_back(i);

        if (is.eof())                   // fine: end of file
                return res;

        if (is.fail()) {                // we failed to read an int; was it the terminator?
                is.clear();     // reset the state to good()
                is.unget();     // put the non-digit back into the stream
                string s;
                if (cin>>s && s==terminator)
                        return res;
                cin.setstate(ios_base::failbit);        // add fail() to cin's state
        }

        return res;
}

auto v = read_ints(cin,"stop");
```

10.5 I/O of User-Defined Types

In addition to the I/O of built-in types and standard **strings**, the **iostream** library allows programmers to define I/O for their own types. For example, consider a simple type **Entry** that we might use to represent entries in a telephone book:

```
struct Entry {
        string name;
        int number;
};
```

We can define a simple output operator to write an **Entry** using a *{"name",number}* format similar to the one we use for initialization in code:

```
ostream& operator<<(ostream& os, const Entry& e)
{
        return os << "{\"" << e.name << "\", " << e.number << "}";
}
```

A user-defined output operator takes its output stream (by reference) as its first argument and returns it as its result.

The corresponding input operator is more complicated because it has to check for correct formatting and deal with errors:

```
istream& operator>>(istream& is, Entry& e)
        // read { "name" , number } pair. Note: formatted with { " " , and }
{
        char c, c2;
        if (is>>c && c=='{' && is>>c2 && c2=='"') { // start with a { "
                string name;                     // the default value of a string is the empty string: ""
                while (is.get(c) && c!='"')      // anything before a " is part of the name
                        name+=c;

                if (is>>c && c==',') {
                        int number = 0;
                        if (is>>number>>c && c=='}') { // read the number and a }
                                e = {name,number};     // assign to the entry
                                return is;
                        }
                }
        }
        is.setstate(ios_base::failbit);          // register the failure in the stream
        return is;
}
```

An input operation returns a reference to its **istream** that can be used to test if the operation succeeded. For example, when used as a condition, **is>>c** means "Did we succeed at reading a **char** from **is** into **c**?"

The **is>>c** skips whitespace by default, but **is.get(c)** does not, so this **Entry**-input operator ignores (skips) whitespace outside the name string, but not within it. For example:

```
{ "John Marwood Cleese", 123456        }
{"Michael Edward Palin", 987654}
```

We can read such a pair of values from input into an **Entry** like this:

```
for (Entry ee; cin>>ee; )   // read from cin into ee
      cout << ee << '\n';   // write ee to cout
```

The output is:

```
{"John Marwood Cleese", 123456}
{"Michael Edward Palin", 987654}
```

See §9.4 for a more systematic technique for recognizing patterns in streams of characters (regular expression matching).

10.6 Formatting

The **iostream** library provides a large set of operations for controlling the format of input and output. The simplest formatting controls are called *manipulators* and are found in **<ios>**, **<istream>**, **<ostream>**, and **<iomanip>** (for manipulators that take arguments). For example, we can output integers as decimal (the default), octal, or hexadecimal numbers:

```
cout << 1234 << ',' << hex << 1234 << ',' << oct << 1234 << '\n';        // print 1234,4d2,2322
```

We can explicitly set the output format for floating-point numbers:

```
constexpr double d = 123.456;

cout << d << "; "                    // use the default format for d
      << scientific << d << "; "     // use 1.123e2 style format for d
      << hexfloat << d << "; "       // use hexadecimal notation for d
      << fixed << d << "; "          // use 123.456 style format for d
      << defaultfloat << d << '\n';  // use the default format for d
```

This produces:

```
123.456; 1.234560e+002; 0x1.edd2f2p+6; 123.456000; 123.456
```

Precision is an integer that determines the number of digits used to display a floating-point number:

- The *general* format (**defaultfloat**) lets the implementation choose a format that presents a value in the style that best preserves the value in the space available. The precision specifies the maximum number of digits.
- The *scientific* format (**scientific**) presents a value with one digit before a decimal point and an exponent. The precision specifies the maximum number of digits after the decimal point.
- The *fixed* format (**fixed**) presents a value as an integer part followed by a decimal point and a fractional part. The precision specifies the maximum number of digits after the decimal point.

Floating-point values are rounded rather than just truncated, and **precision()** doesn't affect integer output. For example:

```
cout.precision(8);
cout << 1234.56789 << ' ' << 1234.56789 << ' ' << 123456 << '\n';

cout.precision(4);
cout << 1234.56789 << ' ' << 1234.56789 << ' ' << 123456 << '\n';
cout << 1234.56789 << '\n';
```

This produces:

```
1234.5679 1234.5679 123456
1235 1235 123456
1235
```

These floating-point manipulators are "sticky"; that is, their effects persist for subsequent floating-point operations.

10.7 File Streams

In <fstream>, the standard library provides streams to and from a file:

- ifstreams for reading from a file
- ofstreams for writing to a file
- fstreams for reading from and writing to a file

For example:

```
ofstream ofs {"target"};          // "o" for "output"
if (!ofs)
        error("couldn't open 'target' for writing");
```

Testing that a file stream has been properly opened is usually done by checking its state.

```
ifstream ifs {"source"};          // "i" for "input"
if (!ifs)
        error("couldn't open 'source' for reading");
```

Assuming that the tests succeeded, ofs can be used as an ordinary ostream (just like cout) and ifs can be used as an ordinary istream (just like cin).

File positioning and more detailed control of the way a file is opened is possible, but beyond the scope of this book.

For the composition of file names and file system manipulation, see §10.10.

10.8 String Streams

In <sstream>, the standard library provides streams to and from a string:

- istringstreams for reading from a string
- ostringstreams for writing to a string
- stringstreams for reading from and writing to a string.

For example:

```
void test()
{
      ostringstream oss;

      oss << "{temperature," << scientific << 123.4567890 << "}";
      cout << oss.str() << '\n';
}
```

The result from an ostringstream can be read using str(). One common use of an ostringstream is to format before giving the resulting string to a GUI. Similarly, a string received from a GUI can be read using formatted input operations (§10.3) by putting it into an istringstream.

A stringstream can be used for both reading and writing. For example, we can define an operation that can convert any type with a string representation into another that can also be represented as a string:

```
template<typename Target =string, typename Source =string>
Target to(Source arg)            // convert Source to Target
{
   stringstream interpreter;
   Target result;

   if (!(interpreter << arg)                    // write arg into stream
      || !(interpreter >> result)               // read result from stream
      || !(interpreter >> std::ws).eof())       // stuff left in stream?
      throw runtime_error{"to<>() failed"};

   return result;
}
```

A function template argument needs to be explicitly mentioned only if it cannot be deduced or if there is no default (§7.2.4), so we can write:

```
auto x1 = to<string,double>(1.2);   // very explicit (and verbose)
auto x2 = to<string>(1.2);          // Source is deduced to double
auto x3 = to<>(1.2);                // Target is defaulted to string; Source is deduced to double
auto x4 = to(1.2);                  // the <> is redundant;
                                    // Target is defaulted to string; Source is deduced to double
```

If all function template arguments are defaulted, the <> can be left out.

I consider this a good example of the generality and ease of use that can be achieved by a combination of language features and standard-library facilities.

10.9 C-style I/O

The C++ standard library also supports the C standard-library I/O, including printf() and scanf(). Many uses of this library are unsafe from a type and security point-of-view, so I don't recommend its use. In particular, it can be difficult to use for safe and convenient input. It does not support user-defined types. If you *don't* use C-style I/O and care about I/O performance, call

```
ios_base::sync_with_stdio(false);        // avoid significant overhead
```

Without that call, iostreams can be significantly slowed down to be compatible with the C-style I/O.

10.10 File System

Most systems have a notion of a *file system* providing access to permanent information stored as *files*. Unfortunately, the properties of file systems and the ways of manipulating them vary greatly. To deal with that, the file system library in <filesystem> offers a uniform interface to most facilities of most file systems. Using <filesystem>, we can portably

- express file system paths and navigate through a file system
- examine file types and the permissions associated with them

The filesystem library can handle unicode, but explaining how is beyond the scope of this book. I recommend the cppreference [Cppreference] and the Boost filesystem documentation [Boost] for detailed information.

Consider an example:

```
path f = "dir/hypothetical.cpp";        // naming a file

assert(exists(f));              // f must exist

if (is_regular_file(f))         // is f an ordinary file?
    cout << f << " is a file; its size is " << file_size(f) << '\n';
```

Note that a program manipulating a file system is usually running on a computer together with other programs. Thus, the contents of a file system can change between two commands. For example, even though we first of all carefully asserted that f existed, that may no longer be true when on the next line, we ask if f is a regular file.

A path is quite a complicated class, capable of handling the native character sets and conventions of many operating systems. In particular, it can handle file names from command lines as presented by main(); for example:

```
int main(int argc, char* argv[])
{
        if (argc < 2) {
                cerr << "arguments expected\n";
                return 1;
        }

        path p {argv[1]};       // create a path from the command line

        cout << p << " " << exists(p) << '\n';          // note: a path can be printed like a string
        // ...
}
```

A path is not checked for validity until it is used. Even then, its validity depends on the conventions of the system on which the program runs.

Naturally, a path can be used to open a file

```
void use(path p)
{
      ofstream f {p};
      if (!f) error("bad file name: ", p);
      f << "Hello, file!";
}
```

In addition to path, <filesystem> offers types for traversing directories and inquiring about the properties of the files found:

File System Types (partial)	
path	A directory path
filesystem_error	A file system exception
directory_entry	A directory entry
directory_iterator	For iterating over a directory
recursive_directory_iterator	For iterating over a directory and its subdirectories

Consider a simple, but not completely unrealistic, example:

```
void print_directory(path p)
try
{
      if (is_directory(p)) {
            cout << p << ":\n";
            for (const directory_entry& x : directory_iterator{p})
                  cout << "    " << x.path() << '\n';
      }
}
catch (const filesystem_error& ex) {
      cerr << ex.what() << '\n';
}
```

A string can be implicitly converted to a path so we can exercise print_directory like this:

```
void use()
{
      print_directory(".");       // current directory
      print_directory("..");      // parent directory
      print_directory("/");       // Unix root directory
      print_directory("c:");      // Windows volume C

      for (string s; cin>>s; )
            print_directory(s);
}
```

Had I wanted to list subdirectories also, I would have said recursive_directory_iterator{p}. Had I wanted to print entries in lexicographical order, I would have copied the paths into a vector and sorted that before printing.

Class path offers many common and useful operations:

Path Operations (partial) p and p2 are paths	
value_type	Character type used by the native encoding of the filesystem: char on POSIX, wchar_t on Windows
string_type	std::basic_string<value_type>
const_iterator	A const BidirectionalIterator with a value_type of path
iterator	Alias for const_iterator
p=p2	Assign p2 to p
p/=p2	p and p2 concatenated using the file-name separator (by default /)
p+=p2	p and p2 concatenated (no separator)
p.native()	The native format of p
p.string()	p in the native format of p as a string
p.generic_string()	p in the generic format as a string
p.filename()	The filename part of p
p.stem()	The stem part of p
p.extension()	The file extension part of p
p.begin()	The beginning of p's element sequence
p.end()	The end of p's element sequence
p==p2, p!=p2	Equality and inequality for p and p2
p<p2, p<=p2, p>p2, p>=p2	Lexicographical comparisons
is>>p, os<<p	Stream I/O to/from p
u8path(s)	A path from a UTF-8 encoded source s

For example:

```
void test(path p)
{
     if (is_directory(p)) {
          cout << p << ":\n";
          for (const directory_entry& x : directory_iterator(p)) {
               const path& f = x;     // refer to the path part of a directory entry
               if (f.extension() == ".exe")
                    cout << f.stem() << " is a Windows executable\n";
               else {
                    string n = f.extension().string();
                    if (n == ".cpp" || n == ".C" || n == ".cxx")
                         cout << f.stem() << " is a C++ source file\n";
               }
          }
     }
}
```

We use a path as a string (e.g., f.extension) and we can extract strings of various types from a path (e.g., f.extension().string()).

Note that naming conventions, natural languages, and string encodings are rich in complexity. The filesystem-library abstractions offer portability and great simplification.

File System Operations (partial) p, p1, and p2 are paths; e is an error_code; b is a bool indicating success or failure	
exists(p)	Does p refer to an existing file system object?
copy(p1,p2)	Copy files or directories from p1 to p2; report errors as exceptions
copy(p1,p2,e)	Copy files or directories; report errors as error codes
b=copy_file(p1,p2)	Copy file contents from p1 to p2; report errors as exceptions
b=create_directory(p)	Create new directory named p; all intermediate directories on p must exist
b=create_directories(p)	Create new directory named p; create all intermediate directories on p
p=current_path()	p is the current working directory
current_path(p)	Make p the current working directory
s=file_size(p)	s is the number of bytes in p
b=remove(p)	Remove p if it is a file or an empty directory

Many operations have overloads that take extra arguments, such as operating systems permissions. The handling of such is far beyond the scope of this book, so look them up if you need them.

Like copy(), all operations come in two versions:

- The basic version as listed in the table, e.g., exists(p). The function will throw filesystem_error if the operation failed.
- A version with an extra error_code argument, e.g., exists(p,e). Check e to see if the operations succeeded.

We use the error codes when operations are expected to fail frequently in normal use and the throwing operations when an error is considered exceptional.

Often, using an inquiry function is the simplest and most straightforward approach to examining the properties of a file. The <filesystem> library knows about a few common kinds of files and classifies the rest as "other":

File types f Is a path or a file_status	
is_block_file(f)	Is f a block device?
is_character_file(f)	Is f a character device?
is_directory(f)	Is f a directory?
is_empty(f)	Is f an empty file or directory?
is_fifo(f)	Is f a named pipe?
is_other(f)	Is f some other kind of file?
is_regular_file(f)	Is f a regular (ordinary) file?
is_socket(f)	Is f a named IPC socket?
is_symlink(f)	Is f a symbolic link?
status_known(f)	Is f's file status known?

10.11 Advice

[1] iostreams are type-safe, type-sensitive, and extensible; §10.1.
[2] Use character-level input only when you have to; §10.3; [CG: SL.io.1].
[3] When reading, always consider ill-formed input; §10.3; [CG: SL.io.2].
[4] Avoid endl (if you don't know what endl is, you haven't missed anything); [CG: SL.io.50].
[5] Define << and >> for user-defined types with values that have meaningful textual representations; §10.1, §10.2, §10.3.
[6] Use cout for normal output and cerr for errors; §10.1.
[7] There are iostreams for ordinary characters and wide characters, and you can define an iostream for any kind of character; §10.1.
[8] Binary I/O is supported; §10.1.
[9] There are standard iostreams for standard I/O streams, files, and strings; §10.2, §10.3, §10.7, §10.8.
[10] Chain << operations for a terser notation; §10.2.
[11] Chain >> operations for a terser notation; §10.3.
[12] Input into strings does not overflow; §10.3.
[13] By default >> skips initial whitespace; §10.3.
[14] Use the stream state fail to handle potentially recoverable I/O errors; §10.4.
[15] You can define << and >> operators for your own types; §10.5.
[16] You don't need to modify istream or ostream to add new << and >> operators; §10.5.
[17] Use manipulators to control formatting; §10.6.
[18] precision() specifications apply to all following floating-point output operations; §10.6.
[19] Floating-point format specifications (e.g., scientific) apply to all following floating-point output operations; §10.6.
[20] #include <ios> when using standard manipulators; §10.6.
[21] #include <iomanip> when using standard manipulators taking arguments; §10.6.
[22] Don't try to copy a file stream.
[23] Remember to check that a file stream is attached to a file before using it; §10.7.
[24] Use stringstreams for in-memory formatting; §10.8.
[25] You can define conversions between any two types that both have string representation; §10.8.
[26] C-style I/O is not type-safe; §10.9.
[27] Unless you use printf-family functions call ios_base::sync_with_stdio(false); §10.9; [CG: SL.io.10].
[28] Prefer <filesystem> to direct use of a specific operating system interfaces; §10.10.

11

Containers

It was new.
It was singular.
It was simple.
It must succeed!
– H. Nelson

- Introduction
- vector
  Elements; Range Checking
- list
- map
- unordered_map
- Container Overview
- Advice

11.1 Introduction

Most computing involves creating collections of values and then manipulating such collections. Reading characters into a string and printing out the string is a simple example. A class with the main purpose of holding objects is commonly called a *container*. Providing suitable containers for a given task and supporting them with useful fundamental operations are important steps in the construction of any program.

To illustrate the standard-library containers, consider a simple program for keeping names and telephone numbers. This is the kind of program for which different approaches appear "simple and obvious" to people of different backgrounds. The Entry class from §10.5 can be used to hold a simple phone book entry. Here, we deliberately ignore many real-world complexities, such as the fact that many phone numbers do not have a simple representation as a 32-bit int.

11.2 vector

The most useful standard-library container is vector. A vector is a sequence of elements of a given type. The elements are stored contiguously in memory. A typical implementation of vector (§4.2.2, §5.2) will consist of a handle holding pointers to the first element, one-past-the-last element, and one-past-the-last allocated space (§12.1) (or the equivalent information represented as a pointer plus offsets):

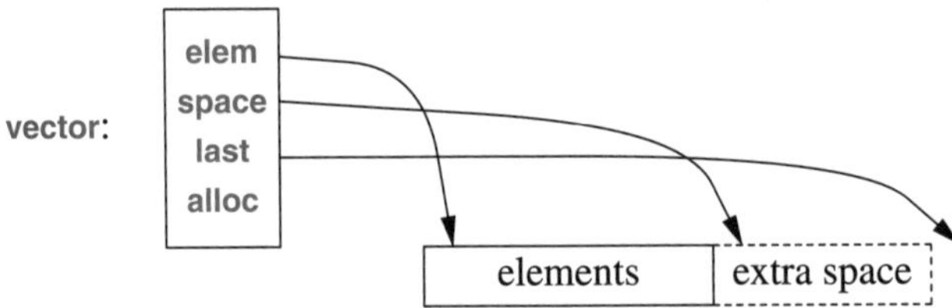

In addition, it holds an allocator (here, alloc), from which the vector can acquire memory for its elements. The default allocator uses new and delete to acquire and release memory (§13.6).

We can initialize a vector with a set of values of its element type:

```
vector<Entry> phone_book = {
	{"David Hume",123456},
	{"Karl Popper",234567},
	{"Bertrand Arthur William Russell",345678}
};
```

Elements can be accessed through subscripting. So, assuming that we have defined << for Entry, we can write:

```
void print_book(const vector<Entry>& book)
{
	for (int i = 0; i!=book.size(); ++i)
		cout << book[i] << '\n';
}
```

As usual, indexing starts at 0 so that book[0] holds the entry for David Hume. The vector member function size() gives the number of elements.

The elements of a vector constitute a range, so we can use a range-for loop (§1.7):

```
void print_book(const vector<Entry>& book)
{
	for (const auto& x : book)	// for "auto" see §1.4
		cout << x << '\n';
}
```

When we define a vector, we give it an initial size (initial number of elements):

```
vector<int> v1 = {1, 2, 3, 4};		// size is 4
vector<string> v2;			// size is 0
vector<Shape*> v3(23);			// size is 23; initial element value: nullptr
vector<double> v4(32,9.9);		// size is 32; initial element value: 9.9
```

An explicit size is enclosed in ordinary parentheses, for example, (23), and by default, the elements are initialized to the element type's default value (e.g., nullptr for pointers and 0 for numbers). If you don't want the default value, you can specify one as a second argument (e.g., 9.9 for the 32 elements of v4).

The initial size can be changed. One of the most useful operations on a vector is push_back(), which adds a new element at the end of a vector, increasing its size by one. For example, assuming that we have defined >> for Entry, we can write:

```
void input()
{
      for (Entry e; cin>>e; )
            phone_book.push_back(e);
}
```

This reads Entrys from the standard input into phone_book until either the end-of-input (e.g., the end of a file) is reached or the input operation encounters a format error.

The standard-library vector is implemented so that growing a vector by repeated push_back()s is efficient. To show how, consider an elaboration of the simple Vector from (Chapter 4 and Chapter 6) using the representation indicated in the diagram above:

```
template<typename T>
class Vector {
      T* elem;         // pointer to first element
      T* space;        // pointer to first unused (and uninitialized) slot
      T* last;         // pointer to last slot
public:
      // ...
      int size();                          // number of elements (space-elem)
      int capacity();                      // number of slots available for elements (last-elem)
      // ...
      void reserve(int newsz);             // increase capacity() to newsz
      // ...
      void push_back(const T& t);          // copy t into Vector
      void push_back(T&& t);               // move t into Vector
};
```

The standard-library vector has members capacity(), reserve(), and push_back(). The reserve() is used by users of vector and other vector members to make room for more elements. It may have to allocate new memory and when it does, it moves the elements to the new allocation.

Given capacity() and reserve(), implementing push_back() is trivial:

```
template<typename T>
void Vector<T>::push_back(const T& t)
{
      if (capacity()<size()+1)                  // make sure we have space for t
            reserve(size()==0?8:2*size());      // double the capacity
      new(space) T{t};                          // initialize *space to t
      ++space;
}
```

Now allocation and relocation of elements happens only infrequently. I used to use reserve() to try to improve performance, but that turned out to be a waste of effort: the heuristic used by vector is on average better than my guesses, so now I only explicitly use reserve() to avoid reallocation of elements when I want to use pointers to elements.

A vector can be copied in assignments and initializations. For example:

```
vector<Entry> book2 = phone_book;
```

Copying and moving of vectors are implemented by constructors and assignment operators as described in §5.2. Assigning a vector involves copying its elements. Thus, after the initialization of book2, book2 and phone_book hold separate copies of every Entry in the phone book. When a vector holds many elements, such innocent-looking assignments and initializations can be expensive. Where copying is undesirable, references or pointers (§1.7) or move operations (§5.2.2) should be used.

The standard-library vector is very flexible and efficient. Use it as your default container; that is, use it unless you have a solid reason to use some other container. If you avoid vector because of concerns about "efficiency," measure. Our intuition is most fallible in matters of the performance of container uses.

11.2.1 Elements

Like all standard-library containers, vector is a container of elements of some type T, that is, a vector<T>. Just about any type qualifies as an element type: built-in numeric types (such as char, int, and double), user-defined types (such as string, Entry, list<int>, and Matrix<double,2>), and pointers (such as const char*, Shape*, and double*). When you insert a new element, its value is copied into the container. For example, when you put an integer with the value 7 into a container, the resulting element really has the value 7. The element is not a reference or a pointer to some object containing 7. This makes for nice, compact containers with fast access. For people who care about memory sizes and run-time performance this is critical.

If you have a class hierarchy (§4.5) that relies on virtual functions to get polymorphic behavior, do not store objects directly in a container. Instead store a pointer (or a smart pointer; §13.2.1). For example:

```
vector<Shape> vs;                   // No, don't - there is no room for a Circle or a Smiley
vector<Shape*> vps;                 // better, but see §4.5.3
vector<unique_ptr<Shape>> vups;     // OK
```

11.2.2 Range Checking

The standard-library vector does not guarantee range checking. For example:

```
void silly(vector<Entry>& book)
{
        int i = book[book.size()].number;        // book.size() is out of range
        // ...
}
```

That initialization is likely to place some random value in i rather than giving an error. This is undesirable, and out-of-range errors are a common problem. Consequently, I often use a simple range-checking adaptation of vector:

```
template<typename T>
class Vec : public std::vector<T> {
public:
     using vector<T>::vector;                    // use the constructors from vector (under the name Vec)

     T& operator[](int i)                        // range check
          { return vector<T>::at(i); }

     const T& operator[](int i) const            // range check const objects; §4.2.1
          { return vector<T>::at(i); }
};
```

Vec inherits everything from vector except for the subscript operations that it redefines to do range checking. The at() operation is a vector subscript operation that throws an exception of type out_of_range if its argument is out of the vector's range (§3.5.1).

For Vec, an out-of-range access will throw an exception that the user can catch. For example:

```
void checked(Vec<Entry>& book)
{
     try {
          book[book.size()] = {"Joe",999999};      // will throw an exception
          // ...
     }
     catch (out_of_range&) {
          cerr << "range error\n";
     }
}
```

The exception will be thrown, and then caught (§3.5.1). If the user doesn't catch an exception, the program will terminate in a well-defined manner rather than proceeding or failing in an undefined manner. One way to minimize surprises from uncaught exceptions is to use a main() with a try-block as its body. For example:

```
int main()
try {
     // your code
}
catch (out_of_range&) {
     cerr << "range error\n";
}
catch (...) {
     cerr << "unknown exception thrown\n";
}
```

This provides default exception handlers so that if we fail to catch some exception, an error message is printed on the standard error-diagnostic output stream cerr (§10.2).

Why doesn't the standard guarantee range checking? Many performance-critical applications use vectors and checking all subscripting implies a cost on the order of 10%. Obviously, that cost can vary dramatically depending on hardware, optimizers, and an application's use of subscripting. However, experience shows that such overhead can lead people to prefer the far more unsafe built-in arrays. Even the mere fear of such overhead can lead to disuse. At least vector is easily range checked at debug time and we can build checked versions on top of the unchecked default. Some implementations save you the bother of defining Vec (or equivalent) by providing a range-checked version of vector (e.g., as a compiler option).

A range-for avoids range errors at no cost by accessing elements through iterators in the range [begin():end()). As long as their iterator arguments are valid, the standard-library algorithms do the same to ensure the absence of range errors.

If you can use vector::at() directly in your code, you don't need my Vec workaround. Furthermore, some standard libraries have range-checked vector implementations that offer more complete checking than Vec.

11.3 list

The standard library offers a doubly-linked list called list:

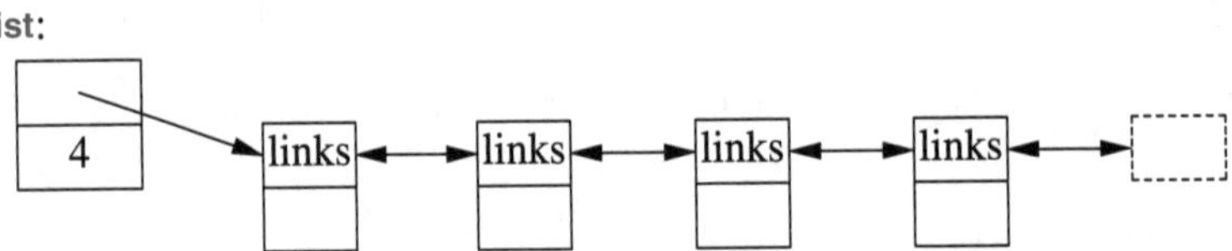

We use a list for sequences where we want to insert and delete elements without moving other elements. Insertion and deletion of phone book entries could be common, so a list could be appropriate for representing a simple phone book. For example:

```
list<Entry> phone_book = {
      {"David Hume",123456},
      {"Karl Popper",234567},
      {"Bertrand Arthur William Russell",345678}
};
```

When we use a linked list, we tend not to access elements using subscripting the way we commonly do for vectors. Instead, we might search the list looking for an element with a given value. To do this, we take advantage of the fact that a list is a sequence as described in Chapter 12:

```
int get_number(const string& s)
{
      for (const auto& x : phone_book)
            if (x.name==s)
                  return x.number;
      return 0;   // use 0 to represent "number not found"
}
```

The search for s starts at the beginning of the list and proceeds until s is found or the end of phone_book is reached.

Sometimes, we need to identify an element in a list. For example, we may want to delete an element or insert a new element before it. To do that we use an *iterator*: a list iterator identifies an element of a list and can be used to iterate through a list (hence its name). Every standard-library container provides the functions begin() and end(), which return an iterator to the first and to one-past-the-last element, respectively (Chapter 12). Using iterators explicitly, we can – less elegantly – write the get_number() function like this:

```
int get_number(const string& s)
{
      for (auto p = phone_book.begin(); p!=phone_book.end(); ++p)
            if (p->name==s)
                  return p->number;
      return 0;  // use 0 to represent "number not found"
}
```

In fact, this is roughly the way the terser and less error-prone range-for loop is implemented by the compiler. Given an iterator p, *p is the element to which it refers, ++p advances p to refer to the next element, and when p refers to a class with a member m, then p->m is equivalent to (*p).m.

Adding elements to a list and removing elements from a list is easy:

```
void f(const Entry& ee, list<Entry>::iterator p, list<Entry>::iterator q)
{
      phone_book.insert(p,ee);        // add ee before the element referred to by p
      phone_book.erase(q);            // remove the element referred to by q
}
```

For a list, insert(p,elem) inserts an element with a copy of the value elem before the element pointed to by p. Here, p may be an iterator pointing one-beyond-the-end of the list. Conversely, erase(p) removes the element pointed to by p and destroys it.

These list examples could be written identically using vector and (surprisingly, unless you understand machine architecture) perform better with a small vector than with a small list. When all we want is a sequence of elements, we have a choice between using a vector and a list. Unless you have a reason not to, use a vector. A vector performs better for traversal (e.g., find() and count()) and for sorting and searching (e.g., sort() and equal_range(); §12.6, §13.4.3).

The standard library also offers a singly-linked list called forward_list:

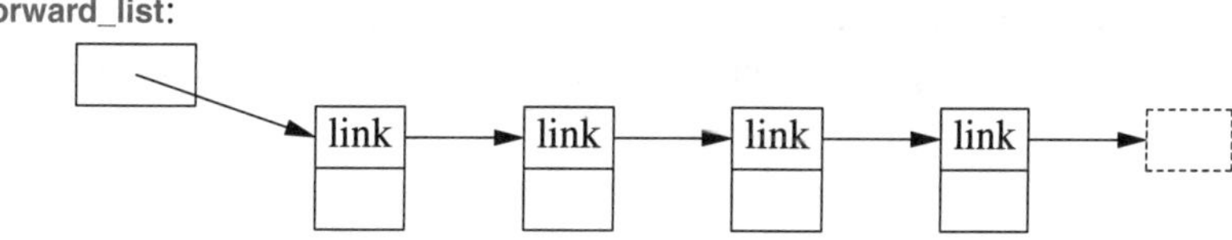

A forward_list differs from a list by only allowing forward iteration. The point of that is to save space. There is no need to keep a predecessor pointer in each link and the size of an empty forward_list is just one pointer. A forward_list doesn't even keep its number of elements. If you need the element count, count. If you can't afford to count, you probably shouldn't use a forward_list.

11.4 map

Writing code to look up a name in a list of *(name,number)* pairs is quite tedious. In addition, a linear search is inefficient for all but the shortest lists. The standard library offers a balanced binary search tree (usually, a red-black tree) called map:

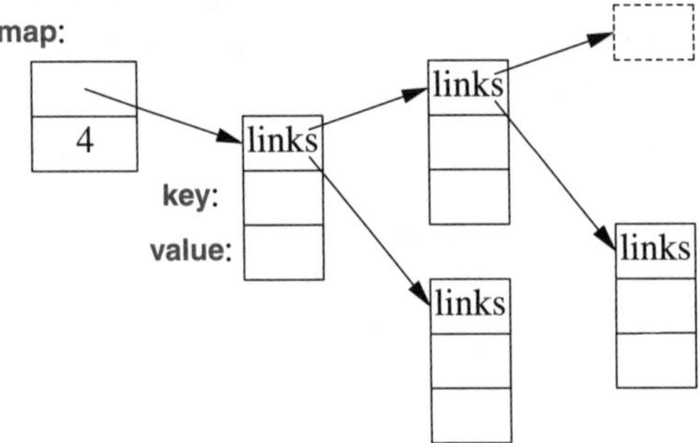

In other contexts, a map is known as an associative array or a dictionary. It is implemented as a balanced binary tree.

The standard-library map is a container of pairs of values optimized for lookup. We can use the same initializer as for vector and list (§11.2, §11.3):

```
map<string,int> phone_book {
        {"David Hume",123456},
        {"Karl Popper",234567},
        {"Bertrand Arthur William Russell",345678}
};
```

When indexed by a value of its first type (called the *key*), a map returns the corresponding value of the second type (called the *value* or the *mapped type*). For example:

```
int get_number(const string& s)
{
        return phone_book[s];
}
```

In other words, subscripting a map is essentially the lookup we called get_number(). If a key isn't found, it is entered into the map with a default value for its value. The default value for an integer type is 0; the value I just happened to choose represents an invalid telephone number.

If we wanted to avoid entering invalid numbers into our phone book, we could use find() and insert() instead of [ ].

11.5 unordered_map

The cost of a map lookup is O(log(n)) where n is the number of elements in the map. That's pretty good. For example, for a map with 1,000,000 elements, we perform only about 20 comparisons and indirections to find an element. However, in many cases, we can do better by using a hashed lookup rather than a comparison using an ordering function, such as <. The standard-library hashed containers are referred to as "unordered" because they don't require an ordering function:

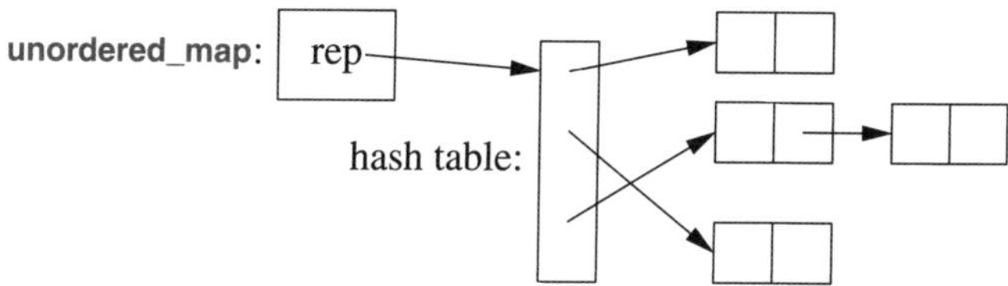

For example, we can use an unordered_map from <unordered_map> for our phone book:

```
unordered_map<string,int> phone_book {
      {"David Hume",123456},
      {"Karl Popper",234567},
      {"Bertrand Arthur William Russell",345678}
};
```

Like for a map, we can subscript an unordered_map:

```
int get_number(const string& s)
{
      return phone_book[s];
}
```

The standard library provides a default hash function for strings as well as for other built-in and standard-library types. If necessary, you can provide your own (§5.4.6). Possibly, the most common need for a "custom" hash function comes when we want an unordered container of one of our own types. A hash function is often provided as a function object (§6.3.2). For example:

```
struct Record {
      string name;
      int product_code;
      // ...
};

struct Rhash {       // a hash function for Record
      size_t operator()(const Record& r) const
      {
            return hash<string>()(r.name) ^ hash<int>()(r.product_code);
      }
};

unordered_set<Record,Rhash> my_set; // set of Records using Rhash for lookup
```

Designing good hash functions is an art and sometimes requires knowledge of the data to which it will be applied. Creating a new hash function by combining existing hash functions using exclusive-or (^) is simple and often very effective.

We can avoid explicitly passing the hash operation by defining it as a specialization of the standard-library hash:

```
namespace std { // make a hash function for Record

    template<> struct hash<Record> {
        using argument_type = Record;
        using result_type = std::size_t;

        size_t operator()(const Record& r) const
        {
            return hash<string>()(r.name) ^ hash<int>()(r.product_code);
        }
    };
}
```

Note the differences between a map and an unordered_map:

- A map requires an ordering function (the default is <) and yields an ordered sequence.
- A unordered_map requires and an equality function (the default is ==); it does not maintain an order among its elements.

Given a good hash function, an unordered_map is much faster than a map for large containers. However, the worst-case behavior of an unordered_map with a poor hash function is far worse than that of a map.

11.6 Container Overview

The standard library provides some of the most general and useful container types to allow the programmer to select a container that best serves the needs of an application:

Standard Container Summary	
vector<T>	A variable-size vector (§11.2)
list<T>	A doubly-linked list (§11.3)
forward_list<T>	A singly-linked list
deque<T>	A double-ended queue
set<T>	A set (a map with just a key and no value)
multiset<T>	A set in which a value can occur many times
map<K,V>	An associative array (§11.4)
multimap<K,V>	A map in which a key can occur many times
unordered_map<K,V>	A map using a hashed lookup (§11.5)
unordered_multimap<K,V>	A multimap using a hashed lookup
unordered_set<T>	A set using a hashed lookup
unordered_multiset<T>	A multiset using a hashed lookup

The unordered containers are optimized for lookup with a key (often a string); in other words, they are implemented using hash tables.

The containers are defined in namespace std and presented in headers <vector>, <list>, <map>, etc. (§8.3). In addition, the standard library provides container adaptors queue<T>, stack<T>, and priority_queue<T>. Look them up if you need them. The standard library also provides more specialized container-like types, such as array<T,N> (§13.4.1) and bitset<N> (§13.4.2).

The standard containers and their basic operations are designed to be similar from a notational point of view. Furthermore, the meanings of the operations are equivalent for the various containers. Basic operations apply to every kind of container for which they make sense and can be efficiently implemented:

Standard Container Operations (partial)	
value_type	The type of an element
p=c.begin()	p points to first element of c; also cbegin() for an iterator to const
p=c.end()	p points to one-past-the-last element of c; also cend() for an iterator to const
k=c.size()	k is the number of elements in c
c.empty()	Is c empty?
k=c.capacity()	k is the number of elements that c can hold without a new allocation
c.reserve(k)	Make the capacity k
c.resize(k)	Make the number of elements k; added elements has the value value_type{}
c[k]	The kth element of c; no range checking
c.at(k)	The kth element of c; if out of range, throw out_of_range
c.push_back(x)	Add x at the end of c; increase the size of c by one
c.emplace_back(a)	Add value_type{a} at the end of c; increase the size of c by one
q=c.insert(p,x)	Add x before p in c
q=c.erase(p)	Remove element at p from c
c=c2	Assignment
b=(c==c2), also !=	Equality of all elements of c and c2; b==true if equal
x=(c<c2), also <=, >, >=	Lexicographical order of c and c2: x<0 if less than, x==0 if equal, and 0<x if greater than

This notational and semantic uniformity enables programmers to provide new container types that can be used in a very similar manner to the standard ones. The range-checked vector, Vector (§3.5.2, Chapter 4), is an example of that. The uniformity of container interfaces allows us to specify algorithms independently of individual container types. However, each has strengths and weaknesses. For example, subscripting and traversing a vector is cheap and easy. On the other hand, vector elements are moved when we insert or remove elements; list has exactly the opposite properties. Please note that a vector is usually more efficient than a list for short sequences of small elements (even for insert() and erase()). I recommend the standard-library vector as the default type for sequences of elements: you need a reason to choose another.

Consider the singly-linked list, forward_list, a container optimized for the empty sequence (§11.3). An empty forward_list occupies just one word, whereas an empty vector occupy three. Empty sequences, and sequences with only an element or two, are surprisingly common and useful.

An emplace operation, such as emplace_back() takes arguments for an element's constructor and builds the object in a newly allocated space in the container, rather than copying an object into the container. For example, for a vector<pair<int,string>> we could write:

```
v.push_back(pair{1,"copy or move"));     // make a pair and move it into v
v.emplace_back(1,"build in place");      // buid a pair in v
```

11.7 Advice

[1] An STL container defines a sequence; §11.2.
[2] STL containers are resource handles; §11.2, §11.3, §11.4, §11.5.
[3] Use vector as your default container; §11.2, §11.6; [CG: SL.con.2].
[4] For simple traversals of a container, use a range-for loop or a begin/end pair of iterators; §11.2, §11.3.
[5] Use reserve() to avoid invalidating pointers and iterators to elements; §11.2.
[6] Don't assume performance benefits from reserve() without measurement; §11.2.
[7] Use push_back() or resize() on a container rather than realloc() on an array; §11.2.
[8] Don't use iterators into a resized vector; §11.2.
[9] Do not assume that [ ] range checks; §11.2.
[10] Use at() when you need guaranteed range checks; §11.2; [CG: SL.con.3].
[11] Use range-for and standard-library algorithms for cost-free avoidance of range errors; §11.2.2.
[12] Elements are copied into a container; §11.2.1.
[13] To preserve polymorphic behavior of elements, store pointers; §11.2.1.
[14] Insertion operations, such as insert() and push_back(), are often surprisingly efficient on a vector; §11.3.
[15] Use forward_list for sequences that are usually empty; §11.6.
[16] When it comes to performance, don't trust your intuition: measure; §11.2.
[17] A map is usually implemented as a red-black tree; §11.4.
[18] An unordered_map is a hash table; §11.5.
[19] Pass a container by reference and return a container by value; §11.2.
[20] For a container, use the ()-initializer syntax for sizes and the {}-initializer syntax for lists of elements; §4.2.3, §11.2.
[21] Prefer compact and contiguous data structures; §11.3.
[22] A list is relatively expensive to traverse; §11.3.
[23] Use unordered containers if you need fast lookup for large amounts of data; §11.5.
[24] Use ordered associative containers (e.g., map and set) if you need to iterate over their elements in order; §11.4.
[25] Use unordered containers for element types with no natural order (e.g., no reasonable <); §11.4.
[26] Experiment to check that you have an acceptable hash function; §11.5.
[27] A hash function obtained by combining standard hash functions for elements using the exclusive-or operator (^) is often good; §11.5.
[28] Know your standard-library containers and prefer them to handcrafted data structures; §11.6.

12

Algorithms

Do not multiply entities beyond necessity.
– William Occam

- Introduction
- Use of Iterators
- Iterator Types
- Stream Iterators
- Predicates
- Algorithm Overview
- Concepts
- Container Algorithms
- Parallel Algorithms
- Advice

12.1 Introduction

A data structure, such as a list or a vector, is not very useful on its own. To use one, we need operations for basic access such as adding and removing elements (as is provided for `list` and `vector`). Furthermore, we rarely just store objects in a container. We sort them, print them, extract subsets, remove elements, search for objects, etc. Consequently, the standard library provides the most common algorithms for containers in addition to providing the most common container types. For example, we can simply and efficiently sort a `vector` of `Entry`s and place a copy of each unique `vector` element on a `list`:

```
void f(vector<Entry>& vec, list<Entry>& lst)
{
     sort(vec.begin(),vec.end());                         // use < for order
     unique_copy(vec.begin(),vec.end(),lst.begin());      // don't copy adjacent equal elements
}
```

For this to work, less than (<) and equal (==) must be defined for Entrys. For example:

```
bool operator<(const Entry& x, const Entry& y)     // less than
{
        return x.name<y.name;            // order Entries by their names
}
```

A standard algorithm is expressed in terms of (half-open) sequences of elements. A *sequence* is represented by a pair of iterators specifying the first element and the one-beyond-the-last element:

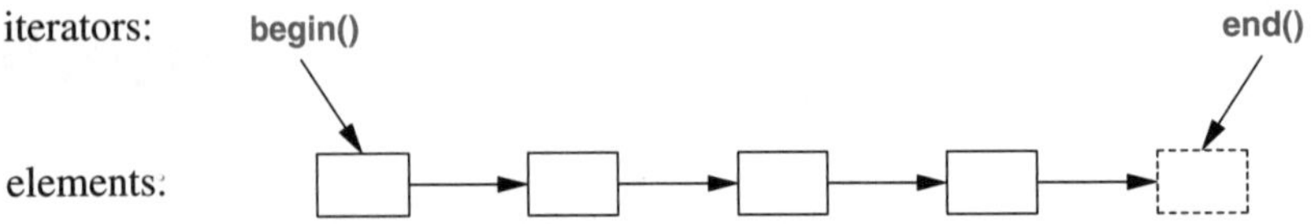

In the example, sort() sorts the sequence defined by the pair of iterators vec.begin() and vec.end(), which just happens to be all the elements of a vector. For writing (output), you need only to specify the first element to be written. If more than one element is written, the elements following that initial element will be overwritten. Thus, to avoid errors, lst must have at least as many elements as there are unique values in vec.

If we wanted to place the unique elements in a new container, we could have written:

```
list<Entry> f(vector<Entry>& vec)
{
        list<Entry> res;
        sort(vec.begin(),vec.end());
        unique_copy(vec.begin(),vec.end(),back_inserter(res));        // append to res
        return res;
}
```

The call back_inserter(res) constructs an iterator for res that adds elements at the end of a container, extending the container to make room for them. This saves us from first having to allocate a fixed amount of space and then filling it. Thus, the standard containers plus back_inserter()s eliminate the need to use error-prone, explicit C-style memory management using realloc(). The standard-library list has a move constructor (§5.2.2) that makes returning res by value efficient (even for lists of thousands of elements).

If you find the pair-of-iterators style of code, such as sort(vec.begin(),vec.end()), tedious, you can define container versions of the algorithms and write sort(vec) (§12.8).

12.2 Use of Iterators

For a container, a few iterators referring to useful elements can be obtained; begin() and end() are the best examples of this. In addition, many algorithms return iterators. For example, the standard algorithm find looks for a value in a sequence and returns an iterator to the element found:

```
bool has_c(const string& s, char c)      // does s contain the character c?
{
     auto p = find(s.begin(),s.end(),c);
     if (p!=s.end())
          return true;
     else
          return false;
}
```

Like many standard-library search algorithms, find returns end() to indicate "not found." An equivalent, shorter, definition of has_c() is:

```
bool has_c(const string& s, char c)      // does s contain the character c?
{
     return find(s.begin(),s.end(),c)!=s.end();
}
```

A more interesting exercise would be to find the location of all occurrences of a character in a string. We can return the set of occurrences as a vector of string iterators. Returning a vector is efficient because vector provides move semantics (§5.2.1). Assuming that we would like to modify the locations found, we pass a non-const string:

```
vector<string::iterator> find_all(string& s, char c)      // find all occurrences of c in s
{
     vector<string::iterator> res;
     for (auto p = s.begin(); p!=s.end(); ++p)
          if (*p==c)
               res.push_back(p);
     return res;
}
```

We iterate through the string using a conventional loop, moving the iterator p forward one element at a time using ++ and looking at the elements using the dereference operator *. We could test find_all() like this:

```
void test()
{
     string m {"Mary had a little lamb"};
     for (auto p : find_all(m,'a'))
          if (*p!='a')
               cerr << "a bug!\n";
}
```

That call of find_all() could be graphically represented like this:

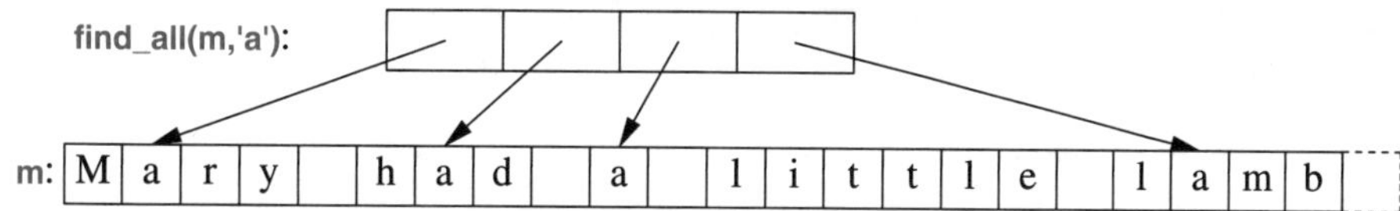

Iterators and standard algorithms work equivalently on every standard container for which their use makes sense. Consequently, we could generalize find_all():

```
template<typename C, typename V>
vector<typename C::iterator> find_all(C& c, V v)          // find all occurrences of v in c
{
     vector<typename C::iterator> res;
     for (auto p = c.begin(); p!=c.end(); ++p)
          if (*p==v)
               res.push_back(p);
     return res;
}
```

The typename is needed to inform the compiler that C's iterator is supposed to be a type and not a value of some type, say, the integer 7. We can hide this implementation detail by introducing a type alias (§6.4.2) for Iterator:

```
template<typename T>
using Iterator = typename T::iterator;          // T's iterator

template<typename C, typename V>
vector<Iterator<C>> find_all(C& c, V v)          // find all occurrences of v in c
{
     vector<Iterator<C>> res;
     for (auto p = c.begin(); p!=c.end(); ++p)
          if (*p==v)
               res.push_back(p);
     return res;
}
```

We can now write:

```
void test()
{
     string m {"Mary had a little lamb"};

     for (auto p : find_all(m,'a'))          // p is a string::iterator
          if (*p!='a')
               cerr << "string bug!\n";

     list<double> ld {1.1, 2.2, 3.3, 1.1};
     for (auto p : find_all(ld,1.1))          // p is a list<double>::iterator
          if (*p!=1.1)
               cerr << "list bug!\n";

     vector<string> vs { "red", "blue", "green", "green", "orange", "green" };
     for (auto p : find_all(vs,"red"))          // p is a vector<string>::iterator
          if (*p!="red")
               cerr << "vector bug!\n";
```

```
    for (auto p : find_all(vs,"green"))
        *p = "vert";
}
```

Iterators are used to separate algorithms and containers. An algorithm operates on its data through iterators and knows nothing about the container in which the elements are stored. Conversely, a container knows nothing about the algorithms operating on its elements; all it does is to supply iterators upon request (e.g., begin() and end()). This model of separation between data storage and algorithm delivers very general and flexible software.

12.3 Iterator Types

What are iterators really? Any particular iterator is an object of some type. There are, however, many different iterator types, because an iterator needs to hold the information necessary for doing its job for a particular container type. These iterator types can be as different as the containers and the specialized needs they serve. For example, a vector's iterator could be an ordinary pointer, because a pointer is quite a reasonable way of referring to an element of a vector:

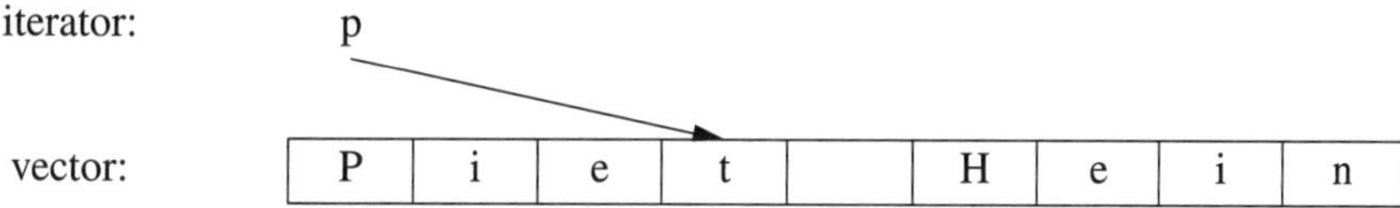

Alternatively, a vector iterator could be implemented as a pointer to the vector plus an index:

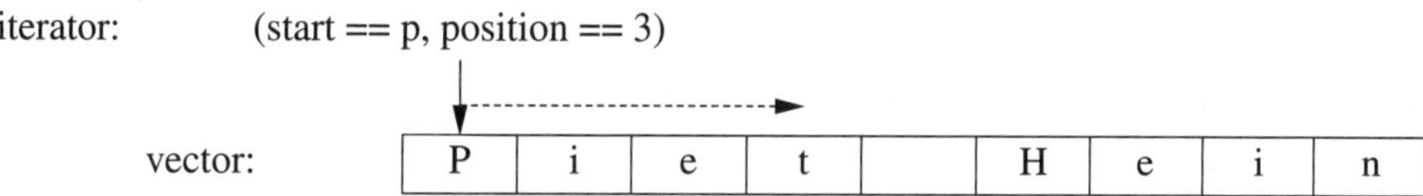

Using such an iterator would allow range checking.

A list iterator must be something more complicated than a simple pointer to an element because an element of a list in general does not know where the next element of that list is. Thus, a list iterator might be a pointer to a link:

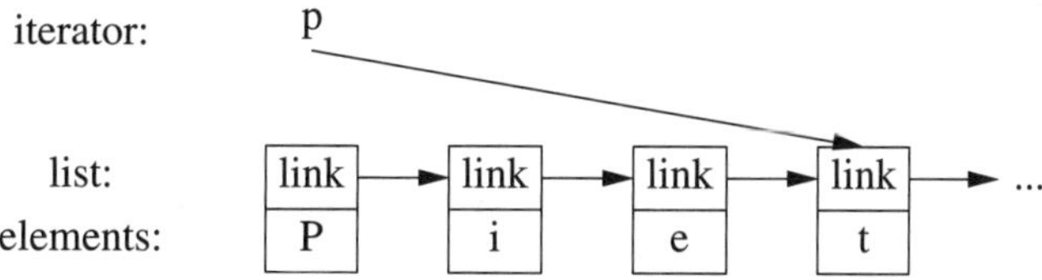

What is common for all iterators is their semantics and the naming of their operations. For example, applying ++ to any iterator yields an iterator that refers to the next element. Similarly, * yields the element to which the iterator refers. In fact, any object that obeys a few simple rules like these is an iterator – *Iterator* is a concept (§7.2, §12.7). Furthermore, users rarely need to know the type of a specific iterator; each container "knows" its iterator types and makes them available under the conventional names iterator and const_iterator. For example, list<Entry>::iterator is the general iterator type for list<Entry>. We rarely have to worry about the details of how that type is defined.

12.4 Stream Iterators

Iterators are a general and useful concept for dealing with sequences of elements in containers. However, containers are not the only place where we find sequences of elements. For example, an input stream produces a sequence of values, and we write a sequence of values to an output stream. Consequently, the notion of iterators can be usefully applied to input and output.

To make an ostream_iterator, we need to specify which stream will be used and the type of objects written to it. For example:

```
ostream_iterator<string> oo {cout};        // write strings to cout
```

The effect of assigning to *oo is to write the assigned value to cout. For example:

```
int main()
{
     *oo = "Hello, ";      // meaning cout<<"Hello, "
     ++oo;
     *oo = "world!\n";     // meaning cout<<"world!\n"
}
```

This is yet another way of writing the canonical message to standard output. The ++oo is done to mimic writing into an array through a pointer.

Similarly, an istream_iterator is something that allows us to treat an input stream as a read-only container. Again, we must specify the stream to be used and the type of values expected:

```
istream_iterator<string> ii {cin};
```

Input iterators are used in pairs representing a sequence, so we must provide an istream_iterator to indicate the end of input. This is the default istream_iterator:

```
istream_iterator<string> eos {};
```

Typically, istream_iterators and ostream_iterators are not used directly. Instead, they are provided as arguments to algorithms. For example, we can write a simple program to read a file, sort the words read, eliminate duplicates, and write the result to another file:

```
int main()
{
     string from, to;
     cin >> from >> to;                        // get source and target file names

     ifstream is {from};                       // input stream for file "from"
     istream_iterator<string> ii {is};         // input iterator for stream
     istream_iterator<string> eos {};          // input sentinel
```

```
    ofstream os {to};                         // output stream for file "to"
    ostream_iterator<string> oo {os,"\n"};    // output iterator for stream

    vector<string> b {ii,eos};                // b is a vector initialized from input
    sort(b.begin(),b.end());                  // sort the buffer

    unique_copy(b.begin(),b.end(),oo);        // copy buffer to output, discard replicated values

    return !is.eof() || !os;                  // return error state (§1.2.1, §10.4)
}
```

An ifstream is an istream that can be attached to a file, and an ofstream is an ostream that can be attached to a file (§10.7). The ostream_iterator's second argument is used to delimit output values.

Actually, this program is longer than it needs to be. We read the strings into a vector, then we sort() them, and then we write them out, eliminating duplicates. A more elegant solution is not to store duplicates at all. This can be done by keeping the strings in a set, which does not keep duplicates and keeps its elements in order (§11.4). That way, we could replace the two lines using a vector with one using a set and replace unique_copy() with the simpler copy():

```
set<string> b {ii,eos};           // collect strings from input
copy(b.begin(),b.end(),oo);       // copy buffer to output
```

We used the names ii, eos, and oo only once, so we could further reduce the size of the program:

```
int main()
{
    string from, to;
    cin >> from >> to;                 // get source and target file names

    ifstream is {from};                // input stream for file "from"
    ofstream os {to};                  // output stream for file "to"

    set<string> b {istream_iterator<string>{is},istream_iterator<string>{}};    // read input
    copy(b.begin(),b.end(),ostream_iterator<string>{os,"\n"});                  // copy to output

    return !is.eof() || !os;           // return error state (§1.2.1, §10.4)
}
```

It is a matter of taste and experience whether or not this last simplification improves readability.

12.5 Predicates

In the examples so far, the algorithms have simply "built in" the action to be done for each element of a sequence. However, we often want to make that action a parameter to the algorithm. For example, the find algorithm (§12.2, §12.6) provides a convenient way of looking for a specific value. A more general variant looks for an element that fulfills a specified requirement, a *predicate*. For example, we might want to search a map for the first value larger than 42. A map allows us to access its elements as a sequence of *(key,value)* pairs, so we can search a map<string,int>'s sequence for a pair<const string,int> where the int is greater than 42:

```
void f(map<string,int>& m)
{
      auto p = find_if(m.begin(),m.end(),Greater_than{42});
      // ...
}
```

Here, Greater_than is a function object (§6.3.2) holding the value (42) to be compared against:

```
struct Greater_than {
      int val;
      Greater_than(int v) : val{v} { }
      bool operator()(const pair<string,int>& r) const { return r.second>val; }
};
```

Alternatively, we could use a lambda expression (§6.3.2):

```
auto p = find_if(m.begin(), m.end(), [](const auto& r) { return r.second>42; });
```

A predicate should not modify the elements to which it is applied.

12.6 Algorithm Overview

A general definition of an algorithm is "a finite set of rules which gives a sequence of operations for solving a specific set of problems [and] has five important features: Finiteness ... Definiteness ... Input ... Output ... Effectiveness" [Knuth,1968,§1.1]. In the context of the C++ standard library, an algorithm is a function template operating on sequences of elements.

The standard library provides dozens of algorithms. The algorithms are defined in namespace std and presented in the <algorithm> header. These standard-library algorithms all take sequences as inputs. A half-open sequence from b to e is referred to as [b:e). Here are a few examples:

Selected Standard Algorithms <algorithm>	
f=for_each(b,e,f)	For each element x in [b:e) do f(x)
p=find(b,e,x)	p is the first p in [b:e) so that *p==x
p=find_if(b,e,f)	p is the first p in [b:e) so that f(*p)
n=count(b,e,x)	n is the number of elements *q in [b:e) so that *q==x
n=count_if(b,e,f)	n is the number of elements *q in [b:e) so that f(*q)
replace(b,e,v,v2)	Replace elements *q in [b:e) so that *q==v with v2
replace_if(b,e,f,v2)	Replace elements *q in [b:e) so that f(*q) with v2
p=copy(b,e,out)	Copy [b:e) to [out:p)
p=copy_if(b,e,out,f)	Copy elements *q from [b:e) so that f(*q) to [out:p)
p=move(b,e,out)	Move [b:e) to [out:p)
p=unique_copy(b,e,out)	Copy [b:e) to [out:p); don't copy adjacent duplicates
sort(b,e)	Sort elements of [b:e) using < as the sorting criterion
sort(b,e,f)	Sort elements of [b:e) using f as the sorting criterion
(p1,p2)=equal_range(b,e,v)	[p1:p2) is the subsequence of the sorted sequence [b:e) with the value v; basically a binary search for v

Selected Standard Algorithms <algorithm> (continued)	
p=merge(b,e,b2,e2,out)	Merge two sorted sequences [b:e) and [b2:e2) into [out:p)
p=merge(b,e,b2,e2,out,f)	Merge two sorted sequences [b:e) and [b2:e2) into [out:p) using f as the comparison

These algorithms, and many more (e.g., §14.3), can be applied to elements of containers, strings, and built-in arrays.

Some algorithms, such as replace() and sort(), modify element values, but no algorithm adds or subtracts elements of a container. The reason is that a sequence does not identify the container that holds the elements of the sequence. To add or delete elements, you need something that knows about the container (e.g., a back_inserter; §12.1) or directly refers to the container itself (e.g., push_back() or erase(); §11.2).

Lambdas are very common as operations passed as arguments. For example:

```
vector<int> v = {0,1,2,3,4,5};
for_each(v.begin(),v.end(),[](int& x){ x=x*x; });          // v=={0,1,4,9,16,25}
```

The standard-library algorithms tend to be more carefully designed, specified, and implemented than the average hand-crafted loop, so know them and use them in preference to code written in the bare language.

12.7 Concepts (C++20)

In C++20, the standard-library algorithms will be specified using concepts (Chapter 7). The preliminary work on this can be found in the Ranges Technical Specification [RangesTS]. Implementations can be found on the Web. For C++20, the ranges concepts are defined in <ranges>.

Range is a generalization of the C++98 sequences defined by begin()/end() pairs. Range is a concept specifying what it takes to be a sequence of elements. It can be defined by

- A {begin,end} pair of iterators
- A {begin,n} pair, where begin is an iterator and n is the number of elements
- A {begin,pred} pair, where begin is an iterator and pred is a predicate; if pred(p) is true for the iterator p, we have reached the end of the sequence. This allows us to have infinite sequences and sequences that are generated "on the fly."

This Range concept is what allows us to say sort(v) rather than sort(v.begin(),v.end()) as we had to using the STL since 1994. For example:

```
template<BoundedRange R>
    requires Sortable<R>
void sort(R& r)
{
    return sort(begin(r),end(r));
}
```

The relation for Sortable is defaulted to less.

In general, where a standard-library algorithm requires a sequence defined by a pair of iterators, C++20 will allow a Range as a notationally simpler alternative.

In addition to Range, C++20 offers many useful concepts. These concepts are found in the headers <ranges>, <iterator>, and <concepts>.

Core language concepts <concepts>	
Same<T,U>	T is the same type as U
DerivedFrom<T,U>	T is derived from U
ConvertibleTo<T,U>	A T can be converted to a U
CommonReference<T,U>	T and U share a common reference type
Common<T,U>	T and U share a common type
Integral<T>	T is an integral type
SignedIntegral<T>	T is a signed integral type
UnsignedIntegral<T>	T is an unsigned integral type
Assignable<T,U>	A U can be assigned to a T
SwappableWith<T,U>	A T can be swapped with a U
Swappable<T>	SwappableWith<T,T>

Common is important for specifying algorithms that should work with a variety of related types while still being mathematically sound. Common<T,U> is a type C that we can use for comparing a T with a U by first converting both to Cs. For example, we would like to compare a std::string with a C-style string (a char*) and an int with a double, but not a std::string with an int. To ensure that we specialize common_type_t, used in the definition of Common, suitably:

```
using common_type_t<std::string,char*> = std::string;
using common_type_t<double,int> = double;
```

The definition of Common is a bit tricky but solves a hard fundamental problem. Fortunately, we don't need to define a common_type_t specialization unless we want to use operations on mixes of types for which a library doesn't (yet) have suitable definitions. Common or CommonReference is used in the definitions of most concepts and algorithms that can compare values of different types.

The concepts related to comparison are strongly influenced by [Stepanov,2009].

Comparison concepts <concepts>	
Boolean<T>	A T can be used as a Boolean
WeaklyEqualityComparableWith<T,U>	A T and a U can be compared for equality using == and !=
WeaklyEqualityComparable<T>	WeaklyEqualityComparableWith<T,T>
EqualityComparableWith<T,U>	A T and a U can be compared for equivalence using ==
EqualityComparable<T>	EqualityComparableWith<T,T>
StrictTotallyOrderedWith<T,U>	A T and a U can be compared using <, <=, >, and >= yielding a total order
StrictTotallyOrdered<T>	StrictTotallyOrderedWith<T,T>

The use of both WeaklyEqualityComparableWith and WeaklyEqualityComparable shows a (so far) missed opportunity to overload.

Object concepts <concepts>	
Destructible<T>	A T can be destroyed and have its address taken with unary &
Constructible<T,Args>	A T can be constructed from an argument list of type Args
DefaultConstructible<T>	A T can be default constructed
MoveConstructible<T>	A T can be move constructed
CopyConstructible<T>	A T can be copy constructed and move constructed
Movable<T>	MoveConstructable<T>, Assignable<T&,T>, and Swapable<T>
Copyable<T>	CopyConstructable<T>, Moveable<T>, and Assignable<T, const T&>
Semiregular<T>	Copyable<T> and DefaultConstructable<T>
Regular<T>	SemiRegular<T> and EqualityComparable<T>

Regular is the ideal for types. A Regular type works roughly like an int and simplifies much of our thinking about how to use a type (§7.2). The lack of default == for classes means that most classes start out as SemiRegular even though most could and should be Regular.

Callable concepts <concepts>	
Invocable<F,Args>	An F can be invoked with an argument list of type Args
InvocableRegular<F,Args>	Invocable<F,Args> and is equality preserving
Predicate<F,Args>	An F can be invoked with an argument list of type Args returning a bool
Relation<F,T,U>	Predicate<F,T,U>
StrictWeakOrder<F,T,U>	A Relation<F,T,U> that provides strict weak ordering

A function f() is *equality preserving* if x==y implies that f(x)==f(y).

Strict weak ordering is what the standard library usually assumes for comparisons, such as <; look it up if you feel the need to know.

Relation and StrictWeakOrder differ only in semantics. We can't (currently) represent that in code so the names simply express our intent.

Iterator concepts <iterators>	
Iterator<I>	An I can be incremented (++) and dereferenced (*)
Sentinel<S,I>	An S is a sentinel for an Iterator type; that is, S is a predicate on I's value type
SizedSentinel<S,I>	A sentinel S where the - operator can be applied to I
InputIterator<I>	An I is an input iterator; * can be used for reading only
OutputIterator<I>	An I is an output iterator; * can be used for writing only
ForwardIterator<I>	An I is a forward iterator, supporting multi-pass
BidirectionalIterator<I>	An I is a ForwardIterator supporting --
RandomAccessIterator<I>	An I is a BidirectionalIterator supporting +, -, +=, -=, and []
Permutable<I>	An I is a ForwardIterator<I> where I allows us to move and swap elements
Mergeable<I1,I2,R,O>	Can merge sorted sequences defined by I1 and I2 into O using Relation<R>
Sortable<I>	Can sort sequences defined by I using less
Sortable<I,R>	Can sort sequences defined by I using Relation<R>

The different kinds (categories) of iterators are used to select the best algorithm for a given algorithm; see §7.2.2 and §13.9.1. For an example of an **InputIterator**, see §12.4.

The basic idea of a sentinel is that we can iterate over a range starting at an iterator until the predicate becomes true for an element. That way, an iterator **p** and a sentinel **s** define a range **[p:s(∗p))**. For example, we could define a predicate for a sentinel for traversing a C-style string using a pointer as the iterator:

```
[](const char∗ p) {return ∗p==0; }
```

The summary of **Mergeable** and **Sortable** are simplified relative to their definition in C++20.

Range concepts <ranges>	
Range<R>	An **R** is a range with a begin iterator and a sentinel
SizedRange<R>	An **R** is a range that knows its size in constant time
View<R>	An **R** is a range with constant time copy, move, and assignment
BoundedRange<R>	An **R** is a range with identical iterator and sentinel types
InputRange<R>	An **R** is a range whose iterator type satisfies InputIterator
OutputRange<R>	An **R** is a range whose iterator type satisfies OutputIterator
ForwardRange<R>	An **R** is a range whose iterator type satisfies ForwardIterator
BidirectionalRange<R>	An **R** is a range whose iterator type satisfies BidirectionalIterator
RandomAccessRange<R>	An **R** is a range whose iterator type satisfies RandomAccessIterator

There are a few more concepts in **<ranges>**, but this set is a good start.

12.8 Container Algorithms

When we can't wait for Ranges, we can define our own simple range algorithms. For example, we can easily provide the shorthand to say just **sort(v)** instead of **sort(v.begin(),v.end())**:

```
namespace Estd {
      using namespace std;

      template<typename C>
      void sort(C& c)
      {
            sort(c.begin(),c.end());
      }

      template<typename C, typename Pred>
      void sort(C& c, Pred p)
      {
            sort(c.begin(),c.end(),p);
      }

      // ...
}
```

I put the container versions of **sort()** (and other algorithms) into their own namespace **Estd** ("extended std") to avoid interfering with other programmers' uses of namespace std and also to make it easier to replace this stopgap with Ranges.

12.9 Parallel Algorithms

When the same task is to be done to many data items, we can execute it in parallel on each data item provided the computations on different data items are independent:

- *parallel execution*: tasks are done on multiple threads (often running on several processor cores)
- *vectorized execution*: tasks are done on a single thread using vectorization, also known as *SIMD* ("Single Instruction, Multiple Data").

The standard library offers support for both and we can be specific about wanting sequential execution; in <execution>, we find:

- seq: sequential execution
- par: parallel execution (if feasible)
- par_unseq: parallel and/or unsequenced (vectorized) execution (if feasible).

Consider std::sort():

```
sort(v.begin(),v.end());                    // sequential
sort(seq,v.begin(),v.end());                // sequential (same as the default)
sort(par,v.begin(),v.end());                // parallel
sort(par_unseq,v.begin(),v.end());          // parallel and/or vectorized
```

Whether it is worthwhile to parallelize and/or vectorize depends on the algorithm, the number of elements in the sequence, the hardware, and the utilization of that hardware by programs running on it. Consequently, the *execution policy indicators* are just hints. A compiler and/or run-time scheduler will decide how much concurrency to use. This is all nontrivial and the rule against making statements about efficiency without measurement is very important here.

Most standard-library algorithms, including all in the table in §12.6 except equal_range, can be requested to be parallelized and vectorized using par and par_unseq as for sort(). Why not equal_range()? Because so far nobody has come up with a worthwhile parallel algorithm for that.

Many parallel algorithms are used primarily for numeric data; see §14.3.1.

When requesting parallel execution, be sure to avoid data races (§15.2) and deadlock (§15.5).

12.10 Advice

[1] An STL algorithm operates on one or more sequences; §12.1.
[2] An input sequence is half-open and defined by a pair of iterators; §12.1.
[3] When searching, an algorithm usually returns the end of the input sequence to indicate "not found"; §12.2.
[4] Algorithms do not directly add or subtract elements from their argument sequences; §12.2, §12.6.
[5] When writing a loop, consider whether it could be expressed as a general algorithm; §12.2.

[6] Use predicates and other function objects to give standard algorithms a wider range of meanings; §12.5, §12.6.
[7] A predicate must not modify its argument; §12.5.
[8] Know your standard-library algorithms and prefer them to hand-crafted loops; §12.6.
[9] When the pair-of-iterators style becomes tedious, introduce a container/range algorithm; §12.8.

13

Utilities

The time you enjoy wasting is not wasted time.
– Bertrand Russell

- Introduction
- Resource Management
  unique_ptr and shared_ptr; move() and forward()
- Range Checking: span
- Specialized Containers
  array; bitset; pair and tuple
- Alternatives
  variant; optional; any
- Time
- Function Adaption
  Lambdas as Adaptors; mem_fn(); function
- Allocators
- Type Functions
  iterator_traits; Type Predicates; enable_if
- Advice

13.1 Introduction

Not all standard-library components come as part of obviously labeled facilities, such as "containers" or "I/O." This section gives a few examples of small, widely useful components. Such components (classes and templates) are often called *vocabulary types* because they are part of the common vocabulary we use to describe our designs and programs. Such library components often act as building blocks for more powerful library facilities, including other components of the standard library. A function or a type need not be complicated or closely tied to a mass of other functions and types to be useful.

13.2 Resource Management

One of the key tasks of any nontrivial program is to manage resources. A resource is something that must be acquired and later (explicitly or implicitly) released. Examples are memory, locks, sockets, thread handles, and file handles. For a long-running program, failing to release a resource in a timely manner ("a leak") can cause serious performance degradation and possibly even a miserable crash. Even for short programs, a leak can become an embarrassment, say by a resource shortage increasing the run time by orders of magnitude.

The standard library components are designed not to leak resources. To do this, they rely on the basic language support for resource management using constructor/destructor pairs to ensure that a resource doesn't outlive an object responsible for it. The use of a constructor/destructor pair in Vector to manage the lifetime of its elements is an example (§4.2.2) and all standard-library containers are implemented in similar ways. Importantly, this approach interacts correctly with error handling using exceptions. For example, this technique is used for the standard-library lock classes:

```
mutex m; // used to protect access to shared data
// ...
void f()
{
        scoped_lock<mutex> lck {m}; // acquire the mutex m
        // ... manipulate shared data ...
}
```

A thread will not proceed until lck's constructor has acquired the mutex (§15.5). The corresponding destructor releases the resources. So, in this example, scoped_lock's destructor releases the mutex when the thread of control leaves f() (through a return, by "falling off the end of the function," or through an exception throw).

This is an application of RAII (the "Resource Acquisition Is Initialization" technique; §4.2.2). RAII is fundamental to the idiomatic handling of resources in C++. Containers (such as vector and map, string, and iostream) manage their resources (such as file handles and buffers) similarly.

13.2.1 unique_ptr and shared_ptr

The examples so far take care of objects defined in a scope, releasing the resources they acquire at the exit from the scope, but what about objects allocated on the free store? In <memory>, the standard library provides two "smart pointers" to help manage objects on the free store:

[1] unique_ptr to represent unique ownership

[2] shared_ptr to represent shared ownership

The most basic use of these "smart pointers" is to prevent memory leaks caused by careless programming. For example:

```
void f(int i, int j)       // X* vs. unique_ptr<X>
{
        X* p = new X;                    // allocate a new X
        unique_ptr<X> sp {new X};        // allocate a new X and give its pointer to unique_ptr
        // ...
```

```
        if (i<99) throw Z{};             // may throw an exception
        if (j<77) return;                // may return "early"
        // ... use p and sp ..
        delete p;                        // destroy *p
}
```

Here, we "forgot" to delete p if i<99 or if j<77. On the other hand, unique_ptr ensures that its object is properly destroyed whichever way we exit f() (by throwing an exception, by executing return, or by "falling off the end"). Ironically, we could have solved the problem simply by *not* using a pointer and *not* using new:

```
void f(int i, int j)     // use a local variable
{
        X x;
        // ...
}
```

Unfortunately, overuse of new (and of pointers and references) seems to be an increasing problem.

However, when you really need the semantics of pointers, unique_ptr is a very lightweight mechanism with no space or time overhead compared to correct use of a built-in pointer. Its further uses include passing free-store allocated objects in and out of functions:

```
unique_ptr<X> make_X(int i)
        // make an X and immediately give it to a unique_ptr
{
        // ... check i, etc. ...
        return unique_ptr<X>{new X{i}};
}
```

A unique_ptr is a handle to an individual object (or an array) in much the same way that a vector is a handle to a sequence of objects. Both control the lifetime of other objects (using RAII) and both rely on move semantics to make return simple and efficient.

The shared_ptr is similar to unique_ptr except that shared_ptrs are copied rather than moved. The shared_ptrs for an object share ownership of an object; that object is destroyed when the last of its shared_ptrs is destroyed. For example:

```
void f(shared_ptr<fstream>);
void g(shared_ptr<fstream>);

void user(const string& name, ios_base::openmode mode)
{
        shared_ptr<fstream> fp {new fstream(name,mode)};
        if (!*fp)                        // make sure the file was properly opened
                throw No_file{};

        f(fp);
        g(fp);
        // ...
}
```

Now, the file opened by fp's constructor will be closed by the last function to (explicitly or implicitly) destroy a copy of fp. Note that f() or g() may spawn a task holding a copy of fp or in some other way store a copy that outlives user(). Thus, shared_ptr provides a form of garbage collection that respects the destructor-based resource management of the memory-managed objects. This is neither cost free nor exorbitantly expensive, but it does make the lifetime of the shared object hard to predict. Use shared_ptr only if you actually need shared ownership.

Creating an object on the free store and then passing the pointer to it to a smart pointer is a bit verbose. It also allows for mistakes, such as forgetting to pass a pointer to a unique_ptr or giving a pointer to something that is not on the free store to a shared_ptr. To avoid such problems, the standard library (in <memory>) provides functions for constructing an object and returning an appropriate smart pointer, make_shared() and make_unique(). For example:

```
struct S {
        int i;
        string s;
        double d;
        // ...
};

auto p1 = make_shared<S>(1,"Ankh Morpork",4.65);     // p1 is a shared_ptr<S>
auto p2 = make_unique<S>(2,"Oz",7.62);                // p2 is a unique_ptr<S>
```

Now, p2 is a unique_ptr<S> pointing to a free-store-allocated object of type S with the value {2,"Oz"s,7.62}.

Using make_shared() is not just more convenient than separately making an object using new and then passing it to a shared_ptr, it is also notably more efficient because it does not need a separate allocation for the use count that is essential in the implementation of a shared_ptr.

Given unique_ptr and shared_ptr, we can implement a complete "no naked new" policy (§4.2.2) for many programs. However, these "smart pointers" are still conceptually pointers and therefore only my second choice for resource management – after containers and other types that manage their resources at a higher conceptual level. In particular, shared_ptrs do not in themselves provide any rules for which of their owners can read and/or write the shared object. Data races (§15.7) and other forms of confusion are not addressed simply by eliminating the resource management issues.

Where do we use "smart pointers" (such as unique_ptr) rather than resource handles with operations designed specifically for the resource (such as vector or thread)? Unsurprisingly, the answer is "when we need pointer semantics."

- When we share an object, we need pointers (or references) to refer to the shared object, so a shared_ptr becomes the obvious choice (unless there is an obvious single owner).
- When we refer to a polymorphic object in classical object-oriented code (§4.5), we need a pointer (or a reference) because we don't know the exact type of the object referred to (or even its size), so a unique_ptr becomes the obvious choice.
- A shared polymorphic object typically requires shared_ptrs.

We do *not* need to use a pointer to return a collection of objects from a function; a container that is a resource handle will do that simply and efficiently (§5.2.2).

13.2.2 move() and forward()

The choice between moving and copying is mostly implicit (§3.6). A compiler will prefer to move when an object is about to be destroyed (as in a return) because that's assumed to be the simpler and more efficient operation. However, sometimes we must be explicit. For example, a unique_ptr is the sole owner of an object. Consequently, it cannot be copied:

```
void f1()
{
      auto p = make_unique<int>(2);
      auto q = p;              // error: we can't copy a unique_ptr
      // ...
}
```

If you want a unique_ptr elsewhere, you must move it. For example:

```
void f1()
{
      auto p = make_unique<int>(2);
      auto q = move(p);              // p now holds nullptr
      // ...
}
```

Confusingly, std::move() doesn't move anything. Instead, it casts its argument to an rvalue reference, thereby saying that its argument will not be used again and therefore may be moved (§5.2.2). It should have been called something like rvalue_cast. Like other casts, it's error-prone and best avoided. It exists to serve a few essential cases. Consider a simple swap:

```
template <typename T>
void swap(T& a, T& b)
{
      T tmp {move(a)};              // the T constructor sees an rvalue and moves
      a = move(b);                  // the T assignment sees an rvalue and moves
      b = move(tmp);                // the T assignment sees an rvalue and moves
}
```

We don't want to repeatedly copy potentially large objects, so we request moves using std::move().

Like for other casts, there are tempting, but dangerous, uses of std::move(). Consider:

```
string s1 = "Hello";
string s2 = "World";
vector<string> v;
v.push_back(s1);                  // use a "const string&" argument; push_back() will copy
v.push_back(move(s2));            // use a move constructor
```

Here s1 is copied (by push_back()) whereas s2 is moved. This sometimes (only sometimes) makes the push_back() of s2 cheaper. The problem is that a moved-from object is left behind. If we use s2 again, we have a problem:

```
cout << s1[2];          // write 'l'
cout << s2[2];          // crash?
```

I consider this use of std::move() to be too error-prone for widespread use. Don't use it unless you can demonstrate significant and necessary performance improvement. Later maintenance may accidentally lead to unanticipated use of the moved-from object.

The state of a moved-from object is in general unspecified, but all standard-library types leave a moved-from object in a state where it can be destroyed and assigned to. It would be unwise not to follow that lead. For a container (e.g., vector or string), the moved-from state will be "empty." For many types, the default value is a good empty state: meaningful and cheap to establish.

Forwarding arguments is an important use case that requires moves (§7.4.2). We sometimes want to transmit a set of arguments on to another function without changing anything (to achieve "perfect forwarding"):

```
template<typename T, typename... Args>
unique_ptr<T> make_unique(Args&&... args)
{
        return unique_ptr<T>{new T{std::forward<Args>(args)...}};    // forward each argument
}
```

The standard-library forward() differs from the simpler std::move() by correctly handling subtleties to do with lvalue and rvalue (§5.2.2). Use std::forward() exclusively for forwarding and don't forward() something twice; once you have forwarded an object, it's not yours to use anymore.

13.3 Range Checking: gsl::span

Traditionally, range errors have been a major source of serious errors in C and C++ programs. The use of containers (Chapter 11), algorithms (Chapter 12), and range-for has significantly reduced this problem, but more can be done. A key source of range errors is that people pass pointers (raw or smart) and then rely on convention to know the number of elements pointed to. The best advice for code outside resource handles is to assume that at most one object is pointed to [CG: F.22], but without support that advice is unmanageable. The standard-library string_view (§9.3) can help, but that is read-only and for characters only. Most programmers need more.

The Core Guidelines [Stroustrup,2015] offer guidelines and a small Guidelines Support Library [GSL], including a span type for referring to a range of elements. This span is being proposed for the standard, but for now it is just something you can download if needed.

A string_span is basically a (pointer,length) pair denoting a sequence of elements:

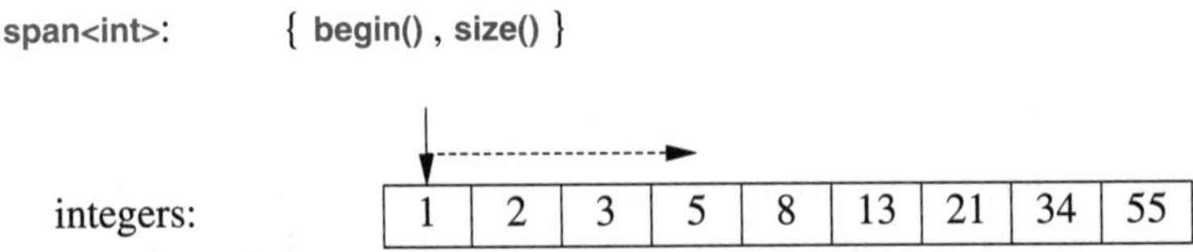

A span gives access to a contiguous sequence of elements. The elements can be stored in many ways, including in vectors and built-in arrays. Like a pointer, a span does not own the characters it points to. In that, it resembles a string_view (§9.3) and an STL pair of iterators (§12.3).

Consider a common interface style:

```
void fpn(int* p, int n)
{
	for (int i = 0; i<n; ++i)
		p[i] = 0;
}
```

We assume that p points to n integers. Unfortunately, this assumption is simply a convention, so we can't use it to write a range-for loop and the compiler cannot implement cheap and effective range checking. Also, our assumption can be wrong:

```
void use(int x)
{
	int a[100];
	fpn(a,100);          // OK
	fpn(a,1000);         // oops, my finger slipped! (range error in fpn)
	fpn(a+10,100);       // range error in fpn
	fpn(a,x);            // suspect, but looks innocent
}
```

We can do better using a span:

```
void fs(span<int> p)
{
	for (int& x : p)
		x = 0;
}
```

We can use fs like this:

```
void use(int x)
{
	int a[100];
	fs(a);                   // implicitly creates a span<int>{a,100}
	fs(a,1000);              // error: span expected
	fs({a+10,100});          // a range error in fs
	fs({a,x});               // obviously suspect
}
```

That is, the common case, creating a span directly from an array, is now safe (the compiler computes the element count) and notationally simple. For other cases, the probability of mistakes is lowered because the programmer has to explicitly compose a span.

The common case where a span is passed along from function to function is simpler than for (pointer,count) interfaces and obviously doesn't require extra checking:

```
void f1(span<int> p);

void f2(span<int> p)
{
	// ...
	f1(p);
}
```

When used for subscripting (e.g., r[i]), range checking is done and a gsl::fail_fast is thrown in case of a range error. Range checks can be suppressed for performance critical code. When span makes it into the standard, I expect that std::span will use contracts [Garcia,2016] [Garcia,2018] to control responses to range violation.

Note that just a single range check is needed for the loop. Thus, for the common case where the body of a function using a span is a loop over the span, range checking is almost free.

A span of characters is supported directly and called gsl::string_span.

13.4 Specialized Containers

The standard library provides several containers that don't fit perfectly into the STL framework (Chapter 11, Chapter 12). Examples are built-in arrays, array, and string. I sometimes refer to those as "almost containers," but that is not quite fair: they hold elements, so they are containers, but each has restrictions or added facilities that make them awkward in the context of the STL. Describing them separately also simplifies the description of the STL.

"Almost Containers"	
T[N]	Built-in array: a fixed-size contiguously allocated sequence of N elements of type T; implicitly converts to a T*
array<T,N>	A fixed-size contiguously allocated sequence of N elements of type T; like the built-in array, but with most problems solved
bitset<N>	A fixed-size sequence of N bits
vector<bool>	A sequence of bits compactly stored in a specialization of vector
pair<T,U>	Two elements of types T and U
tuple<T...>	A sequence of an arbitrary number of elements of arbitrary types
basic_string<C>	A sequence of characters of type C; provides string operations
valarray<T>	An array of numeric values of type T; provides numeric operations

Why does the standard library provide so many containers? They serve common but different (often overlapping) needs. If the standard library didn't provide them, many people would have to design and implement their own. For example:

- pair and tuple are heterogeneous; all other containers are homogeneous (all elements are of the same type).
- array, vector, and tuple elements are contiguously allocated; forward_list and map are linked structures.
- bitset and vector<bool> hold bits and access them through proxy objects; all other standard-library containers can hold a variety of types and access elements directly.
- basic_string requires its elements to be some form of character and to provide string manipulation, such as concatenation and locale-sensitive operations.
- valarray requires its elements to be numbers and to provide numerical operations.

All of these containers can be seen as providing specialized services needed by large communities of programmers. No single container could serve all of these needs because some needs are contradictory, for example, "ability to grow" vs. "guaranteed to be allocated in a fixed location," and "elements do not move when elements are added" vs. "contiguously allocated."

13.4.1 array

An array, defined in <array>, is a fixed-size sequence of elements of a given type where the number of elements is specified at compile time. Thus, an array can be allocated with its elements on the stack, in an object, or in static storage. The elements are allocated in the scope where the array is defined. An array is best understood as a built-in array with its size firmly attached, without implicit, potentially surprising conversions to pointer types, and with a few convenience functions provided. There is no overhead (time or space) involved in using an array compared to using a built-in array. An array does *not* follow the "handle to elements" model of STL containers. Instead, an array directly contains its elements.

An array can be initialized by an initializer list:

```
array<int,3> a1 = {1,2,3};
```

The number of elements in the initializer must be equal to or less than the number of elements specified for the array.

The element count is not optional:

```
array<int> ax = {1,2,3};            // error size not specified
```

The element count must be a constant expression:

```
void f(int n)
{
     array<string,n> aa = {"John's", "Queens' "};        // error: size not a constant expression
     //
}
```

If you need the element count to be a variable, use vector.

When necessary, an array can be explicitly passed to a C-style function that expects a pointer. For example:

```
void f(int* p, int sz);      // C-style interface

void g()
{
     array<int,10> a;

     f(a,a.size());              // error: no conversion
     f(&a[0],a.size());          // C-style use
     f(a.data(),a.size());       // C-style use

     auto p = find(a.begin(),a.end(),777);        // C++/STL-style use
     // ...
}
```

Why would we use an array when vector is so much more flexible? An array is less flexible so it is simpler. Occasionally, there is a significant performance advantage to be had by directly accessing elements allocated on the stack rather than allocating elements on the free store, accessing them indirectly through the vector (a handle), and then deallocating them. On the other hand, the stack is a limited resource (especially on some embedded systems), and stack overflow is nasty.

Why would we use an array when we could use a built-in array? An array knows its size, so it is easy to use with standard-library algorithms, and it can be copied using =. However, my main reason to prefer array is that it saves me from surprising and nasty conversions to pointers. Consider:

```
void h()
{
        Circle a1[10];
        array<Circle,10> a2;
        // ...
        Shape* p1 = a1;        // OK: disaster waiting to happen
        Shape* p2 = a2;        // error: no conversion of array<Circle,10> to Shape*
        p1[3].draw();          // disaster
}
```

The "disaster" comment assumes that sizeof(Shape)<sizeof(Circle), so subscripting a Circle[] through a Shape* gives a wrong offset. All standard containers provide this advantage over built-in arrays.

13.4.2 bitset

Aspects of a system, such as the state of an input stream, are often represented as a set of flags indicating binary conditions such as good/bad, true/false, and on/off. C++ supports the notion of small sets of flags efficiently through bitwise operations on integers (§1.4). Class bitset<N> generalizes this notion by providing operations on a sequence of N bits [0:N), where N is known at compile time. For sets of bits that don't fit into a long long int, using a bitset is much more convenient than using integers directly. For smaller sets, bitset is usually optimized. If you want to name the bits, rather than numbering them, you can use a set (§11.4) or an enumeration (§2.5).

A bitset can be initialized with an integer or a string:

```
bitset<9> bs1 {"110001111"};
bitset<9> bs2 {0b1'1000'1111};      // binary literal using digit separators (§1.4)
```

The usual bitwise operators (§1.4) and the left- and right-shift operators (<< and >>) can be applied:

```
bitset<9> bs3 = ~bs1;          // complement: bs3=="001110000"
bitset<9> bs4 = bs1&bs3;       // all zeros
bitset<9> bs5 = bs1<<2;        // shift left: bs5 = "000111100"
```

The shift operators (here, <<) "shift in" zeros.

The operations to_ullong() and to_string() provide the inverse operations to the constructors. For example, we could write out the binary representation of an int:

```
void binary(int i)
{
        bitset<8*sizeof(int)> b = i;            // assume 8-bit byte (see also §14.7)
        cout << b.to_string() << '\n';          // write out the bits of i
}
```

This prints the bits represented as 1s and 0s from left to right, with the most significant bit leftmost, so that argument 123 would give the output

```
00000000000000000000000001111011
```

For this example, it is simpler to directly use the bitset output operator:

```
void binary2(int i)
{
     bitset<8*sizeof(int)> b = i;       // assume 8-bit byte (see also §14.7)
     cout << b << '\n';                  // write out the bits of i
}
```

13.4.3 pair and tuple

Often, we need some data that is just data; that is, a collection of values, rather than an object of a class with well-defined semantics and an invariant for its value (§3.5.2). In such cases, a simple struct with an appropriate set of appropriately named members is often ideal. Alternatively, we could let the standard library write the definition for us. For example, the standard-library algorithm equal_range returns a pair of iterators specifying a subsequence meeting a predicate:

```
template<typename Forward_iterator, typename T, typename Compare>
     pair<Forward_iterator,Forward_iterator>
     equal_range(Forward_iterator first, Forward_iterator last, const T& val, Compare cmp);
```

Given a sorted sequence [first:last), equal_range() will return the pair representing the subsequence that matches the predicate cmp. We can use that to search in a sorted sequence of Records:

```
auto less = [](const Record& r1, const Record& r2) { return r1.name<r2.name;};     // compare names

void f(const vector<Record>& v)          // assume that v is sorted on its "name" field
{
     auto er = equal_range(v.begin(),v.end(),Record{"Reg"},less);

     for (auto p = er.first; p!=er.second; ++p)      // print all equal records
          cout << *p;                                // assume that << is defined for Record
}
```

The first member of a pair is called first and the second member is called second. This naming is not particularly creative and may look a bit odd at first, but such consistent naming is a boon when we want to write generic code. Where the names first and second are too generic, we can use structured binding (§3.6.3):

```
void f2(const vector<Record>& v)         // assume that v is sorted on its "name" field
{
     auto [first,last] = equal_range(v.begin(),v.end(),Record{"Reg"},less);

     for (auto p = first; p!=last; ++p)       // print all equal records
          cout << *p;                         // assume that << is defined for Record
}
```

The standard-library pair (from <utility>) is quite frequently used in the standard library and elsewhere. A pair provides operators, such as =, ==, and <, if its elements do. Type deduction makes it easy to create a pair without explicitly mentioning its type. For example:

```
void f(vector<string>& v)
{
      pair p1 {v.begin(),2};                  // one way
      auto p2 = make_pair(v.begin(),2);    // another way
      // ...
}
```

Both p1 and p2 are of type pair<vector<string>::iterator,int>.

If you need more than two elements (or less), you can use tuple (from <utility>). A tuple is a heterogeneous sequence of elements; for example:

```
tuple<string,int,double> t1 {"Shark",123,3.14};        // the type is explicitly specified
auto t2 = make_tuple(string{"Herring"},10,1.23);   // the type is deduced to tuple<string,int,double>
tuple t3 {"Cod"s,20,9.99};                                  // the type is deduced to tuple<string,int,double>
```

Older code tends to use make_tuple() because template argument type deduction from constructor arguments is C++17.

Access to tuple members is through a get function template:

```
string s = get<0>(t1);          // get the first element: "Shark"
int x = get<1>(t1);              // get the second element: 123
double d = get<2>(t1);         // get the third element: 3.14
```

The elements of a tuple are numbered (starting with zero) and the indices must be constants.

Accessing members of a tuple by their index is general, ugly, and somewhat error-prone. Fortunately, an element of a tuple with a unique type in that tuple can be "named" by its type:

```
auto s = get<string>(t1);       // get the string: "Shark"
auto x = get<int>(t1);           // get the int: 123
auto d = get<double>(t1);      // get the double: 3.14
```

We can use get<> for writing also:

```
get<string>(t1) = "Tuna";      // write to the string
get<int>(t1) = 7;                   // write to the int
get<double>(t1) = 312;          // write to the double
```

Like pairs, tuples can be assigned and compared if their elements can be. Like tuple elements, pair elements can be accessed using get<>().

Like for pair, structured binding (§3.6.3) can be used for tuple. However, when code doesn't need to be generic, a simple struct with named members often leads to more maintainable code.

13.5 Alternatives

The standard library offers three types to express alternatives:

- variant to represent one of a specified set of alternatives (in <variant>)
- optional to represent a value of a specified type or no value (in <optional>)
- any to represent one of an unbounded set of alternative types (in <any>)

These three types offer related functionality to the user. Unfortunately, they don't offer a unified interface.

13.5.1 variant

A variant<A,B,C> is often a safer and more convenient alternative to explicitly using a union (§2.4). Possibly the simplest example is to return either a value or an error code:

```
variant<string,int> compose_message(istream& s)
{
	string mess;
	// ... read from s and compose message ...
	if (no_problems)
		return mess;		// return a string
	else
		return error_number;	// return an int
}
```

When you assign or initialize a variant with a value, it remembers the type of that value. Later, we can inquire what type the variant holds and extract the value. For example:

```
auto m = compose_message(cin));

if (holds_alternative<string>(m)) {
	cout << m.get<string>();
}
else {
	int err = m.get<int>();
	// ... handle error ...
}
```

This style appeals to some people who dislike exceptions (see §3.5.3), but there are more interesting uses. For example, a simple compiler may need to distinguish between different kind of nodes with different representations:

```
using Node = variant<Expression,Statement,Declaration,Type>;

void check(Node* p)
{
	if (holds_alternative<Expression>(*p)) {
		Expression& e = get<Expression>(*p);
		// ...
	}
	else if (holds_alternative<Statement>(*p)) {
		Statement& s = get<Statement>(*p);
		// ...
	}
	// ... Declaration and Type ...
}
```

This pattern of checking alternatives to decide on the appropriate action is so common and relatively inefficient that it deserves direct support:

```
void check(Node* p)
{
      visit(overloaded {
            [](Expression& e) { /* ... */ },
            [](Statement& s) { /* ... */ },
            // ... Declaration and Type ...
      }, *p);
}
```

This is basically equivalent to a virtual function call, but potentially faster. As with all claims of performance, this "potentially faster" should be verified by measurements when performance is critical. For most uses, the difference in performance is insignificant.

Unfortunately, the overloaded is necessary and not standard. It's a "piece of magic" that builds an overload set from a set of arguments (usually lambdas):

```
template<class... Ts>
struct overloaded : Ts... {
      using Ts::operator()...;
};

template<class... Ts>
      overloaded(Ts...) -> overloaded<Ts...>;   // deduction guide
```

The "visitor" visit then applies () to the overload, which selects the most appropriate lambda to call according to the overload rules.

A *deduction guide* is a mechanism for resolving subtle ambiguities, primarily for constructors of class templates in foundation libraries (§6.2.3).

If we try to access a variant holding a different type than the expected one, bad_variant_access is thrown.

13.5.2 optional

An optional<A> can be seen as a special kind of variant (like a variant<A,nothing>) or as a generalization of the idea of an A* either pointing to an object or being nullptr.

An optional can be useful for functions that may or may not return an object:

```
optional<string> compose_message(istream& s)
{
      string mess;

      // ... read from s and compose message ...

      if (no_problems)
            return mess;
      return {};          // the empty optional
}
```

Given that, we can write

```
if (auto m = compose_message(cin))
      cout << *m;            // note the dereference (*)
else {
      // ... handle error ...
}
```

This appeals to some people who dislike exceptions (see §3.5.3). Note the curious use of *. An optional is treated as a pointer to its object rather than the object itself.

The optional equivalent to nullptr is the empty object, {}. For example:

```
int cat(optional<int> a, optional<int> b)
{
      int res = 0;
      if (a) res+=*a;
      if (b) res+=*b;
      return res;
}

int x = cat(17,19);
int y = cat(17,{});
int z = cat({},{});
```

If we try to access an optional that does not hold a value, the result is undefined; an exception is *not* thrown. Thus, optional is not guaranteed type safe.

13.5.3 any

An any can hold an arbitrary type and know which type (if any) it holds. It is basically an unconstrained version of variant:

```
any compose_message(istream& s)
{
      string mess;

      // ... read from s and compose message ...

      if (no_problems)
            return mess;            // return a string
      else
            return error_number;    // return an int
}
```

When you assign or initialize an any with a value, it remembers the type of that value. Later, we can inquire what type the any holds and extract the value. For example:

```
auto m = compose_message(cin));
string& s = any_cast<string>(m);
cout << s;
```

If we try to access an any holding a different type than the expected one, bad_any_access is thrown. There are also ways of accessing an any that do not rely on exceptions.

13.6 Allocators

By default, standard-library containers allocate space using new. Operators new and delete provide a general free store (also called dynamic memory or heap) that can hold objects of arbitrary size and user-controlled lifetime. This implies time and space overheads that can be eliminated in many special cases. Therefore, the standard-library containers offer the opportunity to install allocators with specific semantics where needed. This has been used to address a wide variety of concerns related to performance (e.g., pool allocators), security (allocators that clean-up memory as part of deletion), per-thread allocation, and non-uniform memory architectures (allocating in specific memories with pointer types to match). This is not the place to discuss these important, but very specialized and often advanced techniques. However, I will give one example motivated by a real-world problem for which a pool allocator was the solution.

An important, long-running system used an event queue (see §15.6) using vectors as events that were passed as shared_ptrs. That way, the last user of an event implicitly deleted it:

```
struct Event {
	vector<int> data = vector<int>(512);
};

list<shared_ptr<Event>> q;

void producer()
{
	for (int n = 0; n!=LOTS; ++n) {
		lock_guard lk {m};		// m is a mutex (§15.5)
		q.push_back(make_shared<Event>());
		cv.notify_one();
	}
}
```

From a logical point of view this worked nicely. It is logically simple, so the code is robust and maintainable. Unfortunately, this led to massive fragmentation. After 100,000 events had been passed among 16 producers and 4 consumers, more than 6GB memory had been consumed.

The traditional solution to fragmentation problems is to rewrite the code to use a pool allocator. A pool allocator is an allocator that manages objects of a single fixed size and allocates space for many objects at a time, rather than using individual allocations. Fortunately, C++17 offers direct support for that. The pool allocator is defined in the pmr (“polymorphic memory resource”) sub-namespace of std:

```
pmr::synchronized_pool_resource pool;			// make a pool

struct Event {
	vector<int> data = vector<int>{512,&pool};	// let Events use the pool
};

list<shared_ptr<Event>> q {&pool};			// let q use the pool
```

```
void producer()
{
      for (int n = 0; n!=LOTS; ++n) {
            scoped_lock lk {m};        // m is a mutex (§15.5)
            q.push_back(allocate_shared<Event,pmr::polymorphic_allocator<Event>>{&pool});
            cv.notify_one();
      }
}
```

Now, after 100,000 events had been passed among 16 producers and 4 consumers, less than 3MB memory had been consumed. That's about a 2000-fold improvement! Naturally, the amount of memory actually in use (as opposed to memory wasted to fragmentation) is unchanged. After eliminating fragmentation, memory use was stable over time so the system could run for months.

Techniques like this have been applied with good effects from the earliest days of C++, but generally they required code to be rewritten to use specialized containers. Now, the standard containers optionally take allocator arguments. The default is for the containers to use new and delete.

13.7 Time

In <chrono>, the standard library provides facilities for dealing with time. For example, here is the basic way of timing something:

```
using namespace std::chrono;        // in sub-namespace std::chrono; see §3.4

auto t0 = high_resolution_clock::now();
do_work();
auto t1 = high_resolution_clock::now();
cout << duration_cast<milliseconds>(t1-t0).count() << "msec\n";
```

The clock returns a time_point (a point in time). Subtracting two time_points gives a duration (a period of time). Various clocks give their results in various units of time (the clock I used measures nanoseconds), so it is usually a good idea to convert a duration into a known unit. That's what duration_cast does.

Don't make statements about "efficiency" of code without first doing time measurements. Guesses about performance are most unreliable.

To simplify notation and minimize errors, <chrono> offers time-unit suffixes (§5.4.4). For example:

```
this_thread::sleep(10ms+33us);      // wait for 10 milliseconds and 33 microseconds
```

The chrono suffixes are defined in namespace std::chrono_literals.

An elegant and efficient extension to <chrono>, supporting longer time intervals (e.g., years and months), calendars, and time zones, is being added to the standard for C++20. It is currently available and in wide production use [Hinnant,2018] [Hinnant,2018b]. You can say things like

```
auto spring_day = apr/7/2018;
cout << weekday(spring_day) << '\n';        // Saturday
```

It even handles leap seconds.

13.8 Function Adaption

When passing a function as a function argument, the type of the argument must exactly match the expectations expressed in the called function's declaration. If the intended argument "almost matches expectations," we have three good alternatives:

- Use a lambda (§13.8.1).
- Use std::mem_fn() to make a function object from a member function (§13.8.2).
- Define the function to accept a std::function (§13.8.3).

There are many other ways, but usually one of these three ways works best.

13.8.1 Lambdas as Adaptors

Consider the classical "draw all shapes" example:

```
void draw_all(vector<Shape*>& v)
{
        for_each(v.begin(),v.end(),[](Shape* p) { p->draw(); });
}
```

Like all standard-library algorithms, for_each() calls its argument using the traditional function call syntax f(x), but Shape's draw() uses the conventional OO notation x->f(). A lambda easily mediates between the two notations.

13.8.2 mem_fn()

Given a member function, the function adaptor mem_fn(mf) produces a function object that can be called as a nonmember function. For example:

```
void draw_all(vector<Shape*>& v)
{
        for_each(v.begin(),v.end(),mem_fn(&Shape::draw));
}
```

Before the introduction of lambdas in C++11, mem_fn() and equivalents were the main way to map from the object-oriented calling style to the functional one.

13.8.3 function

The standard-library function is a type that can hold any object you can invoke using the call operator (). That is, an object of type function is a function object (§6.3.2). For example:

```
int f1(double);
function<int(double)> fct1 {f1};                   // initialize to f1

int f2(string);
function fct2 {f2};                                // fct2's type is function<int(string)>

function fct3 = [](Shape* p) { p->draw(); };       // fct3's type is function<void(Shape*)>
```

For fct2, I let the type of the function be deduced from the initializer: int(string).

Obviously, functions are useful for callbacks, for passing operations as arguments, for passing function objects, etc. However, it may introduce some run-time overhead compared to direct calls, and a function, being an object, does not participate in overloading. If you need to overload function objects (including lambdas), consider overloaded (§13.5.1).

13.9 Type Functions

A *type function* is a function that is evaluated at compile time given a type as its argument or returning a type. The standard library provides a variety of type functions to help library implementers (and programmers in general) to write code that takes advantage of aspects of the language, the standard library, and code in general.

For numerical types, numeric_limits from <limits> presents a variety of useful information (§14.7). For example:

```
constexpr float min = numeric_limits<float>::min();     // smallest positive float
```

Similarly, object sizes can be found by the built-in sizeof operator (§1.4). For example:

```
constexpr int szi = sizeof(int);     // the number of bytes in an int
```

Such type functions are part of C++'s mechanisms for compile-time computation that allow tighter type checking and better performance than would otherwise have been possible. Use of such features is often called *metaprogramming* or (when templates are involved) *template metaprogramming*. Here, I just present the use of two facilities provided by the standard library: iterator_traits (§13.9.1) and type predicates (§13.9.2). Concepts (§7.2) make some of these techniques redundant and simplify many of the rest, but concepts are still not standard or universally available, so the techniques presented here are in wide use.

13.9.1 iterator_traits

The standard-library sort() takes a pair of iterators supposed to define a sequence (Chapter 12). Furthermore, those iterators must offer random access to that sequence, that is, they must be *random-access iterators*. Some containers, such as forward_list, do not offer that. In particular, a forward_list is a singly-linked list so subscripting would be expensive and there is no reasonable way to refer back to a previous element. However, like most containers, forward_list offers *forward iterators* that can be used to traverse the sequence by algorithms and for-statements (§6.2).

The standard library provides a mechanism, iterator_traits, that allows us to check which kind of iterator is provided. Given that, we can improve the range sort() from §12.8 to accept either a vector or a forward_list. For example:

```
void test(vector<string>& v, forward_list<int>& lst)
{
      sort(v);     // sort the vector
      sort(lst);   // sort the singly-linked list
}
```

The techniques needed to make that work are generally useful.

First, I write two helper functions that take an extra argument indicating whether they are to be used for random-access iterators or forward iterators. The version taking random-access iterator arguments is trivial:

```
template<typename Ran>                                           // for random-access iterators
void sort_helper(Ran beg, Ran end, random_access_iterator_tag)   // we can subscript into [beg:end)
{
      sort(beg,end);        // just sort it
}
```

The version for forward iterators simply copies the list into a `vector`, sorts, and copies back:

```
template<typename For>                                   // for forward iterators
void sort_helper(For beg, For end, forward_iterator_tag) // we can traverse [beg:end)
{
      vector<Value_type<For>> v {beg,end};  // initialize a vector from [beg:end)
      sort(v.begin(),v.end());              // use the random access sort
      copy(v.begin(),v.end(),beg);          // copy the elements back
}
```

`Value_type<For>` is the type of `For`'s elements, called it's *value type*. Every standard-library iterator has a member `value_type`. I get the `Value_type<For>` notation by defining a type alias (§6.4.2):

```
template<typename C>
      using Value_type = typename C::value_type;  // C's value type
```

Thus, for a `vector<X>`, `Value_type<X>` is `X`.

The real "type magic" is in the selection of helper functions:

```
template<typename C>
void sort(C& c)
{
      using Iter = Iterator_type<C>;
      sort_helper(c.begin(),c.end(),Iterator_category<Iter>{});
}
```

Here, I use two type functions: `Iterator_type<C>` returns the iterator type of `C` (that is, `C::iterator`) and then `Iterator_category<Iter>{}` constructs a "tag" value indicating the kind of iterator provided:

- `std::random_access_iterator_tag` if `C`'s iterator supports random access
- `std::forward_iterator_tag` if `C`'s iterator supports forward iteration

Given that, we can select between the two sorting algorithms at compile time. This technique, called *tag dispatch*, is one of several used in the standard library and elsewhere to improve flexibility and performance.

We could define `Iterator_type` like this:

```
template<typename C>
      using Iterator_type = typename C::iterator;    // C's iterator type
```

However, to extend this idea to types without member types, such as pointers, the standard-library support for tag dispatch comes in the form of a class template `iterator_traits` from `<iterator>`. The specialization for pointers looks like this:

```
template<class T>
struct iterator_traits<T*> {
      using difference_type = ptrdiff_t;
      using value_type = T;
      using pointer = T*;
      using reference = T&;
      using iterator_category = random_access_iterator_tag;
};
```

We can now write:

```
template<typename Iter>
      using Iterator_category = typename std::iterator_traits<Iter>::iterator_category;   // Iter's category
```

Now an int* can be used as a random-access iterator despite not having a member type; Iterator_category<int*> is random_access_iterator_tag.

Many traits and traits-based techniques will be made redundant by concepts (§7.2). Consider the concepts version of the sort() example:

```
template<RandomAccessIterator Iter>
void sort(Iter p, Iter q);    // use for std::vector and other types supporting random access

template<ForwardIterator Iter>
void sort(Iter p, Iter q)
      // use for std::list and other types supporting just forward traversal
{
      vector<Value_type<Iter>> v {p,q};
      sort(v);                          // use the random-access sort
      copy(v.begin(),v.end(),p);
}

template<Range R>
void sort(R& r)
{
      sort(r.begin(),r.end());          // use the appropriate sort
}
```

Progress happens.

13.9.2 Type Predicates

In <type_traits>, the standard library offers simple type functions, called *type predicates* that answers a fundamental question about types. For example:

```
bool b1 = std::is_arithmetic<int>();        // yes, int is an arithmetic type
bool b2 = std::is_arithmetic<string>();     // no, std::string is not an arithmetic type
```

Other examples are is_class, is_pod, is_literal_type, has_virtual_destructor, and is_base_of. They are most useful when we write templates. For example:

```
template<typename Scalar>
class complex {
      Scalar re, im;
public:
      static_assert(is_arithmetic<Scalar>(), "Sorry, I only support complex of arithmetic types");
      // ...
};
```

To improve readability, the standard library defines template aliases. For example:

```
template<typename T>
      constexpr bool is_arithmetic_v = std::is_arithmetic<T>();
```

I'm no great fan of the _v suffix notation, but the technique for defining aliases is immensely useful. For example, the standard library defines the concept **Regular** (§12.7) like this:

```
template<class T>
      concept Regular = Semiregular<T> && EqualityComparable<T>;
```

13.9.3 enable_if

Obvious ways of using type predicates includes conditions for **static_asserts**, compile-time **ifs**, and **enable_ifs**. The standard-library **enable_if** is a widely used mechanism for conditonally introducing definitions. Consider defining a "smart pointer":

```
template<typename T>
class Smart_pointer {
      // ...
      T& operator*();
      T& operator->();     // -> should work if and only if T is a class
};
```

The -> should be defined if and only if **T** is a class type. For example, **Smart_pointer<vector<T>>** should have ->, but **Smart_pointer<int>** should not.

We cannot use a compile-time **if** because we are not inside a function. Instead, we write

```
template<typename T>
class Smart_pointer {
      // ...
      T& operator*();
      std::enable_if<is_class<T>(),T&> operator->();     // -> is defined if and only if T is a class
};
```

If **is_class<T>()** is **true**, the return type of **operator->()** is **T&**; otherwise, the definition of **operator->()** is ignored.

The syntax of **enable_if** is odd, awkward to use, and will in many cases be rendered redundant by concepts (§7.2). However, **enable_if** is the basis for much current template metaprogramming and for many standard-library components. It relies on a subtle language feature called SFINAE ("Substitution Failure Is Not An Error").

13.10 Advice

[1] A library doesn't have to be large or complicated to be useful; §13.1.
[2] A resource is anything that has to be acquired and (explicitly or implicitly) released; §13.2.
[3] Use resource handles to manage resources (RAII); §13.2; [CG: R.1].
[4] Use unique_ptr to refer to objects of polymorphic type; §13.2.1; [CG: R.20].
[5] Use shared_ptr to refer to shared objects (only); §13.2.1; [CG: R.20].
[6] Prefer resource handles with specific semantics to smart pointers; §13.2.1.
[7] Prefer unique_ptr to shared_ptr; §5.3, §13.2.1.
[8] Use make_unique() to construct unique_ptrs; §13.2.1; [CG: R.22].
[9] Use make_shared() to construct shared_ptrs; §13.2.1; [CG: R.23].
[10] Prefer smart pointers to garbage collection; §5.3, §13.2.1.
[11] Don't use std::move(); §13.2.2; [CG: ES.56].
[12] Use std::forward() exclusively for forwarding; §13.2.2.
[13] Never read from an object after std::move()ing or std::forward()ing it; §13.2.2.
[14] Prefer spans to pointer-plus-count interfaces; §13.3; [CG: F.24].
[15] Use array where you need a sequence with a constexpr size; §13.4.1.
[16] Prefer array over built-in arrays; §13.4.1; [CG: SL.con.2].
[17] Use bitset if you need N bits and N is not necessarily the number of bits in a built-in integer type; §13.4.2.
[18] Don't overuse pair and tuple; named structs often lead to more readable code; §13.4.3.
[19] When using pair, use template argument deduction or make_pair() to avoid redundant type specification; §13.4.3.
[20] When using tuple, use template argument deduction and make_tuple() to avoid redundant type specification; §13.4.3; [CG: T.44].
[21] Prefer variant to explicit use of unions; §13.5.1; [CG: C.181].
[22] Use allocators to prevent memory fragmentation; §13.6.
[23] Time your programs before making claims about efficiency; §13.7.
[24] Use duration_cast to report time measurements with proper units; §13.7.
[25] When specifying a duration, use proper units; §13.7.
[26] Use mem_fn() or a lambda to create function objects that can invoke a member function when called using the traditional function call notation; §13.8.2.
[27] Use function when you need to store something that can be called; §13.8.3.
[28] You can write code to explicitly depend on properties of types; §13.9.
[29] Prefer concepts over traits and enable_if whenever you can; §13.9.
[30] Use aliases and type predicates to simplify notation; §13.9.1, §13.9.2.

14

Numerics

The purpose of computing is insight, not numbers.
– R. W. Hamming

... but for the student,
numbers are often the best road to insight.
– A. Ralston

- Introduction
- Mathematical Functions
- Numerical Algorithms
  Parallel Numerical Algorithms
- Complex Numbers
- Random Numbers
- Vector Arithmetic
- Numeric Limits
- Advice

14.1 Introduction

C++ was not designed primarily with numeric computation in mind. However, numeric computation typically occurs in the context of other work – such as database access, networking, instrument control, graphics, simulation, and financial analysis – so C++ becomes an attractive vehicle for computations that are part of a larger system. Furthermore, numeric methods have come a long way from being simple loops over vectors of floating-point numbers. Where more complex data structures are needed as part of a computation, C++'s strengths become relevant. The net effect is that C++ is widely used for scientific, engineering, financial, and other computation involving sophisticated numerics. Consequently, facilities and techniques supporting such computation have emerged. This chapter describes the parts of the standard library that support numerics.

14.2 Mathematical Functions

In <cmath>, we find the *standard mathematical functions*, such as sqrt(), log(), and sin() for arguments of type float, double, and long double:

Standard Mathematical Functions	
abs(x)	Absolute value
ceil(x)	Smallest integer >= x
floor(x)	Largest integer <= x
sqrt(x)	Square root; x must be non-negative
cos(x)	Cosine
sin(x)	Sine
tan(x)	Tangent
acos(x)	Arccosine; the result is non-negative
asin(x)	Arcsine; the result nearest to 0 is returned
atan(x)	Arctangent
sinh(x)	Hyperbolic sine
cosh(x)	Hyperbolic cosine
tanh(x)	Hyperbolic tangent
exp(x)	Base e exponential
log(x)	Natural logarithm, base e; x must be positive
log10(x)	Base 10 logarithm

The versions for complex (§14.4) are found in <complex>. For each function, the return type is the same as the argument type.

Errors are reported by setting errno from <cerrno> to EDOM for a domain error and to ERANGE for a range error. For example:

```
void f()
{
    errno = 0; // clear old error state
    sqrt(-1);
    if (errno==EDOM)
        cerr << "sqrt() not defined for negative argument";

    errno = 0; // clear old error state
    pow(numeric_limits<double>::max(),2);
    if (errno == ERANGE)
        cerr << "result of pow() too large to represent as a double";
}
```

A few more mathematical functions are found in <cstdlib> and the so-called *special mathematical functions*, such as beta(), rieman_zeta(), and sph_bessel(), are also in <cmath>.

14.3 Numerical Algorithms

In <numeric>, we find a small set of generalized numerical algorithms, such as accumulate().

Numerical Algorithms	
x=accumulate(b,e,i)	x is the sum of i and the elements of [b:e)
x=accumulate(b,e,i,f)	accumulate using f instead of +
x=inner_product(b,e,b2,i)	x is the inner product of [b:e) and [b2:b2+(e−b)), that is, the sum of i and (*p1)*(*p2) for each p1 in [b:e) and the corresponding p2 in [b2:b2+(e−b))
x=inner_product(b,e,b2,i,f,f2)	inner_product using f and f2 instead of + and *
p=partial_sum(b,e,out)	Element i of [out:p) is the sum of elements [b:b+i]
p=partial_sum(b,e,out,f)	partial_sum using f instead of +
p=adjacent_difference(b,e,out)	Element i of [out:p) is *(b+i)−*(b+i−1) for i>0; if e−b>0, then *out is *b
p=adjacent_difference(b,e,out,f)	adjacent_difference using f instead of −
iota(b,e,v)	For each element in [b:e) assign ++v; thus the sequence becomes v+1, v+2, ...
x=gcd(n,m)	x is the greatest common denominator of integers n and m
x=lcm(n,m)	x is the least common multiple of integers n and m

These algorithms generalize common operations such as computing a sum by letting them apply to all kinds of sequences. They also make the operation applied to elements of those sequences a parameter. For each algorithm, the general version is supplemented by a version applying the most common operator for that algorithm. For example:

```
list<double> lst {1, 2, 3, 4, 5, 9999.99999};
auto s = accumulate(lst.begin(),lst.end(),0.0);      // calculate the sum: 10014.9999
```

These algorithms work for every standard-library sequence and can have operations supplied as arguments (§14.3).

14.3.1 Parallel Algorithms

In <numeric>, the numerical algorithms have parallel versions (§12.9) that are slightly different:

Parallel Numerical Algorithms	
x=reduce(b,e,v)	x=accumulate(b,e,v), except out of order
x=reduce(b,e)	x=reduce(b,e,V{}), where V is b's value type
x=reduce(pol,b,e,v)	x=reduce(b,e,v) with execution policy pol
x=reduce(pol,b,e)	x=reduce(pol,b,e,V{}), where V is b's value type
p=exclusive_scan(pol,b,e,out)	p=partial_sum(b,e,out) according to pol, excludes the ith input element from the ith sum
p=inclusive_scan(pol,b,e,out)	p=partial_sum(b,e,out) according to pol includes the ith input element in the ith sum

Parallel Numerical Algorithms (continued)	
p=transform_reduce(pol,b,e,f,v)	f(x) for each x in [b:e), then reduce
p=transform_exclusive_scan(pol,b,e,out,f,v)	f(x) for each x in [b:e), then exclusive_scan
p=transform_inclusive_scan(pol,b,e,out,f,v)	f(x) for each x in [b:e), then inclusive_scan

For simplicity, I left out the versions of these algorithms that take functor arguments, rather than just using + and =. Except for reduce(), I also left out the versions with default policy (sequential) and default value.

Just as for the parallel algorithms in <algorithm> (§12.9), we can specify an execution policy:

```
vector<double> v {1, 2, 3, 4, 5, 9999.99999};
auto s = reduce(v.begin(),v.end());          // calculate the sum using a double as the accumulator

vector<double> large;
// ... fill large with lots of values ...
auto s2 = reduce(par_unseq,large.begin(),large.end()); // calculate the sum using available parallelism
```

The parallel algorithms (e.g., reduce()) differ from the sequential ones (e.g., accumulate()) by allowing operations on elements in unspecified order.

14.4 Complex Numbers

The standard library supports a family of complex number types along the lines of the complex class described in §4.2.1. To support complex numbers where the scalars are single-precision floating-point numbers (floats), double-precision floating-point numbers (doubles), etc., the standard library complex is a template:

```
template<typename Scalar>
class complex {
public:
     complex(const Scalar& re ={}, const Scalar& im ={});    // default function arguments; see §3.6.1
     // ...
};
```

The usual arithmetic operations and the most common mathematical functions are supported for complex numbers. For example:

```
void f(complex<float> fl, complex<double> db)
{
     complex<long double> ld {fl+sqrt(db)};
     db += fl*3;
     fl = pow(1/fl,2);
     // ...
}
```

The sqrt() and pow() (exponentiation) functions are among the usual mathematical functions defined in <complex> (§14.2).

14.5 Random Numbers

Random numbers are useful in many contexts, such as testing, games, simulation, and security. The diversity of application areas is reflected in the wide selection of random number generators provided by the standard library in <random>. A random number generator consists of two parts:

[1] An *engine* that produces a sequence of random or pseudo-random values

[2] A *distribution* that maps those values into a mathematical distribution in a range

Examples of distributions are uniform_int_distribution (where all integers produced are equally likely), normal_distribution ("the bell curve"), and exponential_distribution (exponential growth); each for some specified range. For example:

```
using my_engine = default_random_engine;                // type of engine
using my_distribution = uniform_int_distribution<>;     // type of distribution

my_engine re {};                                        // the default engine
my_distribution one_to_six {1,6};                       // distribution that maps to the ints 1..6
auto die = [](){ return one_to_six(re); }               // make a generator

int x = die();                                          // roll the die: x becomes a value in [1:6]
```

Thanks to its uncompromising attention to generality and performance, one expert has deemed the standard-library random number component "what every random number library wants to be when it grows up." However, it can hardly be deemed "novice friendly." The using statements and the lambda make what is being done a bit more obvious.

For novices (of any background) the fully general interface to the random number library can be a serious obstacle. A simple uniform random number generator is often sufficient to get started. For example:

```
Rand_int rnd {1,10};     // make a random number generator for [1:10]
int x = rnd();           // x is a number in [1:10]
```

So, how could we get that? We have to get something that, like die(), combines an engine with a distribution inside a class Rand_int:

```
class Rand_int {
public:
      Rand_int(int low, int high) :dist{low,high} { }
      int operator()() { return dist(re); }          // draw an int
      void seed(int s) { re.seed(s); }               // choose new random engine seed
private:
      default_random_engine re;
      uniform_int_distribution<> dist;
};
```

That definition is still "expert level," but the *use* of Rand_int() is manageable in the first week of a C++ course for novices. For example:

```
int main()
{
	constexpr int max = 9;
	Rand_int rnd {0,max};                 // make a uniform random number generator

	vector<int> histogram(max+1);         // make a vector of appropriate size
	for (int i=0; i!=200; ++i)
		++histogram[rnd()];           // fill histogram with the frequencies of numbers [0:max]

	for (int i = 0; i!=histogram.size(); ++i) {    // write out a bar graph
		cout << i << '\t';
		for (int j=0; j!=histogram[i]; ++j) cout << '*';
		cout << endl;
	}
}
```

The output is a (reassuringly boring) uniform distribution (with reasonable statistical variation):

```
0	*********************
1	****************
2	*******************
3	********************
4	****************
5	***********************
6	**************************
7	***********
8	**********************
9	*************************
```

There is no standard graphics library for C++, so I use "ASCII graphics." Obviously, there are lots of open source and commercial graphics and GUI libraries for C++, but in this book I restrict myself to ISO standard facilities.

14.6 Vector Arithmetic

The vector described in §11.2 was designed to be a general mechanism for holding values, to be flexible, and to fit into the architecture of containers, iterators, and algorithms. However, it does not support mathematical vector operations. Adding such operations to vector would be easy, but its generality and flexibility preclude optimizations that are often considered essential for serious numerical work. Consequently, the standard library provides (in <valarray>) a vector-like template, called valarray, that is less general and more amenable to optimization for numerical computation:

```
template<typename T>
class valarray {
	// ...
};
```

The usual arithmetic operations and the most common mathematical functions are supported for valarrays. For example:

```
void f(valarray<double>& a1, valarray<double>& a2)
{
      valarray<double> a = a1*3.14+a2/a1;          // numeric array operators *, +, /, and =
      a2 += a1*3.14;
      a = abs(a);
      double d = a2[7];
      // ...
}
```

In addition to arithmetic operations, valarray offers stride access to help implement multidimensional computations.

14.7 Numeric Limits

In <limits>, the standard library provides classes that describe the properties of built-in types – such as the maximum exponent of a float or the number of bytes in an int. For example, we can assert that a char is signed:

```
static_assert(numeric_limits<char>::is_signed,"unsigned characters!");
static_assert(100000<numeric_limits<int>::max(),"small ints!");
```

Note that the second assert (only) works because numeric_limits<int>::max() is a constexpr function (§1.6).

14.8 Advice

[1] Numerical problems are often subtle. If you are not 100% certain about the mathematical aspects of a numerical problem, either take expert advice, experiment, or do both; §14.1.

[2] Don't try to do serious numeric computation using only the bare language; use libraries; §14.1.

[3] Consider accumulate(), inner_product(), partial_sum(), and adjacent_difference() before you write a loop to compute a value from a sequence; §14.3.

[4] Use std::complex for complex arithmetic; §14.4.

[5] Bind an engine to a distribution to get a random number generator; §14.5.

[6] Be careful that your random numbers are sufficiently random; §14.5.

[7] Don't use the C standard-library rand(); it isn't insufficiently random for real uses; §14.5.

[8] Use valarray for numeric computation when run-time efficiency is more important than flexibility with respect to operations and element types; §14.6.

[9] Properties of numeric types are accessible through numeric_limits; §14.7.

[10] Use numeric_limits to check that the numeric types are adequate for their use; §14.7.

15

Concurrency

Keep it simple:
as simple as possible,
but no simpler.
– A. Einstein

- Introduction
- Tasks and threads
- Passing Arguments
- Returning Results
- Sharing Data
- Waiting for Events
- Communicating Tasks
    future and promise; packaged_task; async()
- Advice

15.1 Introduction

Concurrency – the execution of several tasks simultaneously – is widely used to improve throughput (by using several processors for a single computation) or to improve responsiveness (by allowing one part of a program to progress while another is waiting for a response). All modern programming languages provide support for this. The support provided by the C++ standard library is a portable and type-safe variant of what has been used in C++ for more than 20 years and is almost universally supported by modern hardware. The standard-library support is primarily aimed at supporting systems-level concurrency rather than directly providing sophisticated higher-level concurrency models; those can be supplied as libraries built using the standard-library facilities.

The standard library directly supports concurrent execution of multiple threads in a single address space. To allow that, C++ provides a suitable memory model and a set of atomic operations. The atomic operations allow lock-free programming [Dechev,2010]. The memory model ensures that as long as a programmer avoids data races (uncontrolled concurrent access to mutable data), everything works as one would naively expect. However, most users will see concurrency only in terms of the standard library and libraries built on top of that. This section briefly gives examples of the main standard-library concurrency support facilities: threads, mutexes, lock() operations, packaged_tasks, and futures. These features are built directly upon what operating systems offer and do not incur performance penalties compared with those. Neither do they guarantee significant performance improvements compared to what the operating system offers.

Do not consider concurrency a panacea. If a task can be done sequentially, it is often simpler and faster to do so.

As an alternative to using explicit concurrency features, we can often use a parallel algorithm to exploit multiple execution engines for better performance (§12.9, §14.3.1).

15.2 Tasks and threads

We call a computation that can potentially be executed concurrently with other computations a *task*. A *thread* is the system-level representation of a task in a program. A task to be executed concurrently with other tasks is launched by constructing a std::thread (found in <thread>) with the task as its argument. A task is a function or a function object:

```
void f();                   // function

struct F {                  // function object
      void operator()();    // F's call operator (§6.3.2)
};

void user()
{
      thread t1 {f};        // f() executes in separate thread
      thread t2 {F()};      // F()() executes in separate thread

      t1.join();            // wait for t1
      t2.join();            // wait for t2
}
```

The join()s ensure that we don't exit user() until the threads have completed. To "join" a thread means to "wait for the thread to terminate."

Threads of a program share a single address space. In this, threads differ from processes, which generally do not directly share data. Since threads share an address space, they can communicate through shared objects (§15.5). Such communication is typically controlled by locks or other mechanisms to prevent data races (uncontrolled concurrent access to a variable).

Programming concurrent tasks can be *very* tricky. Consider possible implementations of the tasks f (a function) and F (a function object):

```
void f()
{
      cout << "Hello ";
}
```

```
struct F {
      void operator()() { cout << "Parallel World!\n"; }
};
```

This is an example of a bad error: here, `f` and `F()` each use the object `cout` without any form of synchronization. The resulting output would be unpredictable and could vary between different executions of the program because the order of execution of the individual operations in the two tasks is not defined. The program may produce "odd" output, such as

```
PaHerallllel o World!
```

Only a specific guarantee in the standard saves us from a data race within the definition of `ostream` that could lead to a crash.

When defining tasks of a concurrent program, our aim is to keep tasks completely separate except where they communicate in simple and obvious ways. The simplest way of thinking of a concurrent task is as a function that happens to run concurrently with its caller. For that to work, we just have to pass arguments, get a result back, and make sure that there is no use of shared data in between (no data races).

15.3 Passing Arguments

Typically, a task needs data to work upon. We can easily pass data (or pointers or references to the data) as arguments. Consider:

```
void f(vector<double>& v);      // function: do something with v

struct F {                      // function object: do something with v
      vector<double>& v;
      F(vector<double>& vv) :v{vv} { }
      void operator()();        // application operator; §6.3.2
};

int main()
{
      vector<double> some_vec {1,2,3,4,5,6,7,8,9};
      vector<double> vec2 {10,11,12,13,14};

      thread t1 {f,ref(some_vec)};    // f(some_vec) executes in a separate thread
      thread t2 {F{vec2}};            // F(vec2)() executes in a separate thread

      t1.join();
      t2.join();
}
```

Obviously, `F{vec2}` saves a reference to the argument vector in `F`. `F` can now use that vector and hopefully no other task accesses `vec2` while `F` is executing. Passing `vec2` by value would eliminate that risk.

The initialization with `{f,ref(some_vec)}` uses a `thread` variadic template constructor that can accept an arbitrary sequence of arguments (§7.4). The `ref()` is a type function from `<functional>` that unfortunately is needed to tell the variadic template to treat some_vec as a reference, rather than as an object. Without that ref(), some_vec would be passed by value. The compiler checks that the first argument can be invoked given the following arguments and builds the necessary function object to pass to the thread. Thus, if F::operator()() and f() perform the same algorithm, the handling of the two tasks are roughly equivalent: in both cases, a function object is constructed for the thread to execute.

15.4 Returning Results

In the example in §15.3, I pass the arguments by non-const reference. I only do that if I expect the task to modify the value of the data referred to (§1.7). That's a somewhat sneaky, but not uncommon, way of returning a result. A less obscure technique is to pass the input data by const reference and to pass the location of a place to deposit the result as a separate argument:

```
void f(const vector<double>& v, double* res);        // take input from v; place result in *res

class F {
public:
     F(const vector<double>& vv, double* p) :v{vv}, res{p} { }
     void operator()();                    // place result in *res
private:
     const vector<double>& v;               // source of input
     double* res;                          // target for output
};

double g(const vector<double>&); // use return value

void user(vector<double>& vec1, vector<double> vec2, vector<double> vec3)
{
     double res1;
     double res2;
     double res3;

     thread t1 {f,cref(vec1),&res1};              // f(vec1,&res1) executes in a separate thread
     thread t2 {F{vec2,&res2}};                   // F{vec2,&res2}() executes in a separate thread
     thread t3 { [&](){ res3 = g(vec3); } };      // capture local variables by reference

     t1.join();
     t2.join();
     t3.join();

     cout << res1 << ' ' << res2 << ' ' << res3 << '\n';
}
```

This works and the technique is very common, but I don't consider returning results through references particularly elegant, so I return to this topic in §15.7.1.

15.5 Sharing Data

Sometimes tasks need to share data. In that case, the access has to be synchronized so that at most one task at a time has access. Experienced programmers will recognize this as a simplification (e.g., there is no problem with many tasks simultaneously reading immutable data), but consider how to ensure that at most one task at a time has access to a given set of objects.

The fundamental element of the solution is a mutex, a "mutual exclusion object." A thread acquires a mutex using a lock() operation:

```
mutex m; // controlling mutex
int sh;     // shared data

void f()
{
     scoped_lock lck {m};           // acquire mutex
     sh += 7;                       // manipulate shared data
}    // release mutex implicitly
```

The type of lck is deduced to be scoped_lock<mutex> (§6.2.3). The scoped_lock's constructor acquires the mutex (through a call m.lock()). If another thread has already acquired the mutex, the thread waits ("blocks") until the other thread completes its access. Once a thread has completed its access to the shared data, the scoped_lock releases the mutex (with a call m.unlock()). When a mutex is released, threads waiting for it resume executing ("are woken up"). The mutual exclusion and locking facilities are found in <mutex>.

Note the use of RAII (§5.3). Use of resource handles, such as scoped_lock and unique_lock (§15.6), is simpler and far safer than explicitly locking and unlocking mutexes.

The correspondence between the shared data and a mutex is conventional: the programmer simply has to know which mutex is supposed to correspond to which data. Obviously, this is error-prone, and equally obviously we try to make the correspondence clear through various language means. For example:

```
class Record {
public:
     mutex rm;
     // ...
};
```

It doesn't take a genius to guess that for a Record called rec, you are supposed to acquire rec.rm before accessing the rest of rec, though a comment or a better name might have helped the reader.

It is not uncommon to need to simultaneously access several resources to perform some action. This can lead to deadlock. For example, if thread1 acquires mutex1 and then tries to acquire mutex2 while thread2 acquires mutex2 and then tries to acquire mutex1, then neither task will ever proceed further. The scoped_lock helps by enabling us to acquire several locks simultaneously:

```
void f()
{
     scoped_lock lck {mutex1,mutex2,mutex3};    // acquire all three locks
     // ... manipulate shared data ...
} // implicitly release all mutexes
```

This scoped_lock will proceed only after acquiring all its mutexes arguments and will never block ("go to sleep") while holding a mutex. The destructor for scoped_lock ensures that the mutexes are released when a thread leaves the scope.

Communicating through shared data is pretty low level. In particular, the programmer has to devise ways of knowing what work has and has not been done by various tasks. In that regard, use of shared data is inferior to the notion of call and return. On the other hand, some people are convinced that sharing must be more efficient than copying arguments and returns. That can indeed be so when large amounts of data are involved, but locking and unlocking are relatively expensive operations. On the other hand, modern machines are very good at copying data, especially compact data, such as vector elements. So don't choose shared data for communication because of "efficiency" without thought and preferably not without measurement.

The basic mutex allows one thread at a time to access data. One of the most common ways of sharing data is among many readers and a single writer. This "reader-writer lock" idiom is supported be shared_mutex. A reader will acquire the mutex "shared" so that other readers can still gain access, whereas a writer will demand exclusive access. For example:

```
shared_mutex mx;          // a mutex that can be shared

void reader()
{
        shared_lock lck {mx};          // willing to share access with other readers
        // ... read ...
}

void writer()
{
        unique_lock lck {mx};          // needs exclusive (unique) access
        // ... write ...
}
```

15.6 Waiting for Events

Sometimes, a thread needs to wait for some kind of external event, such as another thread completing a task or a certain amount of time having passed. The simplest "event" is simply time passing. Using the time facilities found in <chrono> I can write:

```
using namespace std::chrono;       // see §13.7

auto t0 = high_resolution_clock::now();
this_thread::sleep_for(milliseconds{20});
auto t1 = high_resolution_clock::now();

cout << duration_cast<nanoseconds>(t1-t0).count() << " nanoseconds passed\n";
```

Note that I didn't even have to launch a thread; by default, this_thread refers to the one and only thread.

I used duration_cast to adjust the clock's units to the nanoseconds I wanted.

The basic support for communicating using external events is provided by condition_variables found in <condition_variable>. A condition_variable is a mechanism allowing one thread to wait for another. In particular, it allows a thread to wait for some *condition* (often called an *event*) to occur as the result of work done by other threads.

Using condition_variables supports many forms of elegant and efficient sharing but can be rather tricky. Consider the classical example of two threads communicating by passing messages through a queue. For simplicity, I declare the queue and the mechanism for avoiding race conditions on that queue global to the producer and consumer:

```
class Message {     // object to be communicated
     // ...
};

queue<Message> mqueue;              // the queue of messages
condition_variable mcond;           // the variable communicating events
mutex mmutex;                       // for synchronizing access to mcond
```

The types queue, condition_variable, and mutex are provided by the standard library.

The consumer() reads and processes Messages:

```
void consumer()
{
     while(true) {
          unique_lock lck {mmutex};          // acquire mmutex
          mcond.wait(lck,[] { return !mqueue.empty(); });    // release lck and wait;
                                                              // re-acquire lck upon wakeup
                                                              // don't wake up unless mqueue is non-empty
          auto m = mqueue.front();           // get the message
          mqueue.pop();
          lck.unlock();                      // release lck
          // ... process m ...
     }
}
```

Here, I explicitly protect the operations on the queue and on the condition_variable with a unique_lock on the mutex. Waiting on condition_variable releases its lock argument until the wait is over (so that the queue is non-empty) and then reacquires it. The explicit check of the condition, here !mqueue.empty(), protects against waking up just to find that some other task has "gotten there first" so that the condition no longer holds.

I used a unique_lock rather than a scoped_lock for two reasons:

- We need to pass the lock to the condition_variable's wait(). A scoped_lock cannot be copied, but a unique_lock can be.
- We want to unlock the mutex protecting the condition variable before processing the message. A unique_lock offers operations, such as lock() and unlock(), for low-level control of synchronization.

On the other hand, unique_lock can only handle a single mutex.

The corresponding producer looks like this:

```
void producer()
{
     while(true) {
          Message m;
          // ... fill the message ...
          scoped_lock lck {mmutex};          // protect operations
          mqueue.push(m);
          mcond.notify_one();                // notify
     }                                       // release lock (at end of scope)
}
```

15.7 Communicating Tasks

The standard library provides a few facilities to allow programmers to operate at the conceptual level of tasks (work to potentially be done concurrently) rather than directly at the lower level of threads and locks:

- future and promise for returning a value from a task spawned on a separate thread
- packaged_task to help launch tasks and connect up the mechanisms for returning a result
- async() for launching of a task in a manner very similar to calling a function

These facilities are found in <future>.

15.7.1 future and promise

The important point about future and promise is that they enable a transfer of a value between two tasks without explicit use of a lock; "the system" implements the transfer efficiently. The basic idea is simple: when a task wants to pass a value to another, it puts the value into a promise. Somehow, the implementation makes that value appear in the corresponding future, from which it can be read (typically by the launcher of the task). We can represent this graphically:

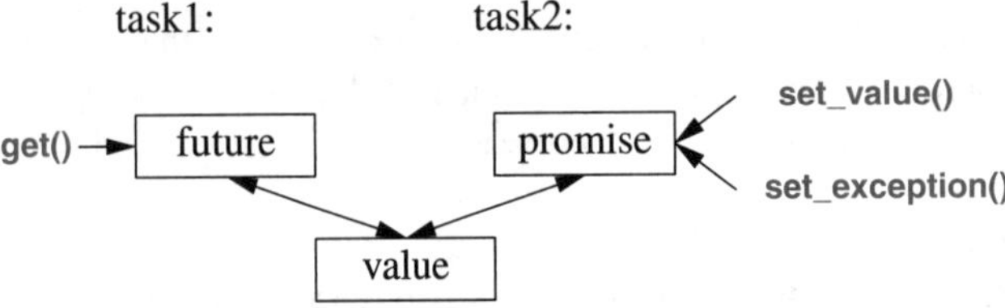

If we have a future<X> called fx, we can get() a value of type X from it:

```
X v = fx.get(); // if necessary, wait for the value to get computed
```

If the value isn't there yet, our thread is blocked until it arrives. If the value couldn't be computed, get() might throw an exception (from the system or transmitted from the task from which we were trying to get() the value).

The main purpose of a promise is to provide simple "put" operations (called set_value() and set_exception()) to match future's get(). The names "future" and "promise" are historical; please don't blame or credit me. They are yet another fertile source of puns.

If you have a promise and need to send a result of type X to a future, you can do one of two things: pass a value or pass an exception. For example:

```
void f(promise<X>& px)  // a task: place the result in px
{
     // ...
     try {
          X res;
          // ... compute a value for res ...
          px.set_value(res);
     }
     catch (...) {              // oops: couldn't compute res
          px.set_exception(current_exception());          // pass the exception to the future's thread
     }
}
```

The current_exception() refers to the caught exception.

To deal with an exception transmitted through a future, the caller of get() must be prepared to catch it somewhere. For example:

```
void g(future<X>& fx)              // a task: get the result from fx
{
     // ...
     try {
          X v = fx.get();  // if necessary, wait for the value to get computed
          // ... use v ...
     }
     catch (...) {              // oops: someone couldn't compute v
          // ... handle error ...
     }
}
```

If the error doesn't need to be handled by g() itself, the code reduces to the minimal:

```
void g(future<X>& fx)              // a task: get the result from fx
{
     // ...
     X v = fx.get();  // if necessary, wait for the value to get computed
     // ... use v ...
}
```

15.7.2 packaged_task

How do we get a future into the task that needs a result and the corresponding promise into the thread that should produce that result? The packaged_task type is provided to simplify setting up tasks connected with futures and promises to be run on threads. A packaged_task provides wrapper code to put the return value or exception from the task into a promise (like the code shown in

§15.7.1). If you ask it by calling get_future, a packaged_task will give you the future corresponding to its promise. For example, we can set up two tasks to each add half of the elements of a vector<double> using the standard-library accumulate() (§14.3):

```
double accum(double* beg, double* end, double init)
      // compute the sum of [beg:end) starting with the initial value init
{
      return accumulate(beg,end,init);
}

double comp2(vector<double>& v)
{
      using Task_type = double(double*,double*,double);                    // type of task

      packaged_task<Task_type> pt0 {accum};                                // package the task (i.e., accum)
      packaged_task<Task_type> pt1 {accum};

      future<double> f0 {pt0.get_future()};                                // get hold of pt0's future
      future<double> f1 {pt1.get_future()};                                // get hold of pt1's future

      double* first = &v[0];
      thread t1 {move(pt0),first,first+v.size()/2,0};                      // start a thread for pt0
      thread t2 {move(pt1),first+v.size()/2,first+v.size(),0};             // start a thread for pt1

      // ...

      return f0.get()+f1.get();                                            // get the results
}
```

The packaged_task template takes the type of the task as its template argument (here Task_type, an alias for double(double*,double*,double)) and the task as its constructor argument (here, accum). The move() operations are needed because a packaged_task cannot be copied. The reason that a packaged_task cannot be copied is that it is a resource handle: it owns its promise and is (indirectly) responsible for whatever resources its task may own.

Please note the absence of explicit mention of locks in this code: we are able to concentrate on tasks to be done, rather than on the mechanisms used to manage their communication. The two tasks will be run on separate threads and thus potentially in parallel.

15.7.3 async()

The line of thinking I have pursued in this chapter is the one I believe to be the simplest yet still among the most powerful: treat a task as a function that may happen to run concurrently with other tasks. It is far from the only model supported by the C++ standard library, but it serves well for a wide range of needs. More subtle and tricky models (e.g., styles of programming relying on shared memory), can be used as needed.

To launch tasks to potentially run asynchronously, we can use async():

```
double comp4(vector<double>& v)
     // spawn many tasks if v is large enough
{
     if (v.size()<10000)          // is it worth using concurrency?
          return accum(v.begin(),v.end(),0.0);

     auto v0 = &v[0];
     auto sz = v.size();

     auto f0 = async(accum,v0,v0+sz/4,0.0);                // first quarter
     auto f1 = async(accum,v0+sz/4,v0+sz/2,0.0);           // second quarter
     auto f2 = async(accum,v0+sz/2,v0+sz*3/4,0.0);         // third quarter
     auto f3 = async(accum,v0+sz*3/4,v0+sz,0.0);           // fourth quarter

     return f0.get()+f1.get()+f2.get()+f3.get(); // collect and combine the results
}
```

Basically, async() separates the "call part" of a function call from the "get the result part" and separates both from the actual execution of the task. Using async(), you don't have to think about threads and locks. Instead, you think just in terms of tasks that potentially compute their results asynchronously. There is an obvious limitation: don't even think of using async() for tasks that share resources needing locking. With async() you don't even know how many threads will be used because that's up to async() to decide based on what it knows about the system resources available at the time of a call. For example, async() may check whether any idle cores (processors) are available before deciding how many threads to use.

Using a guess about the cost of computation relative to the cost of launching a thread, such as v.size()<10000, is very primitive and prone to gross mistakes about performance. However, this is not the place for a proper discussion about how to manage threads. Don't take this estimate as more than a simple and probably poor guess.

It is rarely necessary to manually parallelize a standard-library algorithm, such as accumulate(), because the parallel algorithms, such as reduce(par_unseq,/*...*/), usually do a better job at that (§14.3.1). However, the technique is general.

Please note that async() is not just a mechanism specialized for parallel computation for increased performance. For example, it can also be used to spawn a task for getting information from a user, leaving the "main program" active with something else (§15.7.3).

15.8 Advice

[1] Use concurrency to improve responsiveness or to improve throughput; §15.1.
[2] Work at the highest level of abstraction that you can afford; §15.1.
[3] Consider processes as an alternative to threads; §15.1.
[4] The standard-library concurrency facilities are type safe; §15.1.
[5] The memory model exists to save most programmers from having to think about the machine architecture level of computers; §15.1.

[6] The memory model makes memory appear roughly as naively expected; §15.1.
[7] Atomics allow for lock-free programming; §15.1.
[8] Leave lock-free programming to experts; §15.1.
[9] Sometimes, a sequential solution is simpler and faster than a concurrent solution; §15.1.
[10] Avoid data races; §15.1, §15.2.
[11] Prefer parallel algorithms to direct use of concurrency; §15.1, §15.7.3.
[12] A thread is a type-safe interface to a system thread; §15.2.
[13] Use join() to wait for a thread to complete; §15.2.
[14] Avoid explicitly shared data whenever you can; §15.2.
[15] Prefer RAII to explicit lock/unlock; §15.5; [CG: CP.20].
[16] Use scoped_lock to manage mutexes; §15.5.
[17] Use scoped_lock to acquire multiple locks; §15.5; [CG: CP.21].
[18] Use shared_lock to implement reader-write locks; §15.5;
[19] Define a mutex together with the data it protects; §15.5; [CG: CP.50].
[20] Use condition_variables to manage communication among threads; §15.6.
[21] Use unique_lock (rather than scoped_lock) when you need to copy a lock or need lower-level manipulation of synchronization; §15.6.
[22] Use unique_lock (rather than scoped_lock) with condition_variables; §15.6.
[23] Don't wait without a condition; §15.6; [CG: CP.42].
[24] Minimize time spent in a critical section; §15.6 [CG: CP.43].
[25] Think in terms of tasks that can be executed concurrently, rather than directly in terms of threads; §15.7.
[26] Value simplicity; §15.7.
[27] Prefer packaged_task and futures over direct use of threads and mutexes; §15.7.
[28] Return a result using a promise and get a result from a future; §15.7.1; [CG: CP.60].
[29] Use packaged_tasks to handle exceptions thrown by tasks and to arrange for value return; §15.7.2.
[30] Use a packaged_task and a future to express a request to an external service and wait for its response; §15.7.2.
[31] Use async() to launch simple tasks; §15.7.3; [CG: CP.61].

16

History and Compatibility

Hurry Slowly
(festina lente).
– Octavius, Caesar Augustus

- History
  Timeline; The Early Years; The ISO C++ Standards; Standards and Programming Style C++ Use
- C++ Feature Evolution
  C++11 Language Features; C++14 Language Features; C++17 Language Features; C++11 Standard-Library Components; C++14 Standard-Library Components; C++17 Standard-Library Components; Removed and Deprecated Features
- C/C++ Compatibility
  C and C++ Are Siblings; Compatibility Problems
- Bibliography
- Advice

16.1 History

I invented C++, wrote its early definitions, and produced its first implementation. I chose and formulated the design criteria for C++, designed its major language features, developed or helped to develop many of the early libraries, and for 25 years was responsible for the processing of extension proposals in the C++ standards committee.

C++ was designed to provide Simula's facilities for program organization [Dahl,1970] together with C's efficiency and flexibility for systems programming [Kernighan,1978]. Simula was the initial source of C++'s abstraction mechanisms. The class concept (with derived classes and virtual functions) was borrowed from it. However, templates and exceptions came to C++ later with different sources of inspiration.

The evolution of C++ was always in the context of its use. I spent a lot of time listening to users and seeking out the opinions of experienced programmers. In particular, my colleagues at AT&T Bell Laboratories were essential for the growth of C++ during its first decade.

This section is a brief overview; it does not try to mention every language feature and library component. Furthermore, it does not go into details. For more information, and in particular for more names of people who contributed, see my two papers from the ACM History of Programming Languages conferences [Stroustrup,1993] [Stroustrup,2007] and my *Design and Evolution of C++* book (known as "D&E") [Stroustrup,1994]. They describe the design and evolution of C++ in detail and document influences from other programming languages.

Most of the documents produced as part of the ISO C++ standards effort are available online [WG21]. In my FAQ, I try to maintain a connection between the standard facilities and the people who proposed and refined those facilities [Stroustrup,2010]. C++ is not the work of a faceless, anonymous committee or of a supposedly omnipotent "dictator for life"; it is the work of many dedicated, experienced, hard-working individuals.

16.1.1 Timeline

The work that led to C++ started in the fall of 1979 under the name "C with Classes." Here is a simplified timeline:

1979 Work on "C with Classes" started. The initial feature set included classes and derived classes, public/private access control, constructors and destructors, and function declarations with argument checking. The first library supported non-preemptive concurrent tasks and random number generators.

1984 "C with Classes" was renamed to C++. By then, C++ had acquired virtual functions, function and operator overloading, references, and the I/O stream and complex number libraries.

1985 First commercial release of C++ (October 14). The library included I/O streams, complex numbers, and tasks (non-preemptive scheduling).

1985 *The C++ Programming Language* ("TC++PL," October 14) [Stroustrup,1986].

1989 *The Annotated C++ Reference Manual* ("the ARM") [Ellis,1989].

1991 *The C++ Programming Language, Second Edition* [Stroustrup,1991], presenting generic programming using templates and error handling based on exceptions, including the "Resource Acquisition Is Initialization" (RAII) general resource-management idiom.

1997 *The C++ Programming Language, Third Edition* [Stroustrup,1997] introduced ISO C++, including namespaces, `dynamic_cast`, and many refinements of templates. The standard library added the STL framework of generic containers and algorithms.

1998 ISO C++ standard [C++,1998].

2002 Work on a revised standard, colloquially named C++0x, started.

2003 A "bug fix" revision of the ISO C++ standard was issued. A C++ Technical Report introduced new standard-library components, such as regular expressions, unordered containers (hash tables), and resource management pointers, which later became part of C++11.

2006 An ISO C++ Technical Report on Performance addressed questions of cost, predictability, and techniques, mostly related to embedded systems programming [C++,2004].

2011 ISO C++11 standard [C++,2011]. It provided uniform initialization, move semantics, types deduced from initializers (auto), range-for, variadic template arguments, lambda expressions, type aliases, a memory model suitable for concurrency, and much more. The standard library added several components, including threads, locks, and most of the components from the 2003 Technical Report.

2013 The first complete C++11 implementations emerged.

2013 *The C++ Programming Language, Fourth Edition* introduced C++11.

2014 ISO C++14 standard [C++,2014] completing C++11 with variable templates, digit separators, generic lambdas, and a few standard-library improvements. The first C++14 implementations were completed.

2015 The C++ Core Guidelines projects started [Stroustrup,2015].

2015 The concepts TS was approved.

2017 ISO C++17 standard [C++,2017] offering a diverse set of new features, including order of evaluation guarantees, structured bindings, fold expressions, a file system library, parallel algorithms, and variant and optional types. The first C++17 implementations were completed.

2017 The modules TS and the Ranges TS were approved.

2020 ISO C++20 standard (scheduled).

During development, C++11 was known as C++0x. As is not uncommon in large projects, we were overly optimistic about the completion date. Towards the end, we joked that the 'x' in C++0x was hexadecimal so that C++0x became C++0B. On the other hand, the committee shipped C++14 and C++17 on time, as did the major compiler providers.

16.1.2 The Early Years

I originally designed and implemented the language because I wanted to distribute the services of a UNIX kernel across multiprocessors and local-area networks (what are now known as multicores and clusters). For that, I needed to precisely specify parts of a system and how they communicated. Simula [Dahl,1970] would have been ideal for that, except for performance considerations. I also needed to deal directly with hardware and provide high-performance concurrent programming mechanisms for which C would have been ideal, except for its weak support for modularity and type checking. The result of adding Simula-style classes to C (Classic C; §16.3.1), "C with Classes," was used for major projects in which its facilities for writing programs that use minimal time and space were severely tested. It lacked operator overloading, references, virtual functions, templates, exceptions, and many, many details [Stroustrup,1982]. The first use of C++ outside a research organization started in July 1983.

The name C++ (pronounced "see plus plus") was coined by Rick Mascitti in the summer of 1983 and chosen as the replacement for "C with Classes" by me. The name signifies the evolutionary nature of the changes from C; "++" is the C increment operator. The slightly shorter name "C+" is a syntax error; it had also been used as the name of an unrelated language. Connoisseurs of C semantics find C++ inferior to ++C. The language was not called D, because it was an extension of C, because it did not attempt to remedy problems by removing features, and because there already existed several would-be C successors named D. For yet another interpretation of the name C++, see the appendix of [Orwell,1949].

C++ was designed primarily so that my friends and I would not have to program in assembler, C, or various then-fashionable high-level languages. Its main purpose was to make writing good programs easier and more pleasant for the individual programmer. In the early years, there was no C++ paper design; design, documentation, and implementation went on simultaneously. There was no "C++ project" either, or a "C++ design committee." Throughout, C++ evolved to cope with problems encountered by users and as a result of discussions among my friends, my colleagues, and me.

The very first design of C++ (then called "C with Classes") included function declarations with argument type checking and implicit conversions, classes with the public/private distinction between the interface and the implementation, derived classes, and constructors and destructors. I used macros to provide primitive parameterization [Stroustrup,1982]. This was in non-experimental use by mid-1980. Late that year, I was able to present a set of language facilities supporting a coherent set of programming styles. In retrospect, I consider the introduction of constructors and destructors most significant. In the terminology of the time [Stroustrup,1979]:

A "new function" creates the execution environment for the member functions and the "delete function" reverses that.

Soon after, "new function' and "delete function' were renamed "constructor" and "destructor." Here is the root of C++'s strategies for resource management (causing a demand for exceptions) and the key to many techniques for making user code short and clear. If there were other languages at the time that supported multiple constructors capable of executing general code, I didn't (and don't) know of them. Destructors were new in C++.

C++ was released commercially in October 1985. By then, I had added inlining (§1.3, §4.2.1), consts (§1.6), function overloading (§1.3), references (§1.7), operator overloading (§4.2.1), and virtual functions (§4.4). Of these features, support for run-time polymorphism in the form of virtual functions was by far the most controversial. I knew its worth from Simula but found it impossible to convince most people in the systems programming world of its value. Systems programmers tended to view indirect function calls with suspicion, and people acquainted with other languages supporting object-oriented programming had a hard time believing that virtual functions could be fast enough to be useful in systems code. Conversely, many programmers with an object-oriented background had (and many still have) a hard time getting used to the idea that you use virtual function calls only to express a choice that must be made at run time. The resistance to virtual functions may be related to a resistance to the idea that you can get better systems through more regular structure of code supported by a programming language. Many C programmers seem convinced that what really matters is complete flexibility and careful individual crafting of every detail of a program. My view was (and is) that we need every bit of help we can get from languages and tools: the inherent complexity of the systems we are trying to build is always at the edge of what we can express.

Early documents (e.g., [Stroustrup,1985] and [Stroustrup,1994]) described C++ like this:

C++ is a general-purpose programming language that

- *is a better C*
- *supports data abstraction*
- *supports object-oriented programming*

Note *not* "C++ is an object-oriented programming language." Here, "supports data abstraction" refers to information hiding, classes that are not part of class hierarchies, and generic programming.

Initially, generic programming was poorly supported through the use of macros [Stroustrup,1982]. Templates and concepts came much later.

Much of the design of C++ was done on the blackboards of my colleagues. In the early years, the feedback from Stu Feldman, Alexander Fraser, Steve Johnson, Brian Kernighan, Doug McIlroy, and Dennis Ritchie was invaluable.

In the second half of the 1980s, I continued to add language features in response to user comments. The most important of those were templates [Stroustrup,1988] and exception handling [Koenig,1990], which were considered experimental at the time the standards effort started. In the design of templates, I was forced to decide among flexibility, efficiency, and early type checking. At the time, nobody knew how to simultaneously get all three. To compete with C-style code for demanding systems applications, I felt that I had to choose the first two properties. In retrospect, I think the choice was the correct one, and the search for better type checking of templates continues [DosReis,2006] [Gregor,2006] [Sutton,2011] [Stroustrup,2012a]. The design of exceptions focused on multilevel propagation of exceptions, the passing of arbitrary information to an error handler, and the integration between exceptions and resource management by using local objects with destructors to represent and release resources. I clumsily named that critical technique *Resource Acquisition Is Initialization* and others soon reduced that to the acronym *RAII* (§4.2.2).

I generalized C++'s inheritance mechanisms to support multiple base classes [Stroustrup,1987]. This was called *multiple inheritance* and was considered difficult and controversial. I considered it far less important than templates or exceptions. Multiple inheritance of abstract classes (often called *interfaces*) is now universal in languages supporting static type checking and object-oriented programming.

The C++ language evolved hand-in-hand with some of the key library facilities. For example, I designed the complex [Stroustrup,1984], vector, stack, and (I/O) stream classes [Stroustrup,1985] together with the operator overloading mechanisms. The first string and list classes were developed by Jonathan Shopiro and me as part of the same effort. Jonathan's string and list classes were the first to see extensive use as part of a library. The string class from the standard C++ library has its roots in these early efforts. The task library described in [Stroustrup,1987b] was part of the first "C with Classes" program ever written in 1980. It provided coroutines and a scheduler. I wrote it and its associated classes to support Simula-style simulations. Unfortunately, we had to wait until 2011 (30 years!) to get concurrency support standardized and universally available (Chapter 15). Coroutines are likely to be part of C++20 [CoroutinesTS]. The development of the template facility was influenced by a variety of `vector`, `map`, `list`, and `sort` templates devised by Andrew Koenig, Alex Stepanov, me, and others.

The most important innovation in the 1998 standard library was the STL, a framework of algorithms and containers (Chapter 11, Chapter 12). It was the work of Alex Stepanov (with Dave Musser, Meng Lee, and others) based on more than a decade's work on generic programming. The STL has been massively influential within the C++ community and beyond.

C++ grew up in an environment with a multitude of established and experimental programming languages (e.g., Ada [Ichbiah,1979], Algol 68 [Woodward,1974], and ML [Paulson,1996]). At the time, I was comfortable in about 25 languages, and their influences on C++ are documented in [Stroustrup,1994] and [Stroustrup,2007]. However, the determining influences always came from the applications I encountered. It was a deliberate policy to have the development of C++ "problem driven" rather than imitative.

16.1.3 The ISO C++ Standards

The explosive growth of C++ use caused some changes. Sometime during 1987, it became clear that formal standardization of C++ was inevitable and that we needed to start preparing the ground for a standardization effort [Stroustrup,1994]. The result was a conscious effort to maintain contact between implementers of C++ compilers and their major users. This was done through paper and electronic mail and through face-to-face meetings at C++ conferences and elsewhere.

AT&T Bell Labs made a major contribution to C++ and its wider community by allowing me to share drafts of revised versions of the C++ reference manual with implementers and users. Because many of those people worked for companies that could be seen as competing with AT&T, the significance of this contribution should not be underestimated. A less enlightened company could have caused major problems of language fragmentation simply by doing nothing. As it happened, about a hundred individuals from dozens of organizations read and commented on what became the generally accepted reference manual and the base document for the ANSI C++ standardization effort. Their names can be found in *The Annotated C++ Reference Manual* ("the ARM") [Ellis,1989]. The X3J16 committee of ANSI was convened in December 1989 at the initiative of Hewlett-Packard. In June 1991, this ANSI (American national) standardization of C++ became part of an ISO (international) standardization effort for C++. The ISO C++ committee is called WG21. From 1990, these joint C++ standards committees have been the main forum for the evolution of C++ and the refinement of its definition. I served on these committees throughout. In particular, as the chairman of the working group for extensions (later called the evolution group) from 1990 to 2014, I was directly responsible for handling proposals for major changes to C++ and the addition of new language features. An initial draft standard for public review was produced in April 1995. The first ISO C++ standard (ISO/IEC 14882-1998) [C++,1998] was ratified by a 22-0 national vote in 1998. A "bug fix release" of this standard was issued in 2003, so you sometimes hear people refer to C++03, but that is essentially the same language as C++98.

C++11, known for years as C++0x, is the work of the members of WG21. The committee worked under increasingly onerous self-imposed processes and procedures. These processes probably led to a better (and more rigorous) specification, but they also limited innovation [Stroustrup,2007]. An initial draft standard for public review was produced in 2009. The second ISO C++ standard (ISO/IEC 14882-2011) [C++,2011] was ratified by a 21-0 national vote in August 2011.

One reason for the long gap between the two standards is that most members of the committee (including me) were under the mistaken impression that the ISO rules required a "waiting period" after a standard was issued before starting work on new features. Consequently, serious work on new language features did not start until 2002. Other reasons included the increased size of modern languages and their foundation libraries. In terms of pages of standards text, the language grew by about 30% and the standard library by about 100%. Much of the increase was due to more detailed specification, rather than new functionality. Also, the work on a new C++ standard obviously had to take great care not to compromise older code through incompatible changes. There are billions of lines of C++ code in use that the committee must not break. Stability over decades is an essential "feature."

C++11 added massively to the standard library and pushed to complete the feature set needed for a programming style that is a synthesis of the "paradigms" and idioms that had proven successful with C++98.

The overall aims for the C++11 effort were:

- Make C++ a better language for systems programming and library building.
- Make C++ easier to teach and learn.

The aims are documented and detailed in [Stroustrup,2007].

A major effort was made to make concurrent systems programming type-safe and portable. This involved a memory model (§15.1) and support for lock-free programming, This was the work of Hans Boehm, Brian McKnight, and others in the concurrency working group. On top of that, we added the threads library.

After C++11, there was wide agreement that 13 years between standards were far too many. Herb Sutter proposed that the committee adopt a policy of shipping on time at fixed intervals, the "train model." I argued strongly for a short interval between standards to minimize the chance of delays because someone insisted on extra time to allow inclusion of "just one more essential feature." We agreed on an ambitious 3-year schedule with the idea that we should alternate between minor and major releases.

C++14 was deliberately a minor release aiming at "completing C++11." This reflects the reality that with a fixed release date, there will be features that we know we want, but can't deliver on time. Also, once in widespread use, gaps in the feature set will inevitably be discovered.

To allow work to progress faster, to allow parallel development of independent features, and to better utilize the enthusiasm and skills of the many volunteers, the committee makes use of the ISO mechanisms of developing and publishing "Technical Specifications" (TSs). That seems to work well for standard-library components, though it can lead to more stages in the development process, and thus delays. For language features, TSs seems to work less well. Possibly the reason is that few significant language features are truly independent, because the work of crafting standards wording isn't all that different between a standard and a TS, and because fewer people can experiment with compiler implementations.

C++17 was meant to be a major release. By "major," I mean containing features that will change the way we think about design and structure our software. By this definition, C++17 was at best a medium release. It included a lot of minor extensions, but the features that would have made dramatic changes (e.g., concepts, modules, and coroutines) were either not ready or became mired in controversy and lack of design direction. As a result, C++17 includes a little bit for everyone, but nothing that will significantly change the life of a C++ programmer who has already absorbed the lessons of C++11 and C++14. I hope that C++20 will be the promised and much-needed major revision, and that the major new features will become widely available well before 2020. The dangers are "Design by committee," feature bloat, lack of consistent style, and short-sighted decisions. In a committee with well over 100 members present at each meeting and more participating online, such undesirable phenomena are almost unavoidable. Making progress toward a simpler-to-use and more coherent language is very hard.

16.1.4 Standards and Style

A standard says what will work, and how. It does not say what constitutes good and effective use. There are significant differences between understanding the technical details of programming language features and using them effectively in combination with other features, libraries, and tools to produce better software. By "better" I mean "more maintainable, less error-prone, and faster."

We need to develop, popularize, and support coherent programming styles. Further, we must support the evolution of older code to these more modern, effective, and coherent styles.

With the growth of the language and its standard library, the problem of popularizing effective programming styles became critical. It is extremely difficult to make large groups of programmers depart from something that works for something better. There are still people who see C++ as a few minor additions to C and people who consider 1980s Object-Oriented programming styles based on massive class hierarchies the pinnacle of development. Many are struggling to use C++11 well in environments with lots of old C++ code. On the other hand, there are also many who enthusiastically overuse novel facilities. For example, some programmers are convinced that only code using massive amounts of template metaprogramming is true C++.

What is *Modern C++*? In 2015, I set out to answer this question by developing a set of coding guidelines supported by articulated rationales. I soon found that I was not alone in grappling with that problem and together with people from many parts of the world, notably from Microsoft, Red Hat, and Facebook, we started the "C++ Core Guidelines" project [Stroustrup,2015]. This is an ambitious project aiming at complete type-safety and complete resource-safety as a base for simpler, faster, and more maintainable code [Stroustrup,2015b]. In addition to specific coding rules with rationales, we back up the guidelines with static analysis tools and a tiny support library. I see something like that as necessary for moving the C++ community at large forward to benefit from the improvements in language features, libraries, and supporting tools.

16.1.5 C++ Use

C++ is now a very widely used programming language. Its user populations grew quickly from one in 1979 to about 400,000 in 1991; that is, the number of users doubled about every 7.5 months for more than a decade. Naturally, the growth rate slowed since that initial growth spurt, but my best estimate is that there are about 4.5 million C++ programmers in 2018 [Kazakova,2015]. Much of that growth happened after 2005 when the exponential explosion of processor speed stopped so that language performance grew in importance. This growth was achieved without formal marketing or an organized user community.

C++ is primarily an industrial language; that is, it is more prominent in industry than in education or programming language research. It grew up in Bell Labs inspired by the varied and stringent needs of telecommunications and of systems programming (including device drivers, networking, and embedded systems). From there, C++ use has spread into essentially every industry: microelectronics, Web applications and infrastructure, operating systems, financial, medical, automobile, aerospace, high-energy physics, biology, energy production, machine learning, video games, graphics, animation, virtual reality, and much more. It is primarily used where problems require C++'s combination of the ability to use hardware effectively and to manage complexity. This seems to be a continuously expanding set of applications [Stroustrup,1993] [Stroustrup,2014].

16.2 C++ Feature Evolution

Here, I list the language features and standard-library components that have been added to C++ for the C++11, C++14, and C++17 standards.

16.2.1 C++11 Language Features

Looking at a list of language features can be quite bewildering. Remember that a language feature is not meant to be used in isolation. In particular, most features that are new in C++11 make no sense in isolation from the framework provided by older features.

[1] Uniform and general initialization using {}-lists (§1.4, §4.2.3)
[2] Type deduction from initializer: auto (§1.4)
[3] Prevention of narrowing (§1.4)
[4] Generalized and guaranteed constant expressions: constexpr (§1.6)
[5] Range-for-statement (§1.7)
[6] Null pointer keyword: nullptr (§1.7)
[7] Scoped and strongly typed enums: enum class (§2.5)
[8] Compile-time assertions: static_assert (§3.5.5)
[9] Language mapping of {}-list to std::initializer_list (§4.2.3)
[10] Rvalue references, enabling move semantics (§5.2.2)
[11] Nested template arguments ending with >> (no space between the >s)
[12] Lambdas (§6.3.2)
[13] Variadic templates (§7.4)
[14] Type and template aliases (§6.4.2)
[15] Unicode characters
[16] long long integer type
[17] Alignment controls: alignas and alignof
[18] The ability to use the type of an expression as a type in a declaration: decltype
[19] Raw string literals (§9.4)
[20] Generalized POD ("Plain Old Data")
[21] Generalized unions
[22] Local classes as template arguments
[23] Suffix return type syntax
[24] A syntax for attributes and two standard attributes: [[carries_dependency]] and [[noreturn]]
[25] Preventing exception propagation: the noexcept specifier (§3.5.1)
[26] Testing for the possibility of a throw in an expression: the noexcept operator.
[27] C99 features: extended integral types (i.e., rules for optional longer integer types); concatenation of narrow/wide strings; __STDC_HOSTED__; _Pragma(X); vararg macros and empty macro arguments
[28] __func__ as the name of a string holding the name of the current function
[29] inline namespaces
[30] Delegating constructors
[31] In-class member initializers (§5.1.3)
[32] Control of defaults: default and delete (§5.1.1)
[33] Explicit conversion operators
[34] User-defined literals (§5.4.4)
[35] More explicit control of template instantiation: extern templates
[36] Default template arguments for function templates

[37] Inheriting constructors
[38] Override controls: override and final (§4.5.1)
[39] A simpler and more general SFINAE (Substitution Failure Is Not An Error) rule
[40] Memory model (§15.1)
[41] Thread-local storage: thread_local

For a more complete description of the changes to C++98 in C++11, see [Stroustrup,2013].

16.2.2 C++14 Language Features

[1] Function return-type deduction; §3.6.2
[2] Improved constexpr functions, e.g., for-loops allowed (§1.6)
[3] Variable templates (§6.4.1)
[4] Binary literals (§1.4)
[5] Digit separators (§1.4)
[6] Generic lambdas (§6.3.3)
[7] More general lambda capture
[8] [[deprecated]] attribute
[9] A few more minor extensions

16.2.3 C++17 Language Features

[1] Guaranteed copy elision (§5.2.2)
[2] Dynamic allocation of over-aligned types
[3] Stricter order of evaluation (§1.4)
[4] UTF-8 literals (u8)
[5] Hexadecimal floating-point literals
[6] Fold expressions (§7.4.1)
[7] Generic value template arguments (auto template parameters)
[8] Class template argument type deduction (§6.2.3)
[9] Compile-time if (§6.4.3)
[10] Selection statements with initializers (§1.8)
[11] constexpr lambdas
[12] inline variables
[13] Structured bindings (§3.6.3)
[14] New standard attributes: [[fallthrough]], [[nodiscard]], and [[maybe_unused]]
[15] std::byte type
[16] Initialization of an enum by a value of its underlying type (§2.5)
[17] A few more minor extensions

16.2.4 C++11 Standard-Library Components

The C++11 additions to the standard library come in two forms: new components (such as the regular expression matching library) and improvements to C++98 components (such as move constructors for containers).

[1] initializer_list constructors for containers (§4.2.3)
[2] Move semantics for containers (§5.2.2, §11.2)
[3] A singly-linked list: forward_list (§11.6)
[4] Hash containers: unordered_map, unordered_multimap, unordered_set, and unordered_multiset (§11.6, §11.5)
[5] Resource management pointers: unique_ptr, shared_ptr, and weak_ptr (§13.2.1)
[6] Concurrency support: thread (§15.2), mutexes (§15.5), locks (§15.5), and condition variables (§15.6)
[7] Higher-level concurrency support: packaged_thread, future, promise, and async() (§15.7)
[8] tuples (§13.4.3)
[9] Regular expressions: regex (§9.4)
[10] Random numbers: distributions and engines (§14.5)
[11] Integer type names, such as int16_t, uint32_t, and int_fast64_t
[12] A fixed-sized contiguous sequence container: array (§13.4.1)
[13] Copying and rethrowing exceptions (§15.7.1)
[14] Error reporting using error codes: system_error
[15] emplace() operations for containers (§11.6)
[16] Wide use of constexpr functions
[17] Systematic use of noexcept functions
[18] Improved function adaptors: function and bind() (§13.8)
[19] string to numeric value conversions
[20] Scoped allocators
[21] Type traits, such as is_integral and is_base_of (§13.9.2)
[22] Time utilities: duration and time_point (§13.7)
[23] Compile-time rational arithmetic: ratio
[24] Abandoning a process: quick_exit
[25] More algorithms, such as move(), copy_if(), and is_sorted() (Chapter 12)
[26] Garbage collection API (§5.3)
[27] Low-level concurrency support: atomics

16.2.5 C++14 Standard-Library Components

[1] shared_mutex (§15.5)
[2] User-defined literals (§5.4.4)
[3] Tuple addressing by type (§13.4.3)
[4] Associative container heterogenous lookup
[5] A few more minor features

16.2.6 C++17 Standard-Library Components

[1] File system (§10.10)
[2] Parallel algorithms (§12.9, §14.3.1)
[3] Mathematical special functions (§14.2)
[4] string_view (§9.3)

[5] any (§13.5.3)
[6] variant (§13.5.1)
[7] optional (§13.5.2)
[8] invoke()
[9] Elementary string conversions: to_chars and from_chars
[10] Polymorphic allocator (§13.6)
[11] A few more minor extensions

16.2.7 Removed and Deprecated Features

There are billions of lines of C++ "out there" and nobody knows exactly what features are in critical use. Consequently, the ISO committee removes older features only reluctantly and after years of warning. However, sometimes troublesome features are removed:

- C++17 finally removed exceptions specifications:

  ```
  void f() throw(X,Y); // C++98; now an error
  ```

  The support facilities for exception specifications, unexcepted_handler, set_unexpected(), get_unexpected(), and unexpected(), are similarly removed. Instead, use noexcept (§3.5.1).
- Trigraphs are no longer supported.
- The auto_ptr is deprecated. Instead, use unique_ptr (§13.2.1).
- The use of the storage specifier register is removed.
- The use of ++ on a bool is removed.
- The C++98 export feature was removed because it was complex and not shipped by the major vendors. Instead, export is used as a keyword for modules (§3.3).
- Generation of copy operations is deprecated for a class with a destructor (§5.1.1).
- Assignment of a string literal to a char* is removed. Instead use const char* or auto.
- Some C++ standard-library function objects and associated functions are deprecated. Most relate to argument binding. Instead use lambdas and function (§13.8).

By deprecating a feature, the standards committee expresses the wish that the feature will go away. However, the committee does not have a mandate to immediately remove a heavily used feature – however redundant or dangerous it may be. Thus, a deprecation is a strong hint to avoid the feature. It may disappear in the future. Compilers are likely to issue warnings for uses of deprecated features. However, deprecated features are part of the standard and history shows that they tend to remain supported "forever" for reasons of compatibility.

16.3 C/C++ Compatibility

With minor exceptions, C++ is a superset of C (meaning C11; [C,2011]). Most differences stem from C++'s greater emphasis on type checking. Well-written C programs tend to be C++ programs as well. A compiler can diagnose every difference between C++ and C. The C99/C++11 incompatibilities are listed in Appendix C of the standard.

16.3.1 C and C++ Are Siblings

Classic C has two main descendants: ISO C and ISO C++. Over the years, these languages have evolved at different paces and in different directions. One result of this is that each language provides support for traditional C-style programming in slightly different ways. The resulting incompatibilities can make life miserable for people who use both C and C++, for people who write in one language using libraries implemented in the other, and for implementers of libraries and tools for C and C++.

How can I call C and C++ siblings? Look at a simplified family tree:

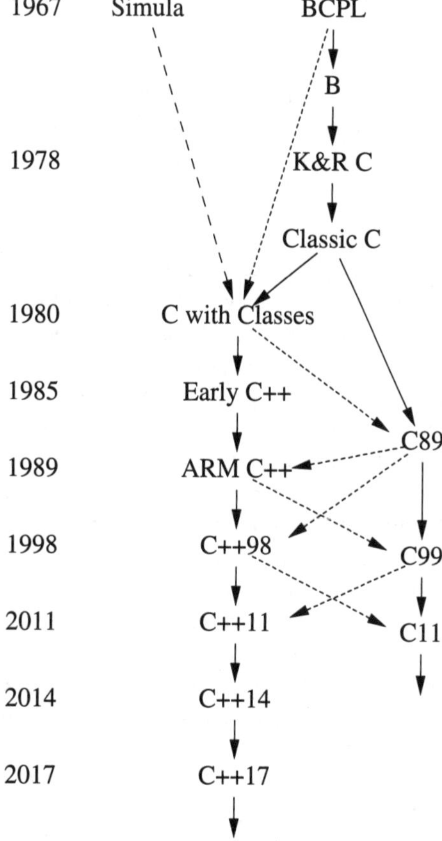

A solid line means a massive inheritance of features, a dashed line a borrowing of major features, and a dotted line a borrowing of minor features. From this, ISO C and ISO C++ emerge as the two major descendants of K&R C [Kernighan,1978], and as siblings. Each carries with it the key aspects of Classic C, and neither is 100% compatible with Classic C. I picked the term "Classic C" from a sticker that used to be affixed to Dennis Ritchie's terminal. It is K&R C plus enumerations and struct assignment. BCPL is defined by [Richards,1980] and C89 by [C1990].

Note that differences between C and C++ are not necessarily the result of changes to C made in C++. In several cases, the incompatibilities arise from features adopted incompatibly into C long after they were common in C++. Examples are the ability to assign a `T*` to a `void*` and the linkage of global `consts` [Stroustrup,2002]. Sometimes, a feature was even incompatibly adopted into C after it was part of the ISO C++ standard, such as details of the meaning of `inline`.

16.3.2 Compatibility Problems

There are many minor incompatibilities between C and C++. All can cause problems for a programmer, but all can be coped with in the context of C++. If nothing else, C code fragments can be compiled as C and linked to using the `extern "C"` mechanism.

The major problems for converting a C program to C++ are likely to be:

- Suboptimal design and programming style.
- A `void*` implicitly converted to a `T*` (that is, converted without a cast).
- C++ keywords, such as `class` and `private`, used as identifiers in C code.
- Incompatible linkage of code fragments compiled as C and fragments compiled as C++.

16.3.2.1 Style Problems

Naturally, a C program is written in a C style, such as the style used in K&R [Kernighan,1988]. This implies widespread use of pointers and arrays, and probably many macros. These facilities are hard to use reliably in a large program. Resource management and error handling are often ad hoc, documented (rather than language and tool supported), and often incompletely documented and adhered to. A simple line-for-line conversion of a C program into a C++ program yields a program that is often a bit better checked. In fact, I have never converted a C program into C++ without finding some bug. However, the fundamental structure is unchanged, and so are the fundamental sources of errors. If you had incomplete error handling, resource leaks, or buffer overflows in the original C program, they will still be there in the C++ version. To obtain major benefits, you must make changes to the fundamental structure of the code:

[1] Don't think of C++ as C with a few features added. C++ can be used that way, but only suboptimally. To get really major advantages from C++ as compared to C, you need to apply different design and implementation styles.

[2] Use the C++ standard library as a teacher of new techniques and programming styles. Note the difference from the C standard library (e.g., `=` rather than `strcpy()` for copying and `==` rather than `strcmp()` for comparing).

[3] Macro substitution is almost never necessary in C++. Use `const` (§1.6), `constexpr` (§1.6), `enum` or `enum class` (§2.5) to define manifest constants, `inline` (§4.2.1) to avoid function-calling overhead, `templates` (Chapter 6) to specify families of functions and types, and `namespaces` (§3.4) to avoid name clashes.

[4] Don't declare a variable before you need it and initialize it immediately. A declaration can occur anywhere a statement can (§1.8), in `for`-statement initializers (§1.7), and in conditions (§4.5.2).

[5] Don't use `malloc()`. The `new` operator (§4.2.2) does the same job better, and instead of `realloc()`, try a `vector` (§4.2.3, §12.1). Don't just replace `malloc()` and `free()` with "naked" `new` and `delete` (§4.2.2).

[6] Avoid void*, unions, and casts, except deep within the implementation of some function or class. Their use limits the support you can get from the type system and can harm performance. In most cases, a cast is an indication of a design error.

[7] If you must use an explicit type conversion, use an appropriate named cast (e.g., static_cast; §16.2.7) for a more precise statement of what you are trying to do.

[8] Minimize the use of arrays and C-style strings. C++ standard-library strings (§9.2), arrays (§13.4.1), and vectors (§11.2) can often be used to write simpler and more maintainable code compared to the traditional C style. In general, try not to build yourself what has already been provided by the standard library.

[9] Avoid pointer arithmetic except in very specialized code (such as a memory manager) and for simple array traversal (e.g., ++p).

[10] Do not assume that something laboriously written in C style (avoiding C++ features such as classes, templates, and exceptions) is more efficient than a shorter alternative (e.g., using standard-library facilities). Often (but of course not always), the opposite is true.

16.3.2.2 void*

In C, a void* may be used as the right-hand operand of an assignment to or initialization of a variable of any pointer type; in C++ it may not. For example:

```
void f(int n)
{
        int* p = malloc(n*sizeof(int));  /* not C++; in C++, allocate using "new" */
        // ...
}
```

This is probably the single most difficult incompatibility to deal with. Note that the implicit conversion of a void* to a different pointer type is *not* in general harmless:

```
char ch;
void* pv = &ch;
int* pi = pv;           // not C++
*pi = 666;              // overwrite ch and other bytes near ch
```

In both languages, cast the result of malloc() to the right type. If you use only C++, avoid malloc().

16.3.2.3 Linkage

C and C++ can (and often are) implemented to use different linkage conventions. The most basic reason for that is C++'s greater emphasis on type checking. A practical reason is that C++ supports overloading, so there can be two global functions called open(). This has to be reflected in the way the linker works.

To give a C++ function C linkage (so that it can be called from a C program fragment) or to allow a C function to be called from a C++ program fragment, declare it extern "C". For example:

```
extern "C" double sqrt(double);
```

Now sqrt(double) can be called from a C or a C++ code fragment. The definition of sqrt(double) can also be compiled as a C function or as a C++ function.

Only one function of a given name in a scope can have C linkage (because C doesn't allow function overloading). A linkage specification does not affect type checking, so the C++ rules for function calls and argument checking still apply to a function declared `extern "C"`.

16.4 Bibliography

[Boost] *The Boost Libraries: free peer-reviewed portable C++ source libraries.* www.boost.org.

[C,1990] X3 Secretariat: *Standard – The C Language.* X3J11/90-013. ISO Standard ISO/IEC 9899-1990. Computer and Business Equipment Manufacturers Association. Washington, DC.

[C,1999] ISO/IEC 9899. *Standard – The C Language.* X3J11/90-013-1999.

[C,2011] ISO/IEC 9899. *Standard – The C Language.* X3J11/90-013-2011.

[C++,1998] ISO/IEC JTC1/SC22/WG21 (editor: Andrew Koenig): *International Standard – The C++ Language.* ISO/IEC 14882:1998.

[C++,2004] ISO/IEC JTC1/SC22/WG21 (editor: Lois Goldtwaite): *Technical Report on C++ Performance.* ISO/IEC TR 18015:2004(E)

[C++Math,2010] *International Standard – Extensions to the C++ Library to Support Mathematical Special Functions.* ISO/IEC 29124:2010.

[C++,2011] ISO/IEC JTC1/SC22/WG21 (editor: Pete Becker): *International Standard – The C++ Language.* ISO/IEC 14882:2011.

[C++,2014] ISO/IEC JTC1/SC22/WG21 (editor: Stefanus du Toit): *International Standard – The C++ Language.* ISO/IEC 14882:2014.

[C++,2017] ISO/IEC JTC1/SC22/WG21 (editor: Richard Smith): *International Standard – The C++ Language.* ISO/IEC 14882:2017.

[ConceptsTS] ISO/IEC JTC1/SC22/WG21 (editor: Gabriel Dos Reis): *Technical Specification: C++ Extensions for Concepts.* ISO/IEC TS 19217:2015.

[CoroutinesTS] ISO/IEC JTC1/SC22/WG21 (editor: Gor Nishanov): *Technical Specification: C++ Extensions for Coroutines.* ISO/IEC TS 22277:2017.

[Cppreference] *Online source for C++ language and standard library facilities.* www.cppreference.com.

[Cox,2007] Russ Cox: *Regular Expression Matching Can Be Simple And Fast.* January 2007. swtch.com/~rsc/regexp/regexp1.html.

[Dahl,1970] O-J. Dahl, B. Myrhaug, and K. Nygaard: *SIMULA Common Base Language.* Norwegian Computing Center S-22. Oslo, Norway. 1970.

[Dechev,2010] D. Dechev, P. Pirkelbauer, and B. Stroustrup: *Understanding and Effectively Preventing the ABA Problem in Descriptor-based Lock-free Designs.* 13th IEEE Computer Society ISORC 2010 Symposium. May 2010.

[DosReis,2006] Gabriel Dos Reis and Bjarne Stroustrup: *Specifying C++ Concepts.* POPL06. January 2006.

[Ellis,1989] Margaret A. Ellis and Bjarne Stroustrup: *The Annotated C++ Reference Manual.* Addison-Wesley. Reading, Massachusetts. 1990. ISBN 0-201-51459-1.

[Garcia,2015] J. Daniel Garcia and B. Stroustrup: *Improving performance and maintainability through refactoring in C++11.* Isocpp.org. August 2015. http://www.stroustrup.com/improving_garcia_stroustrup_2015.pdf.

[Garcia,2016] G. Dos Reis, J. D. Garcia, J. Lakos, A. Meredith, N. Myers, B. Stroustrup: *A Contract Design.* P0380R1. 2016-7-11.

[Garcia,2018] G. Dos Reis, J. D. Garcia, J. Lakos, A. Meredith, N. Myers, B. Stroustrup: *Support for contract based programming in C++.* P0542R4. 2018-4-2.

[Friedl,1997] Jeffrey E. F. Friedl: *Mastering Regular Expressions.* O'Reilly Media. Sebastopol, California. 1997. ISBN 978-1565922570.

[GSL] N. MacIntosh (Editor): *Guidelines Support Library.* https://github.com/microsoft/gsl.

[Gregor,2006] Douglas Gregor et al.: *Concepts: Linguistic Support for Generic Programming in C++.* OOPSLA'06.

[Hinnant,2018] Howard Hinnant: *Date.* https://howardhinnant.github.io/date/date.html. Github. 2018.

[Hinnant,2018b] Howard Hinnant: *Timezones.* https://howardhinnant.github.io/date/tz.html. Github. 2018.

[Ichbiah,1979] Jean D. Ichbiah et al.: *Rationale for the Design of the ADA Programming Language.* SIGPLAN Notices. Vol. 14, No. 6. June 1979.

[Kazakova,2015] Anastasia Kazakova: *Infographic: C/C++ facts.* https://blog.jetbrains.com/clion/2015/07/infographics-cpp-facts-before-clion/ July 2015.

[Kernighan,1978] Brian W. Kernighan and Dennis M. Ritchie: *The C Programming Language.* Prentice Hall. Englewood Cliffs, New Jersey. 1978.

[Kernighan,1988] Brian W. Kernighan and Dennis M. Ritchie: *The C Programming Language, Second Edition.* Prentice-Hall. Englewood Cliffs, New Jersey. 1988. ISBN 0-13-110362-8.

[Knuth,1968] Donald E. Knuth: *The Art of Computer Programming.* Addison-Wesley. Reading, Massachusetts. 1968.

[Koenig,1990] A. R. Koenig and B. Stroustrup: *Exception Handling for C++ (revised).* Proc USENIX C++ Conference. April 1990.

[Maddock,2009] John Maddock: *Boost.Regex.* www.boost.org. 2009. 2017.

[ModulesTS] ISO/IEC JTC1/SC22/WG21 (editor: Gabriel Dos Reis): *Technical Specification: C++ Extensions for Modules.* ISO/IEC TS 21544:2018.

[Orwell,1949] George Orwell: *1984.* Secker and Warburg. London. 1949.

[Paulson,1996] Larry C. Paulson: *ML for the Working Programmer.* Cambridge University Press. Cambridge. 1996.

[RangesTS] ISO/IEC JTC1/SC22/WG21 (editor: Eric Niebler): *Technical Specification: C++ Extensions for Ranges.* ISO/IEC TS 21425:2017. ISBN 0-521-56543-X.

[Richards,1980] Martin Richards and Colin Whitby-Strevens: *BCPL – The Language and Its Compiler.* Cambridge University Press. Cambridge. 1980. ISBN 0-521-21965-5.

[Stepanov,1994] Alexander Stepanov and Meng Lee: *The Standard Template Library*. HP Labs Technical Report HPL-94-34 (R. 1). 1994.

[Stepanov,2009] Alexander Stepanov and Paul McJones: *Elements of Programming*. Addison-Wesley. 2009. ISBN 978-0-321-63537-2.

[Stroustrup,1979] Personal lab notes.

[Stroustrup,1982] B. Stroustrup: *Classes: An Abstract Data Type Facility for the C Language*. Sigplan Notices. January 1982. The first public description of "C with Classes."

[Stroustrup,1984] B. Stroustrup: *Operator Overloading in C++*. Proc. IFIP WG2.4 Conference on System Implementation Languages: Experience & Assessment. September 1984.

[Stroustrup,1985] B. Stroustrup: *An Extensible I/O Facility for C++*. Proc. Summer 1985 USENIX Conference.

[Stroustrup,1986] B. Stroustrup: *The C++ Programming Language*. Addison-Wesley. Reading, Massachusetts. 1986. ISBN 0-201-12078-X.

[Stroustrup,1987] B. Stroustrup: *Multiple Inheritance for C++*. Proc. EUUG Spring Conference. May 1987.

[Stroustrup,1987b] B. Stroustrup and J. Shopiro: *A Set of C Classes for Co-Routine Style Programming*. Proc. USENIX C++ Conference. Santa Fe, New Mexico. November 1987.

[Stroustrup,1988] B. Stroustrup: *Parameterized Types for C++*. Proc. USENIX C++ Conference, Denver, Colorado. 1988.

[Stroustrup,1991] B. Stroustrup: *The C++ Programming Language (Second Edition)*. Addison-Wesley. Reading, Massachusetts. 1991. ISBN 0-201-53992-6.

[Stroustrup,1993] B. Stroustrup: *A History of C++: 1979–1991*. Proc. ACM History of Programming Languages Conference (HOPL-2). ACM Sigplan Notices. Vol 28, No 3. 1993.

[Stroustrup,1994] B. Stroustrup: *The Design and Evolution of C++*. Addison-Wesley. Reading, Massachusetts. 1994. ISBN 0-201-54330-3.

[Stroustrup,1997] B. Stroustrup: *The C++ Programming Language, Third Edition*. Addison-Wesley. Reading, Massachusetts. 1997. ISBN 0-201-88954-4. Hardcover ("Special") Edition. 2000. ISBN 0-201-70073-5.

[Stroustrup,2002] B. Stroustrup: *C and C++: Siblings, C and C++: A Case for Compatibility*, and *C and C++: Case Studies in Compatibility*. The C/C++ Users Journal. July-September 2002. www.stroustrup.com/papers.html.

[Stroustrup,2007] B. Stroustrup: *Evolving a language in and for the real world: C++ 1991-2006*. ACM HOPL-III. June 2007.

[Stroustrup,2009] B. Stroustrup: *Programming – Principles and Practice Using C++*. Addison-Wesley. 2009. ISBN 0-321-54372-6.

[Stroustrup,2010] B. Stroustrup: *The C++11 FAQ*. www.stroustrup.com/C++11FAQ.html.

[Stroustrup,2012a] B. Stroustrup and A. Sutton: *A Concept Design for the STL*. WG21 Technical Report N3351==12-0041. January 2012.

[Stroustrup,2012b] B. Stroustrup: *Software Development for Infrastructure*. Computer. January 2012. doi:10.1109/MC.2011.353.

[Stroustrup,2013] B. Stroustrup: *The C++ Programming Language (Fourth Edition).* Addison-Wesley. 2013. ISBN 0-321-56384-0.

[Stroustrup,2014] B. Stroustrup: C++ Applications. http://www.stroustrup.com/applications.html.

[Stroustrup,2015] B. Stroustrup and H. Sutter: *C++ Core Guidelines.* https://github.com/isocpp/CppCoreGuidelines/blob/master/CppCoreGuidelines.md.

[Stroustrup,2015b] B. Stroustrup, H. Sutter, and G. Dos Reis: *A brief introduction to C++'s model for type- and resource-safety.* Isocpp.org. October 2015. Revised December 2015. http://www.stroustrup.com/resource-model.pdf.

[Sutton,2011] A. Sutton and B. Stroustrup: *Design of Concept Libraries for C++.* Proc. SLE 2011 (International Conference on Software Language Engineering). July 2011.

[WG21] ISO SC22/WG21 The C++ Programming Language Standards Committee: *Document Archive.* www.open-std.org/jtc1/sc22/wg21.

[Williams,2012] Anthony Williams: *C++ Concurrency in Action – Practical Multithreading.* Manning Publications Co. ISBN 978-1933988771.

[Woodward,1974] P. M. Woodward and S. G. Bond: *Algol 68-R Users Guide.* Her Majesty's Stationery Office. London. 1974.

16.5 Advice

[1] The ISO C++ standard [C++,2017] defines C++.

[2] When chosing a style for a new project or when modernizing a code base, rely on the C++ Core Guidelines; §16.1.4.

[3] When learning C++, don't focus on language features in isolation; §16.2.1.

[4] Don't get stuck with decades-old language-feature sets and design techniques; §16.1.4.

[5] Before using a new feature in production code, try it out by writing small programs to test the standards conformance and performance of the implementations you plan to use.

[6] For learning C++, use the most up-to-date and complete implementation of Standard C++ that you can get access to.

[7] The common subset of C and C++ is not the best initial subset of C++ to learn; §16.3.2.1.

[8] Prefer named casts, such as `static_cast` over C-style casts; §16.2.7.

[9] When converting a C program to C++, first make sure that function declarations (prototypes) and standard headers are used consistently; §16.3.2.

[10] When converting a C program to C++, rename variables that are C++ keywords; §16.3.2.

[11] For portability and type safety, if you must use C, write in the common subset of C and C++; §16.3.2.1.

[12] When converting a C program to C++, cast the result of `malloc()` to the proper type or change all uses of `malloc()` to uses of `new`; §16.3.2.2.

[13] When converting from `malloc()` and `free()` to `new` and `delete`, consider using `vector`, `push_back()`, and `reserve()` instead of `realloc()`; §16.3.2.1.

[14] In C++, there are no implicit conversions from ints to enumerations; use explicit type conversion where necessary.
[15] For each standard C header <X.h> that places names in the global namespace, the header <cX> places the names in namespace std.
[16] Use extern "C" when declaring C functions; §16.3.2.3.
[17] Prefer string over C-style strings (direct manipulation of zero-terminated arrays of char).
[18] Prefer iostreams over stdio.
[19] Prefer containers (e.g., vector) over built-in arrays.

I

Index

Knowledge is of two kinds.
We know a subject ourselves,
or we know where
we can find information on it.
– Samuel Johnson

Token

!=
- container 147
- not-equal operator 6

", string literal 3
$, regex 117
%
- modulus operator 6
- remainder operator 6

%=, operator 7
&
- address-of operator 11
- reference to 12

&&, rvalue reference 71
(, regex 117
(), call operator 85
(?: pattern 120
), regex 117
*
- contents-of operator 11
- multiply operator 6
- pointer to 11
- regex 117

*=, scaling operator 7
*? lazy 118
+
- plus operator 6
- regex 117
- string concatenation 111

++, increment operator 7
+=
- operator 7
- string append 112

+? lazy 118
-, minus operator 6
--, decrement operator 7
., regex 117
/, divide operator 6
// comment 2
/=, scaling operator 7
: public 55
<< 75
- output operator 3

<=
- container 147
- less-than-or-equal operator 6

<
- container 147
- less-than operator 6

=
- 0 54
- and == 7

assignment 16
auto 8
container 147
initializer 7
initializer narrowing 8
string assignment 112
==
= and 7
container 147
equal operator 6
string 112
>
container 147
greater-than operator 6
>=
container 147
greater-than-or-equal operator 6
>> 75
template arguments 215
?, regex 117
?? lazy 118
[, regex 117
[]
array 171
array of 11
string 112
\, backslash 3
], regex 117
^, regex 117
{, regex 117
{}
grouping 2
initializer 8
{}? lazy 118
|, regex 117
}, regex 117
~, destructor 51
0
= 54
nullptr NULL 13

A

abs() 188
abstract
class 54
type 54
accumulate() 189
acquisition RAII, resource 164
adaptor, lambda as 180
address, memory 16
address-of operator & 11
adjacent_difference() 189
aims, C++11 213
algorithm 149
container 150, 160
lifting 100
numerical 189
parallel 161
standard library 156
<algorithm> 109, 156
alias
template 184
using 90
alignas 215
alignof 215
allocation 51
allocator new, container 178
almost container 170
alnum, regex 119
alpha, regex 119
[[:alpha:]] letter 119
ANSI C++ 212
any 177
append +=, string 112
argument
constrained 81
constrained template 82
default function 42
default template 98
function 41
passing, function 66
type 82
value 82
arithmetic
conversions, usual 7
operator 6
vector 192
ARM 212
array
array vs. 172
of [] 11
array 171
[] 171
data() 171
initialize 171
size() 171
vs. array 172
vs. vector 171
<array> 109
asin() 188
assembler 210
assert() 40
assertion static_assert 40
Assignable, concept 158
assignment
= 16
=, string 112
copy 66, 69
initialization and 18
move 66, 72
associative array – see map

async() launch 204
at() 141
atan() 188
atan2() 188
AT&T Bell Laboratories 212
auto = 8
auto_ptr, deprecated 218

B

back_inserter() 150
backslash \ 3
bad_variant_access 176
base and derived class 55
basic_string 114
BCPL 219
begin() 75, 143, 147, 150
beginner, book for 1
Bell Laboratories, AT&T 212
beta() 188
bibliography 222
BidirectionalIterator, concept 159
BidirectionalRange, concept 160
binary search 156
binding, structured 45
bit-field, bitset and 172
bitset 172
  and bit-field 172
  and enum 172
blank, regex 119
block
  as function body, try 141
  try 36
body, function 2
book for beginner 1
bool 5
Boolean, concept 158
BoundedRange, concept 160
break 15

C

C 209
  and C++ compatibility 218
  Classic 219
  difference from 218
  K&R 219
  void * assignment, difference from 221
  with Classes 208
  with Classes language features 210
  with Classes standard library 211
C++
  ANSI 212
  compatibility, C and 218
  Core Guidelines 214
  core language 2
  history 207
  ISO 212
  meaning 209
  modern 214
  pronunciation 209
  standard, ISO 2
  standard library 2
  standardization 212
  timeline 208
C++03 212
C++0x, C++11 209, 212
C++11
  aims 213
  C++0x 209, 212
  language features 215
  library components 216
C++14 213
  language features 216
  library components 217
C++17 1, 213
  language features 216
  library components 217
C++20 1, 157, 213
  concepts 94
  contracts 40
  modules 32
C++98 212
  standard library 211
C11 218
C89 and C99 218
C99, C89 and 218
call operator () 85
callback 181
capacity() 139, 147
capture list 87
carries_dependency 215
cast 53
catch
  clause 36
  every exception 141
catch(...) 141
ceil() 188
char 5
character sets, multiple 114
check
  compile-time 40
  run-time 40
checking, cost of range 142
chrono, namespace 179
<chrono> 109, 179, 200
class 48
  abstract 54
  base and derived 55
  concrete 48
  hierarchy 57

scope 9
template 79
Classic C 219
C-library header 110
clock timing 200
<cmath> 109, 188
cntrl, regex 119
code complexity, function and 4
comment, // 2
Common, concept 158
CommonReference, concept 158
common_type_t 158
communication, task 202
comparison 74
operator 6, 74
compatibility, C and C++ 218
compilation
model, template 104
separate 30
compiler 2
compile-time
check 40
computation 181
evaluation 10
complete encapsulation 66
complex 49, 190
<complex> 109, 188, 190
complexity, function and code 4
components
C++11 library 216
C++14 library 217
C++17 library 217
computation, compile-time 181
concatenation +, string 111
concept 81, 94
Assignable 158
based overloading 95
BidirectionalIterator 159
BidirectionalRange 160
Boolean 158
BoundedRange 160
Common 158
CommonReference 158
Constructible 158
ConvertibleTo 158
Copyable 158
CopyConstructible 158
DefaultConstructible 158
DerivedFrom 158
Destructible 158
EqualityComparable 158
ForwardIterator 159
ForwardRange 160
InputIterator 159
InputRange 160
Integral 158
Invocable 159
InvocableRegular 159
Iterator 159
Mergeable 159
Movable 158
MoveConstructible 158
OutputIterator 159
OutputRange 160
Permutable 159
Predicate 159
RandomAccessIterator 159
RandomAccessRange 160
Range 157
Range 160
Regular 158
Relation 159
Same 158
Semiregular 158
Sentinel 159
SignedIntegral 158
SizedRange 160
SizedSentinel 159
Sortable 159
StrictTotallyOrdered 158
StrictWeakOrder 159
support 94
Swappable 158
SwappableWith 158
UnsignedIntegral 158
use 94
View 160
WeaklyEqualityComparable 158
concepts
C++20 94
definition of 97
in <concepts> 158
in <iterator> 158
in <ranges> 158
<concepts>, concepts in 158
concrete
class 48
type 48
concurrency 195
condition, declaration in 61
condition_variable 201
notify_one() 202
wait() 201
<condition_variable> 201
const
immutability 9
member function 50
constant expression 10
const_cast 53
constexpr
function 10
immutability 9

const_iterator 154
constrained
  argument 81
  template 82
  template argument 82
Constructible, concept 158
constructor
  and destructor 210
  copy 66, 69
  default 50
  delegating 215
  explicit 67
  inheriting 216
  initializer-list 52
  invariant and 37
  move 66, 71
container 51, 79, 137
  >= 147
  > 147
  = 147
  == 147
  < 147
  <= 147
  != 147
  algorithm 150, 160
  allocator new 178
  almost 170
  object in 140
  overview 146
  return 151
  sort() 181
  specialized 170
  standard library 146
contents-of operator * 11
contract 40
contracts, C++20 40
conversion 67
  explicit type 53
  narrowing 8
conversions, usual arithmetic 7
ConvertibleTo, concept 158
copy 68
  assignment 66, 69
  constructor 66, 69
  cost of 70
  elision 72
  elision 66
  memberwise 66
copy() 156
Copyable, concept 158
CopyConstructible, concept 158
copy_if() 156
Core Guidelines, C++ 214
core language, C++ 2
coroutine 211
cos() 188
cosh() 188
cost
  of copy 70
  of range checking 142
count() 156
count_if() 155–156
cout, output 3
<cstdlib> 110
C-style
  error handling 188
  string 13

D

\D, regex 119
\d, regex 119
d, regex 119
data race 196
data(), array 171
D&E 208
deadlock 199
deallocation 51
debugging template 100
declaration 5
  function 4
  in condition 61
  interface 29
-declaration, using 34
declarator operator 12
decltype 215
decrement operator -- 7
deduction
  guide 83, 176
  return-type 44
default
  constructor 50
  function argument 42
  member initializer 68
  operations 66
  template argument 98
=default 66
DefaultConstructible, concept 158
definition
  implementation 30
  of concepts 97
delegating constructor 215
=delete 67
delete
  naked 52
  operator 51
deprecated
  auto_ptr 218
  feature 218
deque 146
derived class, base and 55
DerivedFrom, concept 158

Destructible, concept 158
destructor 51, 66
˜ 51
constructor and 210
virtual 59
dictionary – see map
difference
from C 218
from C void ∗ assignment 221
digit, [[:digit:]] 119
digit, regex 119
[[:digit:]] digit 119
-directive, using 35
dispatch, tag 181
distribution, random 191
divide operator / 6
domain error 188
double 5
duck typing 104
duration 179
duration_cast 179
dynamic store 51
dynamic_cast 61
is instance of 62
is kind of 62

E

EDOM 188
element requirements 140
elision, copy 66
emplace_back() 147
empty() 147
enable_if 184
encapsulation, complete 66
end() 75, 143, 147, 150
engine, random 191
enum, bitset and 172
equal operator == 6
equality preserving 159
EqualityComparable, concept 158
equal_range() 156, 173
ERANGE 188
erase() 143, 147
errno 188
error
domain 188
handling 35
handling, C-style 188
range 188
recovery 38
run-time 35
error-code, exception vs 38
essential operations 66
evaluation
compile-time 10
order of 7
example
find_all() 151
Hello, World! 2
Rand_int 191
Vec 141
exception 35
and main() 141
catch every 141
specification, removed 218
vs error-code 38
exclusive_scan() 189
execution policy 161
explicit type conversion 53
explicit constructor 67
exponential_distribution 191
export removed 218
expr() 188
expression
constant 10
lambda 87
requires] 96
extern template 215

F

fabs() 188
facilities, standard library 108
fail_fast 170
feature, deprecated 218
features
C with Classes language 210
C++11 language 215
C++14 language 216
C++17 language 216
file, header 31
final 216
find() 150, 156
find_all() example 151
find_if() 155–156
first, pair member 173
floor() 188
fmod() 188
for
statement 11
statement, range 11
forward() 167
forwarding, perfect 168
ForwardIterator, concept 159
forward_list 146
singly-linked list 143
<forward_list> 109
ForwardRange, concept 160
free store 51
frexp() 188
<fstream> 109

__func__ 215
function 2
 and code complexity 4
 argument 41
 argument, default 42
 argument passing 66
 body 2
 body, try block as 141
 const member 50
 constexpr 10
 declaration 4
 implementation of virtual 56
 mathematical 188
 object 85
 overloading 4
 return value 41
 template 84
 type 181
 value return 66
function 180
 and nullptr 180
fundamental type 5
future
 and promise 202
 member get() 202
<future> 109, 202

G

garbage collection 73
generic programming 93, 210
get<>()
 by index 174
 by type 174
get(), future member 202
graph, regex 119
greater-than operator > 6
greater-than-or-equal operator >= 6
greedy match 118, 121
grouping, {} 2
gsl
 namespace 168
 span 168
Guidelines, C++ Core 214

H

half-open sequence 156
handle 52
 resource 69, 165
hardware, mapping to 16
hash table 144
hash<>, unordered_map 76
header
 C-library 110
 file 31
 standard library 109
heap 51
Hello, World! example 2
hierarchy
 class 57
 navigation 61
history, C++ 207
HOPL 208

I

if statement 14
immutability
 const 9
 constexpr 9
implementation
 definition 30
 inheritance 60
 iterator 153
 of virtual function 56
 string 113
in-class member initialization 215
#include 31
inclusive_scan() 189
increment operator ++ 7
index, get<>() by 174
inheritance 55
 implementation 60
 interface 60
 multiple 211
inheriting constructor 216
initialization
 and assignment 18
 in-class member 215
initialize 52
 array 171
initializer
 = 7
 {} 8
 default member 68
 narrowing, = 8
initializer-list constructor 52
initializer_list 52
inline 49
 namespace 215
inlining 49
inner_product() 189
InputIterator, concept 159
InputRange, concept 160
insert() 143, 147
instantiation 81
instruction, machine 16
int 5
 output bits of 172
Integral, concept 158

interface
  declaration 29
  inheritance 60
invariant 37
  and constructor 37
Invocable, concept 159
InvocableRegular, concept 159
I/O, iterator and 154
<ios> 109
<iostream> 3, 109
iota() 189
is
  instance of, dynamic_cast 62
  kind of, dynamic_cast 62
ISO
  C++ 212
  C++ standard 2
ISO-14882 212
istream_iterator 154
iterator 75, 150
  and I/O 154
  implementation 153
Iterator, concept 159
iterator 143, 154
<iterator> 182
  concepts in 158
iterator_category 182
iterator_traits 181–182
iterator_type 182

J

join(), thread 196

K

key and value 144
K&R C 219

L

\L, regex 119
\l, regex 119
lambda
  as adaptor 180
  expression 87
language
  and library 107
  features, C with Classes 210
  features, C++11 215
  features, C++14 216
  features, C++17 216
launch, async() 204
lazy
  +? 118
  ?? 118
  {}? 118
  *? 118
  match 118, 121
ldexp() 188
leak, resource 62, 72, 164
less-than operator < 6
less-than-or-equal operator <= 6
letter, [[:alpha:]] 119
library
  algorithm, standard 156
  C with Classes standard 211
  C++98 standard 211
  components, C++11 216
  components, C++14 217
  components, C++17 217
  container, standard 146
  facilities, standard 108
  language and 107
  non-standard 107
  standard 107
lifetime, scope and 9
lifting algorithm 100
<limits> 181, 193
linker 2
list
  capture 87
  forward_list singly-linked 143
list 142, 146
literal
  ", string 3
  raw string 116
  suffix, s 113
  suffix, sv 115
  type of string 113
  user-defined 75, 215
literals
  string_literals 113
  string_view_literals 115
local scope 9
lock, reader-writer 200
log() 188
log10() 188
long long 215
lower, regex 119

M

machine instruction 16
main() 2
  exception and 141
make_pair() 173
make_shared() 166
make_tuple() 174
make_unique() 166
management, resource 72, 164

map 144, 146
  and unordered_map 146
<map> 109
mapped type, value 144
mapping to hardware 16
match
  greedy 118, 121
  lazy 118, 121
mathematical
  function 188
  functions, special 188
  functions, standard 188
<math.h> 188
Max Munch rule 118
meaning, C++ 209
member
  function, const 50
  initialization, in-class 215
  initializer, default 68
memberwise copy 66
mem_fn() 180
memory 73
  address 16
<memory> 109, 164, 166
merge() 156
Mergeable, concept 159
minus operator - 6
model, template compilation 104
modern C++ 214
modf() 188
modularity 29
module suport 32
modules, C++20 32
modulus operator % 6
Movable, concept 158
move 71
  assignment 66, 72
  constructor 66, 71
move() 72, 156, 167
MoveConstructible, concept 158
moved-from
  object 72
  state 168
move-only type 167
multi-line pattern 117
multimap 146
multiple
  character sets 114
  inheritance 211
  return-values 44
multiply operator * 6
multiset 146
mutex 199
<mutex> 199

N

\n, newline 3
naked
  delete 52
  new 52
namespace scope 9
namespace 34
  chrono 179
  gsl 168
  inline 215
  pmr 178
  std 3, 35, 109
narrowing
  = initializer 8
  conversion 8
navigation, hierarchy 61
new
  container allocator 178
  naked 52
  operator 51
newline \n 3
noexcept 37
noexcept() 215
non-memory resource 73
non-standard library 107
noreturn 215
normal_distribution 191
notation, regular expression 117
not-equal operator != 6
notify_one(), condition_variable 202
NULL 0, nullptr 13
nullptr 13
  function and 180
  NULL 0 13
number, random 191
<numeric> 189
numerical algorithm 189
numeric_limits 193

O

object 5
  function 85
  in container 140
  moved-from 72
object-oriented programming 57, 210
operations
  default 66
  essential 66
operator
  %= 7
  += 7
  &, address-of 11
  (), call 85
  *, contents-of 11

--, decrement 7
/, divide 6
==, equal 6
>, greater-than 6
>=, greater-than-or-equal 6
++, increment 7
<, less-than 6
<=, less-than-or-equal 6
-, minus 6
%, modulus 6
*, multiply 6
!=, not-equal 6
<<, output 3
+, plus 6
%, remainder 6
/=, scaling 7
*=, scaling 7
arithmetic 6
comparison 6, 74
declarator 12
delete 51
new 51
overloaded 51
user-defined 51
optimization, short-string 113
optional 176
order of evaluation 7
ostream_iterator 154
out_of_range 141
output
bits of int 172
cout 3
operator << 3
OutputIterator, concept 159
OutputRange, concept 160
overloaded operator 51
overloading
concept based 95
function 4
override 55
overview, container 146
ownership 164

P

packaged_task thread 203
pair 173
and structured binding 174
member first 173
member second 173
par 161
parallel algorithm 161
parameterized type 79
partial_sum() 189
par_unseq 161
passing data to task 197
pattern 116
(?: 120
multi-line 117
perfect forwarding 168
Permutable, concept 159
phone_book example 138
plus operator + 6
pmr, namespace 178
pointer 17
smart 164
to * 11
policy, execution 161
polymorphic type 54
pow() 188
precondition 37
predicate 86, 155
type 183
Predicate, concept 159
print, regex 119
procedural programming 2
program 2
programming
generic 93, 210
object-oriented 57, 210
procedural 2
promise
future and 202
member set_exception() 202
member set_value() 202
pronunciation, C++ 209
punct, regex 119
pure virtual 54
purpose, template 93
push_back() 52, 139, 143, 147
push_front() 143

R

R" 116
race, data 196
RAII
and resource management 36
and try-block 40
and try-statement 36
resource acquisition 164
scoped_lock and 199–200
RAII 52
Rand_int example 191
random number 191
random
distribution 191
engine 191
<random> 109, 191
RandomAccessIterator, concept 159
RandomAccessRange, concept 160
range

  - checking, cost of 142
  - checking Vec 140
  - error 188
  - for statement 11
- Range
  - concept 157
  - concept 160
- <ranges> 157
- <ranges>, concepts in 158
- raw string literal 116
- reader-writer lock 200
- recovery, error 38
- reduce() 189
- reference 17
  - &&, rvalue 71
  - rvalue 72
  - to & 12
- regex
  - * 117
  - } 117
  - { 117
  -) 117
  - | 117
  -] 117
  - [117
  - ^ 117
  - ? 117
  - . 117
  - $ 117
  - + 117
  - (117
  - alnum 119
  - alpha 119
  - blank 119
  - cntrl 119
  - d 119
  - \d 119
  - \D 119
  - digit 119
  - graph 119
  - \l 119
  - \L 119
  - lower 119
  - print 119
  - punct 119
  - regular expression 116
  - repetition 118
  - s 119
  - \S 119
  - \s 119
  - space 119
  - \U 119
  - \u 119
  - upper 119
  - w 119
  - \W 119
  - \w 119
  - xdigit 119
- <regex> 109, 116
  - regular expression 116
- regex_iterator 121
- regex_search 116
- regular
  - expression notation 117
  - expression regex 116
  - expression <regex> 116
- Regular, concept 158
- reinterpret_cast 53
- Relation, concept 159
- remainder operator % 6
- removed
  - exception specification 218
  - export 218
- repetition, regex 118
- replace() 156
  - string 112
- replace_if() 156
- requirement, template 94
- requirements, element 140
- requires] expression 96
- reserve() 139, 147
- resize() 147
- resource
  - acquisition RAII 164
  - handle 69, 165
  - leak 62, 72, 164
  - management 72, 164
  - management, RAII and 36
  - non-memory 73
  - retention 73
  - safety 72
- rethrow 38
- return
  - function value 66
  - type, suffix 215
  - value, function 41
- return
  - container 151
  - type, void 3
- returning results from task 198
- return-type deduction 44
- return-values, multiple 44
- riemanzeta() 188
- rule
  - Max Munch 118
  - of zero 67
- run-time
  - check 40
  - error 35
- rvalue
  - reference 72
  - reference && 71

S

s literal suffix 113
\s, regex 119
s, regex 119
\S, regex 119
safety, resource 72
Same, concept 158
scaling
  operator /= 7
  operator *= 7
scope
  and lifetime 9
  class 9
  local 9
  namespace 9
scoped_lock 164
  and RAII 199–200
  unique_lock and 201
scoped_lock() 199
search, binary 156
second, pair member 173
Semiregular, concept 158
Sentinel, concept 159
separate compilation 30
sequence 150
  half-open 156
set 146
<set> 109
set_exception(), promise member 202
set_value(), promise member 202
shared_lock 200
shared_mutex 200
shared_ptr 164
sharing data task 199
short-string optimization 113
SignedIntegral, concept 158
SIMD 161
Simula 207
sin() 188
singly-linked list, forward_list 143
sinh() 188
size of type 6
size() 75, 147
  array 171
SizedRange, concept 160
SizedSentinel, concept 159
sizeof 6
sizeof() 181
size_t 90
smart pointer 164
smatch 116
sort() 149, 156
  container 181
Sortable, concept 159
space, regex 119
span
  gsl 168
  string_view and 168
special mathematical functions 188
specialized container 170
sphbessel() 188
sqrt() 188
<sstream> 109
standard
  ISO C++ 2
  library 107
  library algorithm 156
  library, C++ 2
  library, C with Classes 211
  library, C++98 211
  library container 146
  library facilities 108
  library header 109
  library std 109
  mathematical functions 188
standardization, C++ 212
state, moved-from 168
statement
  for 11
  if 14
  range for 11
  switch 14
  while 14
static_assert 193
  assertion 40
static_cast 53
std
  namespace 3, 35, 109
  standard library 109
<stdexcept> 109
STL 211
store
  dynamic 51
  free 51
StrictTotallyOrdered, concept 158
StrictWeakOrder, concept 159
string
  C-style 13
  literal " 3
  literal, raw 116
  literal, type of 113
  Unicode 114
string 111
  [] 112
  == 112
  append += 112
  assignment = 112
  concatenation + 111
  implementation 113
  replace() 112
  substr() 112
<string> 109, 111

string_literals, literals 113
string_span 170
string_view 114
  and span 168
string_view_literals, literals 115
structured
  binding 45
  binding, pair and 174
  binding, tuple and 174
subclass, superclass and 55
[]subscripting 147
substr(), string 112
suffix 75
  return type 215
  s literal 113
  sv literal 115
superclass and subclass 55
suport, module 32
support, concept 94
sv literal suffix 115
swap() 76
Swappable, concept 158
SwappableWith, concept 158
switch statement 14
synchronized_pool_resource 178

T

table, hash 144
tag dispatch 181
tanh() 188
task
  and thread 196
  communication 202
  passing data to 197
  returning results from 198
  sharing data 199
TC++PL 208
template 79
  alias 184
  argument, constrained 82
  argument, default 98
  arguments, >> 215
  class 79
  compilation model 104
  constrained 82
  debugging 100
  extern 215
  function 84
  purpose 93
  requirement 94
  variadic 100
this 70
thread
  join() 196
  packaged_task 203
  task and 196
<thread> 109, 196
thread_local 216
time 179
timeline, C++ 208
time_point 179
timing, clock 200
to hardware, mapping 16
transform_reduce() 189
translation unit 32
try
  block 36
  block as function body 141
try-block, RAII and 40
try-statement, RAII and 36
tuple 174
  and structured binding 174
type 5
  abstract 54
  argument 82
  concrete 48
  conversion, explicit 53
  function 181
  fundamental 5
  get<>() by 174
  move-only 167
  of string literal 113
  parameterized 79
  polymorphic 54
  predicate 183
  size of 6
typename 79, 152
<type_traits> 183
typing, duck 104

U

\U, regex 119
\u, regex 119
udl 75
Unicode string 114
uniform_int_distribution 191
uninitialized 8
unique_copy() 149, 156
unique_lock 200–201
  and scoped_lock 201
unique_ptr 62, 164
unordered_map 144, 146
  hash<> 76
  map and 146
<unordered_map> 109
unordered_multimap 146
unordered_multiset 146
unordered_set 146
unsigned 5
UnsignedIntegral, concept 158

upper, regex 119
use, concept 94
user-defined
  literal 75, 215
  operator 51
using
  alias 90
  -declaration 34
  -directive 35
usual arithmetic conversions 7
<utility> 109, 173–174

V

valarray 192
<valarray> 192
value 5
  argument 82
  key and 144
  mapped type 144
  return, function 66
valuetype 147
value_type 90
variable 5
variadic template 100
variant 175
Vec
  example 141
  range checking 140
vector arithmetic 192
vector 138, 146
  array vs. 171
<vector> 109
vector<bool> 170
vectorized 161
View, concept 160
virtual 54
  destructor 59
  function, implementation of 56
  function table vtbl 56
  pure 54
void
  * 221
  * assignment, difference from C 221
  return type 3
vtbl, virtual function table 56

W

w, regex 119
\w, regex 119
\W, regex 119
wait(), condition_variable 201
WeaklyEqualityComparable, concept 158
WG21 208
while statement 14

X

X3J16 212
xdigit, regex 119

Z

zero, rule of 67

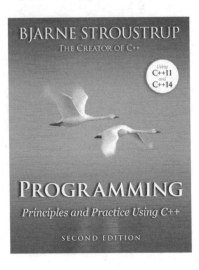